TRACTS

ON

THE SABBATH.

"THE SEVENTH DAY IS THE SABBATH OF THE LORD THY GOD."

NEW YORK:
PUBLISHED BY THE AMERICAN SABBATH TRACT SOCIETY.
No. 9 Spruce Street.
1853.

TABLE OF CONTENTS.

[No. 1.]

REASONS

FOR

INTRODUCING THE SABBATH OF THE FOURTH COMMANDMENT TO THE CONSIDERATION OF THE CHRISTIAN PUBLIC.

NEW YORK:

PUBLISHED BY THE AMERICAN SABBATH TRACT SOCIETY,

No. 9 Spruce-Street.

REASONS

FOR INTRODUCING THE SABBATH OF THE FOURTH COMMANDMENT TO THE CONSIDERATION OF THE CHRISTIAN PUBLIC.

To search for the knowledge of our duty, as subjects of the Divine Government, is of the highest importance to Christians and to all men. "None of us liveth to himself, and no man dieth to himself," but "whether we live or die, we are the Lord's." It behooves us, therefore, to inquire, diligently and prayerfully, what God would have us to do, and how we may best glorify Him and save our generation? We should "seek wisdom as silver, and search for it as for hid treasure;" and we should labor after the knowledge, not only of *some* duties, but of *every* duty. "Obey my voice," is the reiterated mandate of Jehovah. To give full proof of our friendship for Christ, we must "do whatsoever he hath commanded us." Hence the importance of "searching the Scriptures," and of carefully pondering the testimonies of God. All should pursue this course, and feel this responsibility; for "every one of us shall give account of himself unto God." Hence the propriety and necessity, in many cases, of *individuals* dissenting from the views and decisions of *collective bodies*, and of *minorities* dissenting from *majorities*, and protesting against what they discover to be erroneous, unequal, and oppressive, in their resolves and measures—accompanying the same with a particular statement of their reasons. Such a course expresses a determination "not to be partakers of other men's sins," and is often the means of leading to investigation and reform.

This duty is acknowledged, and this privilege is claimed, by the observers of the *seventh day*, in relation to the subject of the Sabbath. Compared with the many who assume the Christian name, we are a *minority*—a *mere remnant*—and our reasons and motives for dissent from the great mass of believers, have been by most but partially, if at all, examined and weighed. Believing, as we do, that we have a full and explicit Divine warrant for our practice, we regard it as our duty to make renewed efforts to sustain the claims of the original Sabbath of God's appointment, enlighten the public mind, disarm our neighbors and fellow Christians of their prejudices, and promote a more thorough and impartial attention to this item of religious practice. The object of this Tract is not to enter fully upon the proofs of our doctrine and practice, but to invite attention to the subject, and impress the reader with the importance of correct views and of being sustained in Sabbath principles and efforts by an explicit warrant from God himself, in order the more effectually to secure the sanctification of this precious institution. Accordingly, we proceed to state some of our Reasons for introducing the Sabbath of the Fourth Commandment to the consideration of the Christian Public.

I. The general concession that the weekly Sabbath is a needful, wise, and valuable institution. Being a weekly rest from secular business and labor, it contributes to the health and vigor both of man and beast, encourages habits of cleanliness and decency, gives opportunity to cultivate the social virtues, makes man acquainted with man, and inspires a mutual regard for the interests of society; and, what is much more, it furnishes a proper and necessary season for mental improvement, public worship and instruction, private meditation and self-examination, the training up of children in the knowledge of God and of Heaven, and the deepening of our impressions of the value of time, and of the importance of preparing for eternity. These and similar considerations sensibly arrest the attention of sober and enlightened Christians, and secure a conscientious regard to the institution. This fact evinces the importance of being able to bring a *divine sanction* for a day so evidently desirable, and so generally esteemed—of being assured that it rests upon no doubtful authority, that it is not a mere human provision or a matter of expediency and accommodation, but that in observing it we are conforming to the clearly-manifested will of God. It is evident, that this consideration will give a value to the institution which can be supplied by no other, and secure a love and respect for it, and a delight in it, which nothing else can so effectually produce. Hence the question is presented, with a high and impressive claim to a true and definite answer, Is any other than the *seventh* day of the week sustained by the important and indisputable sanction of *divine authority?* If this, and this only, be the Sabbath of God's appointment, for general and permanent use, then, by the substitution of another day, the institution is shorn of its chief excellence and force —yea, it is virtually annulled. It no longer exists as

God ordained it, for the express reason that he gave for it. This is a point which it becomes Christians seriously to look at.

. It is not the province of Rulers, Bishops, or Councils, to legislate for the Church, and to bind the consciences of men in this or any other matter. Man's appointment of another day than the one contained in the Divine Enactment, does not make it *the Sabbath of the Lord.* It is only a *human law*, resting on *human authority.* Therefore, all attempts to enforce the observance of such an institution as being of divine authority, are calculated to mislead and ensnare souls. It is "teaching for doctrine the commandments of men." Our faith in this matter "should not stand in the wisdom of men, but in the power of God." The question is not, What day have men judged most proper? and, What reasons for the institution have they deemed the most appropriate? and, What day have civil rulers sanctioned by their decrees and penalties?—but it is, What day has God sanctified and blessed as a day of rest? It is manifest that no man should stop his inquiries until he is able to produce a clear divine warrant for his practice.

III. The fact that there is a lamentable division among professors of religion in regard to the true design of the weekly Sabbath, and the proper day to be observed, evinces the great importance of investigation, and of arriving at a correct knowledge of the Divine Will. This division is not likely to cease till a more general and thorough knowledge of the subject is obtained, and a deeper interest therein is felt. Can it reasonably be supposed that the whole church will become united in the observance of the *first* day of the week, if it is not the Sabbath of the Bible? Will it ever be the case, that God will have no witnesses for his own unrepealed and unadulterated institution? —none that shall call the Sabbath of his own appointment "a delight, the holy of the Lord, honorable, and shall honor him therein?" No—this will never be! Admitting that the Sabbath of the fourth commandment is still binding, there is no doubt that there will ever be a remnant, at least, who will conscientiously observe it. For his great name's sake, God will not suffer this prominent part of his law to be universally corrupted and profaned. And hence, if a preference continues to be given, as it is now, to a day which He has not designated and made holy, there will, of necessity, be a protracted division in the ranks of Zion, and the cause of the Redeemer will, on this account, continue to suffer. The faithful witnesses will unquestionably continue to prophecy, though clothed in sackcloth, and to bear testimony against the innovation. And no earthly power can prevent them. Resolves, and proscriptions, and gibbets, will not wholly suppress their testimony in favor of the Sabbath of the fourth commandment. Therefore, the occasion of the present division must be put away by a general return to the uncorrupted appointment of God, or the same cause for regret and mourning which now exists will continue to afflict the church. Let those who regard the unity and peace of Zion, seriously lay to heart this consequence.

IV. It must be admitted, that in so important a matter as a weekly Sabbath, our great moral Legislator has sufficiently declared his will to enable honest and impartial inquirers to arrive at a true result. If it would be reasonable to expect explicit information of his will concerning any point, it would certainly be reasonable to expect it concerning this, seeing the claims of this law would come in direct contact with the cupidity of men, and sensibly influence the arrangements of business and pleasure—yea, deeply affect the general interests of society. Were the data furnished, from which contemplative and well-disposed minds might *infer* a weekly Sabbath, its observance and its ends could not be extensively secured without an *explicit* warrant. Therefore, if God intended there should be a Sabbath—yea, we might with propriety say, that if he intended his religion and worship should be preserved in the world—he would have given an explicit law upon this subject—one, of course, which could be easily discovered, and the permanent obligation of which could be readily traced.

V. It is an obvious *fact*, that God *has legislated* upon this subject—that he has once made a law for the observance of the *seventh day* as a *weekly Sabbath.* He did this at the close of his creative operations. Excepting marriage, the seventh-day Sabbath is the oldest institution in the world. Moreover, God gave a new edition of this law at the promulgation of the Decalogue upon Mount Sinai, under circumstances of peculiar and awful solemnity and majesty; first pronouncing it, in connection with the other nine commandments, with an audible voice from the Mount, in the hearing of all Israel, amidst thunders, and flames, and tempests; and afterwards writing the *entire ten* on two tables of stone, for a perpetual rule of action. It is obvious, also, that *obedience* to this institution, so solemnly stated and defined, and enforced by so plain and adequate a reason, was regarded as a prominent item of duty, and received his *marked approbation,* whereas *disobedience* received his *marked disapprobation.* It is also clear, that good men throughout the times of the Old Testament were peculiarly zealous for this institution, and sought diligently to prevent its neglect or desecration, and to secure its legitimate advantages. Thus far all is plain, and is generally conceded.

VI. It is a principle which no proficient in the science of Government, *divine* or *human*, will deny, that a law, once enacted and in force, remains in force, unless repealed or amended by the same authority which first enacted it. Hence, if the law respecting the seventh-day weekly Sabbath has not been repealed or amended by the same authority which first enacted it, it still remains in full force and obligation, as originally given. This conclusion is *legitimate*, *necessary*, and *undeniable*. It is obvious to persons of every capacity. And we here declare our deliberate and settled conviction, from a careful and thorough examination of the matter, that there has never been any such repeal or amendment; hence, that our obligation, and that of all men, to keep the Sabbath of the fourth commandment, remains without the least abatement. "Till heaven and earth pass," we believe, according to the declaration of the Saviour, "one jot or one tittle shall in no wise pass from the law, till all be fulfilled." We alledge, then, fearless of successful contradiction, that it *never has been so repealed* or *amended*, and hence *is now binding* upon the entire family of man.

VII. From the nature of the case, and from God's declared will, and procedure in other cases on scriptural record, it is evident that the same divine authority is attached to *the day* of the week to be observed, as belongs to the *institution itself*, so that there is no room to say, that if a *seventh part* of time is observed as a holy rest, it is not essential which day of the week is selected. When God appointed the Passover to be kept on the fourteenth day of the first month at even, the time of keeping it could not be changed to the thirteenth or fifteenth of the month, without disregarding his authority. There was, indeed, a specified case in which those who were not in the prescribed circumstances to keep the fast at the time appointed, might celebrate it on the fourteenth day of the second month at even. But without this express divine provision, no departure from the first arrangement would have been allowable. And when God commanded Saul to slay the Amalekites, without exception, together with the sheep and the cattle, it did not answer for him to spare their king, and "the best of the sheep and the oxen for sacrifice." For this deviation from the course prescribed, God pronounced him a transgressor, and visited him in judgment, declaring that "to obey is better than sacrifice, and to hearken than the fat of rams." So when God instituted a weekly Sabbath, and specified the seventh day for that purpose, assigning a special and appropriate reason, it was manifestly his will that that particular day should be observed; and the substitution of another day, without subsequent instruction to that effect, cannot be reconciled with a due regard for his supreme authority. It is "changing the ordinance, and breaking the everlasting covenant."

VIII. It is evident that the substitution of the *first* day of the week for the *seventh*, as a weekly Sabbath, which has been adopted by the major part of the professors of Christianity, has presented, and continues to present, a formidable obstacle to the conversion of the Jews, and the introduction of the millennium. It is well known, that the Jews as a body are exceedingly tenacious of the Sabbath of the fourth commandment; that, with few exceptions, they have persevered from ancient times in its observance; and that they consider it a prominent article in the religion of their forefathers. This practice has been unbroken in the nation from the time of the giving of the law upon Mount Sinai till the present day. There have been, indeed, many instances of Sabbath-breaking among them, and at present there is reason to believe that the motives which govern them in its observance are sadly deficient. But the *practice itself* is tenaciously adhered to, as required by the unrepealed law of the God of Israel. And, if our views are correct, they have the right of the case, and the majority of Christians have corrupted the law. This, therefore, is a formidable obstacle to their embracing Christianity. To become *first-day* Christians (and such compose a vast majority of professors) they must relinquish or change one of the precepts of the Decalogue, and dissent from a custom held sacred by their ancestors, and deeply venerated by themselves; and that, too, without seeing any *divine warrant* produced for such a departure. This unauthorized practice of keeping the first instead of the seventh day of the week, cannot fail to prove a powerful objection in their view to embracing the gospel of Jesus Christ. It is true that they are tenacious also of other practices enjoined in the Old Testament, which Christians justly regard as obsolete. But as to *these*, we can show authority for their *abrogation*. We can appeal to the New Testament records, and show that the Mosaic *ritual*, "the law of commandments contained in ordinances," which constituted the enmity or separation between Jews and Gentiles, was abolished by the death of Christ—that "he took it out of the way, nailing it to his cross." But the same course cannot be successfully pursued with respect to the seventh-day Sabbath. The Decalogue in which this is found was not included in the abrogated ritual. It is altogether a distinct thing. wherefore the Jews cannot be met in the same way with regard to the weekly Sabbath as they can with regard to the typical observances which had their accomplishment in Christ. Hence the stumbling-block remains. And yet those who observe the first day are generally praying for and expecting the conversion of the Jews, and, in connection therewith, the millennial glory of the church. What an inconsistency is this! While they are praying for their national conversion and return to the land of their forefathers, and are beginning to use some other means for that end, they, by their palpable violation of the law of the fourth commandment, place a most formidable obstacle in their way, and pursue a course calculated to augment their prejudices, confirm their unbelief, and retard the approach of millennial glory. To bring Jews and Gentiles together in the observance of the Sabbath, the one party or the other must materially change their practice. And which is it most reasonable to expect will ultimately be compelled to make the change—the *Jews*, who have the authority of God's example and express precept to sustain them, or the *Gentiles*, who can claim no such authority for a first-day Sabbath? Surely, we need not be at a loss for an answer. It is confidently believed, that this subject has no inconsiderable bearing upon the condition and prospects of the Jews. If a few conversions are now effected among them, what might be expected if Christians would remove the stumbling-blocks which their own errors have placed in their way? Would we enter an effectual plea in behalf of this wonderful and long-neglected people, we know not how we could do it better than to plead for the observance of the Sabbath of the fourth commandment. Let those whose "heart's desire and prayer to God for Israel is," like Paul's, "that they might be saved," give this subject a thorough and impartial consideration, and return to the path of strict obedience.

IX. It is not to be expected, that an effectual check can be put to the sin of Sabbath-breaking, till the duty of keeping the Sabbath is so taught, understood, and practiced, that the sanction of express divine authority can be brought to bear upon it. Though a weekly rest be profitable, both as it respects "the life that now is, and that which is to come," there is much in the carnal views and inclinations of men to oppose it, to resist its restrictions, and to thwart its purposes. Hence powerful considerations and inducements are necessary to suppress its desecration, and insure its proper observance. Not only the *unbelieving world*, but *Christians*, in their present imperfect state, need to have this institution thoroughly guarded to prevent its abuse. If it be considered as resting upon *doubtful authority;* if it be viewed as sustained merely by *inference*, and the *premises* from which the inference is drawn be at best questionable, and do not *necessarily* authorize it; if the principal argument for it be founded on a supposed apostolic example of meeting for public worship on the first day of the week, which is sustained only by *two* passages, while those *very passages* fail to mark it as *a Sabbath*, or to give the least intimation of its having been introduced as *a substitute* for the former Sabbath, and even fail to imply, necessarily, that meetings of this description were *stated* and *general* in the churches in the apostolic age; and if it be found, from subsequent ecclesiastical history, that the first day, called Sunday and Lord's day, was not regarded by Christians in the first centuries after the apostles as *a Sabbath*, nor as *substituted therefore*, but only as a *festival* in commemoration of the resurrection—a *festival* observed in connection with the Sabbath, but not accompanied with a *resting from worldly labor*, till the time of Constantine the Great; yea, if but a part of those who are considered experimental Christians, look upon it *now* as properly *a Sabbath*, or day of *holy rest*, while others regard it merely as a day for *public worship*, and even such as call it a Sabbath conceive, in many instances, that the *strict* observance formerly required is somewhat *modified;* we can easily perceive, that it wants that *explicit sanction*—that *high* and *overpowering authority*—which will be likely to awe the public into obedience—which is necessary, indeed, to give Christians themselves a proper sense of its sanctity, and of the evil of its desecration—to induce them "not to do their own ways, nor to find their own pleasure, nor to speak their own words," in it. In vain do its friends procure for it the resolutions of churches and synods, the essays of the learned, and the decrees of the State; if it fails of being expressly supported by the supreme authority of God, to whom all must render a final and strict account, it will lack the main motive to obedience—it will be unattended with that power which, above all others, acts upon the conscience, and makes men feel their obligation. And as such authority does not pertain to a first-day Sabbath, but is limited to the seventh day, it is manifest that no thorough check to Sabbath desecration can be imposed, till men change their views and practice, and place the institution on its original and proper basis.

X. The power of custom, though sustained by ecclesiastical and civil enactments, and with corresponding forfeitures and penalties, ought not to prevent investigation and discourage reform in this important matter. When the claims of the original Sabbath are plainly presented, many seem to be convinced of their justness; but, at the same time, think that a general return to the observance of the seventh day is impracticable. They alledge that the custom of keeping the first day has been so long and so generally maintained—that it is so intimately wrought into the habits, calculations, and business of life—that it has received such explicit sanction from the civil powers, obedience thereto being required by the authority of the State, and the disobedient being subjected to civil pains and penalties—and that it is so often, ably, and pointedly vindicated by the first ministers, professors, and commentators in the popular churches, that it is in vain to expect a change, and that the cause of Sabbath-keeping is rather retarded than promoted by efforts to change the present custom. And it is highly probable that some, in view of these difficulties, forbear to give the subject a close investigation. But if the same views and modes of reasoning had been adopted in other cases, what would have become of the various reformations which are now established, and even triumphant? What would have become of the whole subject of *Protestantism?* There is nothing more impracticable in a Sabbath reform than in any other reform. In other cases, difficulties which at first seemed insurmountable, have given way to laborious, prayerful, and united efforts. And there is the same reason to believe that they will give way in this, if a proper zeal is once awakened, and the friends of the Sabbath are resolved to examine the subject, build on the foundation of truth, and persevere in their labors, with union and vigor, relying upon the protecting power and blessing of Israel's God. It is manifest that no earthly consideration should impede our investigation of this matter, that no array of opposition and discouragement should daunt us, and that no motives to sit still or pass along with the current of public opinion, if that be not founded in truth, should be suffered to influence us, and detain us in the wilderness of error. The cause of obedience is the cause of God, and we should steadfastly labor to promote it, and trust in him for ultimate victory.

XI. As a consequence of the foregoing principles and facts, we are constrained to regard those who observe the first day of the week, to the neglect of the seventh day, as having sadly deviated from the path of obedience, and we feel ourselves bound to admonish them, and labor respectfully and kindly to reclaim them. We cannot think it *immaterial* what day of the week is observed as a day of rest, when God has specified the seventh, and *no other*, as a weekly Sabbath. We cannot think it a small matter to substitute the first day in the room of the seventh, although it be done in honor of the resurrection of our Lord, and because that event appears to demand equal and even greater commemoration than the work of creation, so long as there is no divine warrant therefor. This appears to us to be making the wisdom of man the foundation of duty, and not the wisdom of God. We discover *two* evils here; first, changing *the day* without order or permission from God; and, secondly, changing *the reason* for the institution, when the Lord hath not spoken. And is not this a departure from the rule of duty? And has not the Lord a controversy with Zion for this? If God had seen fit to substitute the first day for the seventh day, on account of the resurrection, (supposing it to have occurred on the first day, which, however, is not certain,) and to assign another reason than the original one for keeping the Sabbath, he would doubtless have given order to that effect. His not having done so, makes it manifest that he did not see fit to do this, and that he considered the former Sabbath as well adapted to celebrate the work of redemption as it was the work of creation—adapted perfectly to subserve *all the purposes* of a weekly Sabbath. And we find this to be the case by experience. Here, therefore, we rest satisfied with the divine arrangement, and feel deeply the importance of universal conformity thereto. Consequently, our regard for the honor of God, and for the sabbatic institution, induces us to bring this subject in the present form before the Christian public. We do not think that we are justly chargeable with opposing or retarding the practice of Sabbath-keeping, because we protest against keeping the first day of the week as a divine institution, and faithfully present the claims of the original Sabbath. What better course can we take to secure a proper observance of the Sabbath, than to labor to restore it as God originally made it? It is not just to charge us with *Judaizing*—with virtually denying that Christ has come in the flesh and introduced the New Testament dispensation. We might as well be charged with this for maintaining that men should not "have any other God before the Lord," or that they should "not kill," nor "steal." These precepts are in close connection with that requiring the observance of the seventh-day Sabbath, and *stand or fall with it.* The truth of the case is, that the law containing the weekly Sabbath is the law both of the Old Testament and of the New. There is no Christian Sabbath distinct from the Sabbath of the fourth commandment. If this be a correct view—and we see not how it can be gainsayed—we in this respect perform our duty as subjects of God's moral government only when we exhort men to "remember the Sabbath day, to keep it holy," and when we labor to impress them with the annexed fact, that "the seventh day is the Sabbath."

These are some of our Reasons for introducing the subject of the Sabbath, as originally given, to your consideration. And we seriously ask you, whether they are not *sufficient*—whether they are not *adequate* for earnestly and perseveringly inviting investigation and reformation. If there be any blame attached to us in the matter, it is for not having labored more diligently and efficiently in this cause. Are we not clearly bound, by way of promoting inquiry and reform, to bear a more pointed testimony against the evil in question, and to vindicate the claims of the seventh-day Sabbath with more zeal and firmness than ever before? Are we not peculiarly obligated to labor to remove, if possible, the veil which is upon the minds of the great majority of professors of Christianity, correct the false notions received by tradition from 'the Fathers,' and effectually dispel the delusion so extensively prevailing. We do not claim the right of dictating to the consciences of others. "To their own Master they stand or fall." The only ground which we would assume is that which was occupied by the Apostle Paul when he said, "It is written, I have believed, and therefore have I spoken; we also believe, and therefore speak." And also by the Saviour, "Let your light so shine before men, that they may see your good works, and glorify your Father which is in Heaven." And again, "Whatsoever ye would that men should do to you, do ye even so to them; for this is the law and the prophets." Surely, "the Lord hath spoken, and who can but prophesy?" How can we bear to see one of his commandments made void by human tradition?—to see the flock of Jesus divided concerning this question, where union is so necessary and desirable?—to witness the unavoidable interruptions occasioned by the different parties, and the triumph of the adversaries of religion?—to observe those for whom Christ died grossly misled by mistaken teachers, provoking the Most High by neglecting to keep a day which he has made sacred, and transferring the sacredness of his own appointment to an ordinance of men, or, what is still worse, regarding the original institution as annulled, and placing in its stead a day merely of memorial of the resurrection and of worship, divested of the main characteristics of the Sabbath, and resting upon no solid basis—its foundation, at best, being *mere probability* and *conjecture?* Must it not, of necessity, be very painful to us, to see those who are our neighbors, and by profession our fellow Christians, in a case so clear and important, and involving such high and permanent interests, contented with such evidence as they would blush to introduce in relation to almost any other point? How can we bear to see *Protestants*, whose avowed maxim is, that "scriptural authority alone is sufficient to determine matters of faith and duty," dispensing with their own rule, in not requiring expressly a "thus saith the Lord" for their practice, and relying upon far-fetched and inconclusive reasonings, and mere probabilities—yea, in some instances, by their own concession, going out of the Bible to ecclesiastical history, to find a warrant for observing the first day of the week, which warrant itself, even if proof from that source were allowable, is by no means adequate?

Do we talk of reforming the church, while the guilt of disobedience in this matter rests upon the great majority of her members?—while ministers, doctors, and professors of divinity, break one of the commandments of the Decalogue, and teach men so, and the multitude are willingly obedient to their instructions? It is *preposterous!* A thorough reformation cannot be effected under such circumstances, or while things remain thus. It is time that it were more deeply laid to heart, that one of the leading objects of Christ's mission was to "save his people from their sins"—that "he gave himself for us, that he might redeem us from all iniquity, and purify unto himself a peculiar people, zealous of good works"—and that "he that saith, I know him, and keepeth not his commandments, is a liar, and the truth is not in him?" In view of such passages, although it be admitted that occasional mistakes and sins, being repented of, do not absolutely divest men of the Christian character and hopes, it will appear, that obedience to the will of God is an indispensable requisite and all-absorbing consideration; and that, if any man be in Christ, he is verily "a new creature"—that he will be "zealous of good works." One in ancient times, who was eminent for his religious knowledge, observed, "Then shall I not be ashamed, when I have respect unto *all* thy commandments." And this respect, or obedience, which constitutes the moral purity and glory of Christians, and is the test of their discipleship, must be regulated and governed by the precepts of that very law which contains the seventh-day Sabbath. There are, indeed, some precepts peculiar to the gospel, such as "repentance towards God, and faith towards our Lord Jesus Christ," "Baptism," and "the Lord's Supper." Nevertheless, "the commandments of God," so often and so particularly alluded to as the rule of Christian duty, are eminently the precepts of the Decalogue—the "*ten words*" or "*testimonies*" which God spake with his own mouth, and wrote with his own finger, and no one of which has ever been erased from the sacred code, or undergone the least alteration; for "the law of the Lord is *perfect*, converting the soul." The keeping of the weekly Sabbath, therefore, as God appointed it, and has continued it, enters vitally into the matter of holy obedience—the true test of Christianity. If the prescriptions of the fourth commandment are not faithfully adhered to, our obedience is imperfect. We are the proper subjects of reprehension, and may reasonably expect corresponding tokens of Divine displeasure. Sabbath-keeping is peculiarly adapted to serve as a test of loyalty to God, on account of its frequent occurrence, the weekly remission which it requires of secular business, the peremptory call which it makes on us to leave all our own works and ways for the special service of God, and the opportunity which it affords, amidst the common hurry and bustle of this world, to pause and examine our state and prospects for eternity. It is well calculated for this, because it so clearly and so often teaches us that the will of God should govern all our actions. All these and similar considerations, therefore, should combine to fix our attention to the very day of God's appointment, so that we may sensibly feel that we are governed by a divine warrant, and have the sublime pleasure of knowing that we are conforming to the will of God. Taking this course, we not only preserve a good conscience, but tread in the footsteps of God's redeemed flock. We imitate those who, in the times of the Old Testament, "took pleasure in his holy day." We follow the example of the Redeemer himself, who was a strict observer of the Sabbath of the fourth commandment. His vindication of the disciples in the case of "plucking the ears of corn" to satisfy their hunger, which some have thought was a deviation from the strictness originally required, was in perfect accordance with the true intent and meaning of the law, else his obedience would have been imperfect, and thereby the entire prospects of the Christian would have been blasted. Under the circumstances, it was a work of absolute necessity, and therefore not prohibited. As our Lord Jesus Christ was unquestionably a strict observer of the seventh-day Sabbath, it is a commanding motive for a continued observance of it by his followers, there being no substitute appointed.

The Apostles, also, and primitive Christians, were conscientious observers of this institution as originally delivered. The Sabbath so often mentioned in the apostolic records is unquestionably the seventh-day Sabbath. Who will dare deny this? And from ecclesiastical history it appears that the whole Christian church, with very few exceptions at most, kept the seventh-day Sabbath, in obedience to the law contained in the Decalogue, down to the time of Constantine, in the fourth century, and even afterward. So true it is, that we imitate the church in her primitive and purest times, in keeping the Sabbath of the fourth commandment. Under such circumstances, therefore, is it strange that we should strenuously advocate the practice?—that we should adhere to it amidst reproaches, privations, and suffering?—and that we should feel the most ardent desire for the reformation of our brethren who differ from us? The cause is sufficient to demand this deep feeling, this unwearied effort, these prayers and tears, with a vast increase of holy sensibility, tenderness of conscience, and active labor, to promote this branch of obedience. We therefore earnestly, and with all due respect, commend the subject to your notice. Do not pass it by as a matter of little or no consequence. It surely involves much that should be dear to the friends of Jesus, and the advocates of pure morality—to such as would see the church appear "fair as the moon, clear as the sun, and terrible as an army with banners." We entreat you, therefore, for the glory of God, the honor of his law and government, the unity and perfection of the church, your own spiritual attainments and acceptance with God, the conversion and salvation of sinners, the triumph of truth over infidelity, the redemption of the long-neglected house of Israel, the hastening of millennial prosperity, and the recompenses of eternity, to give this subject a most serious consideration, to examine and weigh our proofs and arguments, and, if you find yourselves in error, as we confidently believe you will, to reform. With the high consideration in view, that "wisdom's ways are pleasantness, and all her paths are peace," and that to pursue them "is for your life," we invite and seek your recovery to sound views and practice in this matter. We "long after you in the bowels of Jesus Christ," regarding him as "the Lord of the Sabbath," not to repeal or change the sacred institution, but to protect it, and enforce obedience thereto. Firmly believing that "we are not without law to God, but under the law to Christ," we cannot by any means discharge our own convictions at this eventful period, this remarkable age of attempted reform, without using all the persuasion in our power to promote an investigation of this matter.

We behold with sincere gratification the efforts which have been made, and are being made, in regard to other subjects of special importance to the church and the world. We would cordially coöperate with their respective advocates in securing, as far as practicable, a strict obedience to other moral precepts, and in emancipating the human mind from sin and error. But we cannot forget that God has given a *fourth*, as well as a *first*, a *sixth*, a *seventh*, and a *tenth* commandment, and that it rests upon equal authority with those, and with either of the precepts of the Decalogue; and hence we plead in its behalf. We do this as moral and accountable beings, as Protestants, as Christians, as reformers, and as cotemporaries of our brethren in the nineteenth century, a period so distinguished for its moral and political enterprises, and for its proximity to the time when it shall be said, "The kingdoms of this world are become the kingdom of our Lord and of his Christ." We approach you in the belief that open rebuke is better than secret love"—that "faithful are the wounds of a friend"—and that we "should admonish one another daily, and so much the more as we see the day approaching." We feel bound to exert ourselves in this cause, in the belief that "our labor will not be in vain in the Lord," that the church is "coming up out of the wilderness," and that we live in the dawn of a brighter day, in a period of the world when the scriptures and the providences of God concur in affording the highest encouragement to the faithful advocates of truth and duty. And we do not hesitate to express our expectation, that by the blessing of God upon the well-directed and persevering labors of his people, and the continued and augmenting spirit of inquiry, there will soon be achieved a glorious reformation in respect to the subject of this Tract. God will "overturn, and overturn, and overturn, till He shall come, whose right it is," and "the sanctuary shall be cleansed."

Finally—we enter our testimony in what we deem an important case, in the hope, through grace, of meeting all "the faithful in Christ Jesus in the everlasting rest," of which the rest of the seventh day is a lively and touching type and foretaste.

Published by the American Sabbath Tract Society,
No. 9 Spruce Street, New York.

THE

SABBATH:

ITS MORAL NATURE AND OBSERVANCE

Section I.

THE SABBATH NOT CEREMONIAL.

It is disputed whether the weekly Sabbath is an essential part of what is generally called the Moral Law, which the Holy Ghost declares to be "spiritual —holy, and just, and good;" or whether it is to be classed among the ceremonial institutions, which were "a shadow of things to come." If the latter position can be established, it can be of no use whatever to perpetuate the Institution under the New Dispensation. It can neither be promotive of the spirituality and growth of the body of Christ, nor even conservative of the morals of the community. To suppose that the church cannot enjoy all necessary prosperity, and attain its millennial glory by the use of New Covenant ordinances alone, but must borrow a little help from the abrogated rites of the Old Economy, is most anti-evangelical. Gal. iii. 3. The church needs nothing for the nourishment of its piety, except such means as have the entire sanction of the "better covenant." Moses is dead, and the Lord has buried him. He cannot lead us into the promised inheritance. We have only to follow our Joshua, even Jesus, "the Son who is consecrated forevermore."

Nor can "the weak and beggarly elements" be of service to promote the morals of the community. Where do we find the most elevated and pure morality, that which is refined from all selfishness? We find it only in real Christians. The source, and life, and power of it is the Atonement of their Great High-Priest, and the grace which is by Him. Their obedience to all moral precepts is the obedience of *faith*, even faith in his sacrifice. In proportion as their faith is strong, and their dependence on Him entire, to the exclusion of all reliance upon their own merit, so is their moral conduct irreproachable. It is not by any resort to the "weak and unprofitable commandment," that their morality acquires such excellence. As for that inferior kind of morality, which obtains among unbelievers, however profitable it may be to human society, it is but the mimic representation of that which is practiced by the godly. For its very existence it is dependent on Christianity, from whose influence if it recede, it becomes withered and perishes. Transplanted to a heathen soil, it cannot live. As, therefore, the general morals of the community are traceable to the gospel as their first cause, and are kept in credit only by its nurturing influence, it would be at war with sound reason to suppose, that they could be promoted by such things as are destructive of the purity of the gospel itself. They will be much safer, if left wholly to the nurturing influence of that system, which is declared to be 'complete and faultless,—the power and the wisdom of God.' Wherefore, if the weekly Sabbath was a ceremonial Institution, we have no use for it, either as it respects the church, or the world. It is an injury rather than a benefit.

But if, on the other hand, the Sabbath is a part of God's holy, and just, and good law, to which nothing but the carnal mind refuses subjection, Rom. viii. 7, it must be an institution of lasting value, to dispense with which is dangerous in the extreme. For the transgression of this law is sin, 1 John iii. 4, and the wages of sin is death, Rom. vi. 23.

That the Sabbath was not a ceremonial institution, is proved from the fact that it was given to man before his Apostacy, Gen. ii. 1–3. There he had no need of a Redeemer, for he bore the image of his Maker in righteousness and true holiness. If man in his original state of uprightness had no need of a Redeemer, he certainly had no need of a type of the Redeemer. Types, in such a case, were unmeaning things, or else a source of vexation and horrible forebodings. If he understood their meaning, he could never look upon them, without thinking of the awful ruin into which he must soon be plunged by the fall. But this would both operate as a discouragement to all endeavors at steadfastness, and at the same time would exhibit the All-Benevolent God as marring the happiness of an innocent creature ;—an idea never to be admitted. We conclude, therefore, that the Sabbath, as originally instituted, possessed nothing of a ceremonial character. Typical institutions were introduced *after* the fall, to explain to ruined man the nature of that redemption of which he stood in need, and which in the fulness of the time would be provided for him. They were for his encouragement and consolation :—not to mar his happiness, but to promote it.

To evade the force of this argument, some contend that the Sabbath was not actually instituted and given to man in Paradise ; that the sanctification of it mentioned by Moses, signifies only that appointment then made of the seventh day, to be afterwards solemnized and sanctified by the Jews. But the utter futility of this objection appears from our Savior's declaration that "the Sabbath was made for man." Mark ii 27. If it was made for man, it was made for him *as* man; the very word denoting mankind at large, or rather, referring to the first man as the representative of the whole human race. It was made for him as a human, rational, intelligent creature; for his benefit *as such*, without reference to the particular nation or country to which he might belong. If it was made for his benefit, is it reasonable to suppose that it was, nevertheless, kept in abeyance for twenty-five hundred years? Made for man, and yet not given to him! The world teeming with human beings, and yet the very institution that was designed for their temporal and spiritual welfare, kept from them for more than two thousand years, and then given only to an isolated people forming but a fraction of the human race! The idea is monstrous absurdity. An institution so important to the interests of humanity, of civilization, and of religion, was wanted immediately, as well as at the distance of two thousand years afterwards.

The objection is farther confuted by a consideration of the reason which enforces the institution. The reason is, "that God rested on the seventh day from all his work which he had made." The natural inference is, that the institution existed from the time the reason of it did. Human legislators, it is true, may not enact a law, until long after a good reason exists for doing so; because they may be blind to the existence of such a reason, and slow to discover it. But not so with God. If the work of creation, and his resting from it on the seventh day, is at any period of the world a good reason tnat man should rest on that day, it was a good reason from the beiginning. It was good as soon as there were men to do it. So that what was then their reasonable service, could not have been deferred for twenty-five hundred years. Nay, it may be safely affirmed, that the reason for keeping the Sabbath possessed more cogency at the beginning than it did afterwards. For in after ages sin had marred and defaced the Almighty's work. Nevertheless, if when sin had marred it, there was still good reason for keeping the memorial of it, much more was there good reason for doing so, when it was in all its original glory. In what respect does or did this reason concern the Jews more than any otner part of mankind? Do not Gentiles stand on the same level with them in respect of their being a part of God's creation? Have they not as much interest in creation as the Jews? "Is He the God of the Jews only? Is He not of the Gentiles also?"

The reasons for such institutions as were enjoined on the Jews particularly, were derived from considerations in which they as a people had a special and peculiar interest. Now the Sabbath, it is true, is in one place enforced upon them by a consideration of this kind, viz. their redemption from bondage in Egypt, Deut. v. 15. But while this laid the Jews under a special and peculiar obligation to regard the institution, it does not forbid the idea that they were also under obligations of a general nature, which concern all mankind alike. So too, the Christian church is under a special obligation too keep this sacred day, because of its interest in the blood of redemption. But to infer from this, that the common obligation under which all others are held is canceled, and that none are bound to keep it except the blood-bought church of God, would be in the last degree illogical, as well as unscriptural.

Let it be observed, that the language of the sacred historian: "God blessed the seventh day and sanctified it"—is no more qualified, than that which speaks of his resting. With reference to this, his language is explicit,—"He rested on the seventh day from all his work which he had made." In face of such a declaration, nothing but folly would say, that God did not actually rest on the seventh day of creation, but waited until the Jews were called out of Egypt. God certainly did rest on the seventh day of creation. If the ordinary construction of language is to be employed in reference to this, it must be employed in reference to his blessing and sanctifying it also. Wherefore, as God rested on the seventh day of creation, he blessed and sanctified that day, even that very day on which he rested. "God blessed the seventh day, and sanctified it, because that in *it*, [the very day which he so blessed and sanctified,] he had rested from all his work which God created and made." Gen. ii. 3.

The act of blessing and sanctifying the day can import nothing else than constituting it a Sabbath. For to sanctify, undoubtedly, is to set apart for a holy use. It refers to some line of conduct to be observed by men towards that day. The expression, "God blessed it," must mean that he rendered it a day peculiarly happy and beneficial for man. For whenever God blesses an object, whether it be a person or an inanimate thing—a rational creature or the brute creation—he connects with his blessing certain favors which would otherwise not be bestowed, and renders the object serviceable for the promotion of certain purposes which would not result without his blessing. A few examples will render this perfectly clear. Thus, when he blessed the first human pair, and the brute creation, he bestowed on them the power to be "fruitful and multiply." When the ground receiveth blessing from God, it bringeth forth herbs, meet for them by whom it is dressed. When it is cursed, it bears thorns and briars, Heb. vi. 7, 8. Gen. xxvii. 27. Lev. xxv. 21. Mal. iii. 10. When God blessed Abraham, he bestowed on him a numerous posterity, with Canaan for an inheritance, and counted his faith for righteousness. In blessing Samson, Judges xiii. 24, he endowed him with an heroic spirit, singular valor, miraculous strength of body, and all other gifts and graces necessary to his calling. When he blesses the church, he bestows spiritual blessings in Christ, Eph. i. 3. Numerous other examples might be adduced: but these are sufficient to show, that in connection with the Divine blessing, special favors are always bestowed. We therefore argue, that when it is said, "God blessed the seventh day," it can mean nothing less than that he connected with it favors and benefits above what are connected with any other day, and that he bestows them abundantly upon those who keep it, and delight in it, Isa. lviii. 13. He renders the day serviceable for the promotion of the spiritual and temporal welfare of man. For it can by no means be supposed, that God proposed to render homage to himself, or to bless himself. It must be man, for whom the Sabbath was made, Mark ii. 27, that stands in need of the blessing, and who is bound to make a holy use of the day.

The foregoing remarks are judged sufficient to destroy the notion of the Sabbath being a ceremonial institution. But we will not yet dismiss the subject. If it was a ceremony, why was its importance magnified above all the other ceremonies? Why that pre-eminence and sanctity, which it had above all other types? It rears its head high above all the ritual institutions, and holds this superiority throughout the whole Mosaic Economy. Not only is it counted worthy of being graven by the finger of God upon the stone tablets, thus having the same honor as all the other precepts of the Decalogue, which are confessedly moral; but even where it appears in combination with the ceremonial usages, its great importance as a moral institute directed to the highest ends, is clearly exhibited.

"For first, after the record of the promulgation of the Decalogue, three chapters of judicial statutes follow; but in the midst of these, the people are reminded of the essential importance of the Sabbath, in a manner quite distinct and peculiar. It is associated with the primary duty of worshiping the one true God, as of equal obligation, and indeed as necessary to it. 'Six days shalt thou do thy work, and on the seventh thou shalt rest, * * in all things that I have said unto thee, be circumspect, and make no mention of the name of other gods, neither let it be heard out of thy mouth,' Exod. xxiii. 12, 13. This is sufficiently remarkable.

"Again, after six chapters more concerning the tabernacle and its various sacrifices, the whole communication of the forty days' abode on the mount is concluded with a re-inculcation of the Sabbath-rest, in a manner the most solemn and affecting. 'And the Lord spake unto Moses saying, verily my Sabbath ye shall keep; for it is a sign between me and you throughout your generations, THAT YE MAY KNOW THAT I AM THE LORD THAT DOTH SANCTIFY YOU. Ye shall keep the Sabbath, therefore, for it is holy unto you; every one that defileth it shall surely be put to death; for whosoever doeth any work therein, that soul shall be cut off from among his people. Six days may work be done; but in the seventh is the Sabbath of rest, holy to the Lord; whosoever doeth any work in the Sabbath-day, he shall surely be put to death. Wherefore the children of Israel shall keep the Sabbath, to observe the Sabbath throughout their generations, for a perpetual covenant. It is a sign between me and the children of

Israel forever, for in six days the Lord made heaven and earth, and on the seventh day he rested and was refreshed.' Exod. xxxi. 12—17. Can any thing give dignity to the sacred day, as founded in the essential relation of man to his Maker and Redeemer, if this sublime language does not? Every idea of sanctification, every sense of importance from a sign of a covenant between God and man, every sanction derived from the awful punishment of death, unite to impress upon us the duty; whilst the proportion noted between the working days and the day of rest, and the reason drawn from the order of creation, extend the obligation to every human being."*

This great prominence which the Sabbath had amidst all the ceremonial laws, was equivalent to an intimation that the ritual service must never take the precedence of moral duties; that in the multitude of their offerings and shadowy service, the worshipers must still remember that true holiness does not consist in them, but in something higher; and that all their conformity to the ritual service must proceed upon moral footing, otherwise it is abomination in the sight of God.

But come with me, reader, a little farther, and see how the scriptures magnify the Sabbath at the very time they comparatively underrate the importance of ceremonial observances. Compare carefully Isa. i. 11—14, with chapters lvi. 1—8, and lviii. 13, 14, of the same prophecy. See how in the one case the ritual service is degraded, and in the other the Sabbath is exalted, and the holy keeping of it made the condition on which depends the acceptance of their burnt-offerings and sacrifices. Consider the language of Jeremiah. chap. xvii. 192—7. Read the passage

* Wilson.

with care, and see how all the prosperity of the nation, all the favor of God, is suspended on this one branch of moral obedience; with which compare his language concerning ceremonial observances. "For I spake not unto your fathers, nor commanded them in the day that I brought them out of the land of Egypt, concerning burnt-offerings or sacrifices: But this thing commanded I them, saying, Obey my voice, and I will be your God, and ye shall be my people; and walk ye in all the ways that I have commanded you, that it may be well unto you," Jer. vii. 22, 23. A comparison of these passages shows that Sabbath-breaking stood upon the same level with the breach of all moral precepts, and characterized them as a disobedient and rebellious people; while the neglect of ceremonial observances is classed in a different category. Ezekiel follows in the same strain, chap. xx. 12, 13, 16. In the book of Psalms too, we have the Sabbath and its holy duties and pleasures extolled, Ps. xcii, while ceremonies are depreciated, Ps. l. 8, 14, li. 16, 17. And what was the great reformation which the prophets after the captivity sought to accomplish? Was not Sabbath-breaking the crying sin upon which they dwelt? Look at the holy zeal of Nehemiah. His faithful and searching rebukes proceed not upon their omission of ceremonial duties, but upon their neglect of the great and paramount duty of keeping the Sabbath, Neh. xiii. 15, 21, 22. In view of these scripture references, does the Sabbath look like a ceremony—a shadow—a mere element of the world, weak and beggarly!

Again, if the Sabbath was a part of the ceremonial law, why was Christ at such pains to regulate the manner of observing it? Matt. xii. 1, 13. Why so careful to modify the false usages that obtained?

Why did he lay down distinctions between what is lawful to be done, and what is unlawful? Was this his manner when any thing ceremonial was the subject of dispute? Do we not find him, in such cases, waiving the subject at issue, in order to inculcate matters of lasting importance? How was it in his interview with the Samaritan woman? John iv. Her question in regard to the proper place of worship was merely of a ceremonial nature, yet it had been hotly disputed between her nation and the Jews. Does Jesus become an umpire in the case? No. The ceremonial institutions were about to vanish away; He himself came to end them. Therefore he occupies himself, not in settling the litigated questions that grew out of them, but in preaching great and everlasting truths. In regard to the Moral Law, however, he is at especial pains to vindicate it from all Pharisaic austerities, to remove all false glosses, and to assert its everlasting equity and glory. Witness his admirable exposition of it in his sermon on the mount. Witness too, his exposure of the hypocritical tradition concerning the fifth commandment, Matt. xv. 1—9. With this, his vindication of the Sabbath, his care to purge it from traditional corruptions, is perfectly parallel. But what sane mind ever thought that he proclaimed the fifth commandment to be of a ceremonial nature? Yet, strange to say, the precisely similar course which he took in regard to the Sabbath, has, by some, been made an argument that he abolished it as nothing but a Jewish ceremony.

'But drowning men catch at straws.' In spite of the overwhelming proof that the Sabbath had its origin before ceremonial observances could, with any reason, have been introduced, it is contended that it must have been merely a Mosaic institution, because no mention is made of its observance from the creation down to the time of the exodus of the Israelites from Egypt. It is asked, 'whether men during all that time, though otherwise so wicked, sanctified the Sabbath so universally and perfectly, that not one among them ever needed an excitement to duty, or a reproof for the neglect of it.' But to this question, however triumphantly proposed, we are as ready to answer, No, as the objector himself. That the great mass of men, during all this time, were wicked and sinners before the Lord exceedingly, is admitted. But because they were not particularly reproved for Sabbath-breaking, no more proves that it was not a sin cognizable by the moral law, than the fact of God's winking at the times of the Gentiles' ignorance and idolatry, Acts xvii. 30, proves that their conduct was not cogniza ble as a sin against his law. If God passed over the Sabbath-breaking of those who lived in the first ages of the world without particularly taking notice of it, the same may be said of his carriage towards the Gentile world, in reference to *all* their wickedness for four thousand years. Besides, is not the drunkeness of Noah passed over without reproof? Is not Lot's incest with his daughters?—and Jacob's cheating Esau of the patrimony?—and the plurality of the patriarchs' wives? Were these things not contrary to the Di vine Law, because they were "winked at?" Or, to come to cases still more in point, we observe that the silence of scripture respecting the observance of the Sabbath during the ante-Mosaic age, is no more than what occurs in regard to the period between Moses and the time of David, near four hundred years. Yet who ever doubted that it was observed during all this time? So also the rite of circumcision is not so much as alluded to from a little after the death of Moses, till the days of Jeremiah, a period of eight hundred years or more. Nor is the ordinance of the red heifer once mentioned from the Pentateuch till the close of the Old Testament. But who doubts the constant observance of these ceremonies? The objection, therefore, which is raised from the silence of Scripture, has no force whatever.

But whoever considers the very concise manner in which events are narrated in scripture, and that the history of two thousand years is all compressed within the compass of fifty short chapters, occupying about as many pages, will cease to wonder that no notice is taken of the observance of the Sabbath by the pious patriarchs. This very conciseness is a sufficient solution to a candid mind, without resorting to the supposition that there was no observance of the institution Moreover, any one that peruses with attention the accounts of pious characters contained in the word of God, will see that no express mention is made of their acts of religion, unless something remarkable attaches to them.* Abraham's faith is mentioned, because it was remarkable. So of Abel, of Noah, and of Enoch. But in regard to their observance of the Sabbath in particular, it is not probable that any thing remarkable or extraordinary was connected with it, rendering it of sufficient importance to the world at large to be recorded.

The position that we have taken is, that the Sabbath was instituted in Paradise, when man was innocent; that it was binding before Judaism had any existence. We have seen that the silence of scripture as to any reproof given to the transgressor of it, does not shake this position; that its silence as to any commendation bestowed upon the pious for keeping it, does not shake it; and that its entire silence is no more than what obtains with regard to the Sabbath

* Burnside.

from Moses to David, or with regard to circumcision from Joshua to Jeremiah, or with regard to the red heifer from Moses to the end of the Old Testament Is there any thing yet remaining to weaken the force of our arguments?

In the opinion of our opponents there is one thing more. It is argued, from Ex. xvi., that the Sabbath was first made known to the Israelites in the wilderness, by the falling of the manna. But we can discover nothing in the whole history of the matter, as given by Moses, which intimates that the Sabbath was then made known for the first. On the contrary, the abruptness of the reference implies very strongly the previous knowledge of it. This idea receives strong confirmation from the fact, that when the people were reminded of the institution, nothing was said to them concerning the reason of its being their duty to keep it; which would hardly have been the case. had the subject been then presented to them for the first time. For it is worthy of note, that God condescends to give the reason of this command; a thing which he does not for moral precepts in general. He gives the reason, because man cannot discover it for himself, it being purely a matter of revelation that God made the world in six days, and rested on the seventh. Whereas, other moral precepts are more readily discoverable from the light of nature. Now, if God condescends in any place, and at any time, to give the reason for a command, we might expect it would be at the time of its first promulgation. In Gen. ii., where we suppose the law to be first given, the reason accompanies it; but in the passage now under consideration it does not.

Again, it is nowhere in the context intimated that the object of giving the manna was to make known the Sabbath On the contrary, the declared object of supplying their wants in this miraculous manner, was to make the Israelites know that it was the Lord Jehovah who brought them out of Egypt, v. 6, and not Moses and Aaron, as they intimated, v. 3, to make them know that the Lord was their God, v. 12, and to prove them, whether they would manifest their gratitude for his merciful interposition in their favor, by walking in his law, or no, v. 4. This was the express and primary object. To make known the Sabbath is not even hinted as having been the *subordinate,* much less the *principal* object.

SECTION II.

ARGUMENT FROM THE DECALOGUE.

We commenced this essay with the design of showing that the Sabbath is a necessary part of the immutable law of God—that law which is "holy, and just, and good;" which is "spiritual;" to which nothing is opposed but that which is carnal. Hitherto, we have rested none of our proofs upon the fact, that it was incorporated in the Decalogue; that it is one of the TEN WORDS "which God spake in the Mount, out of the midst of the fire, of the cloud, and of the thick darkness, with a great voice; and he added no more." Deut. v. 22. For to assume that the Decalogue, as such, is the moral law, and that the Sabbath, because it makes a part of it, is therefore everlastingly binding, may not be satisfactory to some of our readers.

That the Decalogue, as such, held a peculiar aspect towards the Jews, different from that which it holds towards any others, is freely admitted. It made a part of their civil code; it was incorporated with their political laws, and, therefore, temporal penalties were annexed, which were inflicted by the civil magistrate. Offences against the most of its precepts were punishable by death, Sabbath-breaking not excepted. Hence some contend that these precepts ought not to be called, by way of eminence, "*the* Moral Law;" that the fact of their having been graven upon stone, and given under circumstances of greater pomp and glory than the other precepts of the Old Testament, constitutes no solid argument for their being so called. The greater glory of their promulgation from the Mount of God, is supposed to be sufficiently accounted for, by considering them as the *Constitution*, or *Grand Platform*, upon which was based the whole of that system which was peculiar to the Jews. The Decalogue, therefore, is supposed to bear about the same relation to the other precepts spoken by Moses, as *constitution* bears to *statute law*. This view is thought to be favored by those passages which call the stone tables "the tables of the Covenant." Heb. ix. 4. Hence, as they say, the Cove nant being abrogated, the tables of the Covenant are set aside also; on the same principle that when a political government is dissolved the constitution is of no farther use.

Upon this seemingly plausible argument we offer the following remarks:

1. Admitting that the Decalogue is the grand constitution of the Jewish polity, and that it has an excellence over the other precepts spoken by Moses, precisely like that of constitution over statute law; still we think it could not, in the nature of things, be any thing less than a code of morals. There was a necessity of the strongest kind, that it should embody all the essential elements of the moral law. For, as obedience to statute law must proceed from constitutional principles, so the obedience of the Israelites to the whole system of Moses must proceed upon moral

footing. Any other obedience than this—any obedience which is of an inferior kind, God does not require, and cannot, consistently with his holy nature. No matter what is the nature of the precepts He gives, obedience to them must be upon moral principle. A love for the great principles of righteousness must regulate it all; for this only is the pledge that they will rigidly, and without deviation, conform to any system that He enjoins upon them. Therefore, the Moral Law, or rather the essential elements of it, go before all the other laws He gave to the children of Israel. If they will keep this law, which they promised to do, Exod. xix. 8, it is a pledge that they will keep all the rest.

2. Though the covenant character of the Decalogue is abolished, by reason of the Sinaitic Covenant being entirely abrogated, the moral character of it remains untouched, and just the same as it was before a covenant was based upon it. Hence, though we are under no covenant obligation to its precepts, we are under a moral obligation to them. The Jews were under a covenant obligation to the Decalogue, brought upon them by the transaction at Sinai. But Jews and Gentiles were alike under moral obligation to its precepts, antecedently to the covenant made at Sinai. Let men learn to distinguish between covenant obligation and moral obligation, and they will have no difficulty on this point.*

3. If the covenant character of the Decalogue is abolished, and all covenant obligation destroyed along with it, of course those temporal penalties which

* "The Decalogue, as to the form of it, and as delivered through the hand and ministry of Moses, only concerned that people (Israel), and was calculated for their use; though, as to the matter of it, and so far as it is of a moral nature, and agrees with the law and light of nature, it is equally binding on the Gentiles."—*Dr. Gill.*

were annexed to its precepts are also abolished. But the moral penalty, the death of the soul, remains to be inflicted upon every impenitent transgressor Hence the Sabbath-breaker, as well as the idolator, the profane swearer, and the adulterer, though not obnoxious to death, as the despiser of Moses' law, is yet obnoxious to the curse of God, and must inherit it by being punished with everlasting destruction from His presence, and from the glory of His power.

What is it then? Not only do the ten commandments possess a moral character, independent of their inscription upon the stone tablets, as the grand constitutional platform of the Jewish Theocracy; but they possess this moral character BECAUSE they compose this constitution. For the constitution, as we have already proved, could not, in the nature of things, be any thing else than a summary of moral precepts. Therefore, as the Sabbath is one of these precepts, it is a part of the moral law, and remains of everlasting force and obligation.

In our defense of the ten commandments, we do *not* "contradistinguish them from the rest by calling the former exclusively *the* moral law, and all the other divine instructions of the Jews, through Moses, *the* ceremonial law." We not only admit, but strongly insist, that moral duties are inculcated elsewhere besides in the Decalogue. "When the Jews are told, Exod. xxii. 22, *Ye shall not afflict any widow or fatherless child*, we need no scholastic definitions to enable us to recognize this as a part of the moral code."* But we *do* suppose that the Decalogue comprises the *elementary principles* of the moral law. We suppose, that whatever moral duty is inculcated elsewhere, it is deducible from one or other of the ten

* Bap. Advocate of Jan. 16, 1841

commandments. We can hardly imagine a single condition in which it is possible for man to be placed in this life, or a relation that he sustains, which is not cognizable by this code.

Our doctrine receives strength from the prominence given to the Decalogue in the New Testament. No small degree of honor is put upon it by the Savior, in his Sermon on the Mount, an important part of that celebrated discourse being occupied with expositions of its precepts, and applications of them to the conduct of men, as the subjects of God's moral government. Again, when the young man came to Christ, and asked, "What good thing shall I do that I may inherit eternal life," he was told to keep the commandments. That by these were meant the precepts of the Decalogue, is evident from the Savior's immediately beginning to quote those precepts. Matt. xix. 16—19. The fact that they were enjoined with reference to *eternal* life, proves conclusively that their bearing was not merely upon the conduct of men as citizens of the Jewish commonwealth, but upon their conduct as moral and accountable creatures.* Again, when the Apostle inculcates those duties which are the mark of love to our neighbor, he quotes the precepts of the second table of the Decalogue. Rom. xiii. 9. It is evident, also, that Paul refers particularly to the Decalogue as the law which convinced him of sin. Rom. vii. 7. For he cites the tenth precept of it, as showing him that strong desire after things forbidden is sin. This is the commandment which, being powerfully applied to his heart, made sin to revive, and he died: ver. 9. Hence he in-

* Christ inculcates only the precepts of the second table of the law, not because they are of more importance than those of the first, but because they are less easily counterfeited. Such duties are by far too weighty to be permanently sustained by the hollow-heartedness of the hypocrite.

cludes the Decalogue, when he speaks of that law which is "spiritual, and holy, and just, and good:" vs. 12, 14; to which the carnal mind, refusing subjection, is therefore enmity against God. Rom. viii 7. One more example. Paul writing, not to Jews, but to converts from among the Gentiles, recognizes the usual arrangement of the Decalogue, and its validity as a rule of duty under the Gospel, when he says, concerning filial obedience, that it is the first commandment which has a promise annexed to it. Eph. vi. 1, 2. In the following verse he states what the promise is, presenting it as a motive to obedience. This proves that no commandment had been changed or dispossessed of its place.

In asserting the importance of the Decalogue, the reader will observe that we do not particularly insist upon the manner and circumstances of its promulgation. We dwell not upon the fact of its having been written with God's own finger upon stone, while Mosaic institutions were engrossed by Moses himself upon parchment. We dwell not upon the thunderings, lightnings, thick clouds, the loud blast of the trumpet, and the voice of Jehovah from the midst of the fire; all which conspire to throw around the ten commandments a glory not belonging to the ceremonial precepts. These things we pass, aware that men will evade the argument from them, by the supposition that they prove nothing more than that kind of superiority which the constitution of a state has over statute law. We can hardly refrain, however, from observing, as we pass, that as the ark was the throne of God, Exod. xxv. 22, Num. vii. 89, xvii. 4, Ps. xcix. 1—it is difficult to conceive how righteousness and judgment were the habitation of his throne, Ps xcvii. 2, if the "ten words" which were there deposited were not designed to be an expression of

His perfections, and the eternal rule of right to His creatures.

But we think we have placed the morality of the Decalogue upon grounds that cannot be successfully disputed. Having thus secured it, we advert to the foregoing circumstances, not as direct proof of the truth of our argument, but as so much collateral evidence. There is one circumstance, however, which ought not to be passed over lightly. The tables of stone were deposited in the ark, and covered over by the mercy seat. On the great day of atonement, when the High Priest entered into the Most Holy, he sprinkled the blood of the sacrifice upon this mercy seat, and upon the floor before it, thus making an atonement for the sins of the people. But did this blood in reality atone for the sins of the people against that law which was concealed under the mercy seat? No. Not only was it no atonement for moral offences, Heb. x. 4, but it was not even an atonement for their political violation of this code. For such violation, in regard to most of its precepts, was a capital crime, and could not be expiated under that covenant. The whole process, therefore, was typical or prefigurative of the grand atonement made for the sins of the world by Jesus Christ, the High-Priest of our profession. Heb. iii. 1. The argument derived from it in favor of the Decalogue is, that what the law by its offerings could not do, God, sending his own son in the likeness of sinful flesh, and for sin, condemned sin in the flesh. Rom. viii. 3. For Christ enters into the Most Holy, even unto Heaven itself, with his own blood, and makes a real atonement for sins. In other words, the legal sacrifices could not reach to sins against the Decalogue, but Christ's sacrifice did, and therefore the superiority of the gospel over the law is fully established. But the whole argument for the superiority of the Christian sacrifice becomes null and void, on the supposition that the atonement had reference to any other law than the Decalogue.

Now if the Decalogue, as a whole, has a claim to be called a summary of the moral law, the Sabbath derives in this way no small degree of authority. For it is a very important part of the Ten Words, standing right in the very heart of them, and bound up along with them; so that, whatever dignity and excellence the rest have, this has also. We are, therefore, driven to the conclusion, that when the Savior says, "One jot or one tittle shall in no wise pass from the law," the Sabbath is alluded to as much as any other precept. That when the Apostle teaches, the law is not made void through faith, Rom. iii. 31, he means, among other things, that the Sabbath is not made void by the gospel, but rather established. That when he says "the law is spiritual," Rom. vii. 14, he means that the Sabbath law, as well as all other precepts, is spiritual; and that none reject it but those who are "carnal, sold under sin."

But we shall hear it objected, that the fourth commandment is not transferred to the New Testament, and re-enacted there, while all the other commandments are. This, however, is taking a wrong view of the case, altogether. The truth is, that no moral precept is re-enacted in the New Testament. What necessity is there for re-enacting laws which never expired? The very notion of re-enacting implies their previous expiration. Wherefore, if those precepts of the moral law which we find in the New Testament are there for no other reason than because they are re-enacted, it follows that they must have expired with the Old Covenant. If they expired with it, they were peculiar to it, and must have had their origin in it. If they were peculiar to it, and originated in it, then all obligation to obey them was merely covenant obligation, while moral or natural obligation is supposed to have had no existence. But this conclusion is an absurdity, and if carried out still farther, leads to multiplied absurdities.

Whatever laws are enacted in the New Testament, are altogether new and peculiar to that covenant of which Jesus is the mediator. They emanated from him in his character of Head of the Church. Baptism is one of them. It is, however, a new institution, peculiar to the New Covenant, and was not brought over from the old. The Lord's Supper is another, yet it is a new Covenant ordinance entirely, and therefore, like baptism, is to be observed only by believers. But as for the *re-enacting* of laws, it is a thing altogether unknown in the New Covenant, and inconsistent with its nature.

The notion of the necessity of re-enacting the Sabbath in the New Testament, arises altogether from supposing that it is a covenant institution or church ordinance. But if it is a church ordinance, it can be binding upon none but believers; on the same principle that the ordinances of the Mosaic church were binding upon none but Jews. Is any one prepared to take this ground? We think not. Those who acknowledge the necessity of any Sabbath whatever, consider the observance of it a duty devolving upon men irrespective of their connection with the church, binding them in the isolated and individual capacity, even though church privileges were altogether out of the question. Were an individual abiding in some lone cavern of the Rocky Mountains, or roaming the uninhabited and trackless wastes of the earth, far, far from scenes of busy life, the law of God still binds him "to remember the Sabbath-day to keep it holy."

The truth is, the Sabbath is not properly an ordinance of either of the covenants. It originated in neither of them, but was in existence long before any covenant was revealed to man. Hence, after the Old Covenant was abrogated, it remained just what it was before. So that if, in the history of the New Covenant, or what is commonly called the New Testament, there was not one word of allusion to the Sabbath in particular, it would not affect the argument in the least.*

* Most writers on this subject, though they admit the morality of the Sabbath, and the claims it has upon all men indiscriminately, appear to reason in a manner entirely different, when they come to contend for a change from the seventh to the first day of the week. Their arguments, which before were predicated upon the nature and fitness of things, and the requirements of God, as the natural Lawgiver of mankind, are suddenly changed and based upon the new dispensation of Jesus Christ. Now this is an inconsistency; but it is one to which they are necessarily driven, in order to give plausibility to the claims of their new Sabbath. The fact that Christ introduced a new dispensation, does not argue a change of the Sabbath, or an institution of a new one, unless it can be proved that the old Sabbath was a church ordinance. If it was, then, as there is a new church state, of course we must look for new church ordinances.

How, then, will it be proved, that the old Sabbath was a church ordinance? Will it be said that the observance of it was indispensable to membership in the Jewish church? Very true. But the same may be said of the laws concerning murder, and theft, and adultery. Yet these were not, properly speaking, church ordinances. Concerning these things men were bound, though no church had ever existed. The sin of murder lay at Cain's door, long before any church was formed. The earth was corrupt before God, and the earth was filled with violence, before the Jews were organized into a church; and the sin of dishonoring his father blackened the character of Ham, long before the fifth commandment was published from Sinai. So, too, the Sabbath was set apart by God sanctifying it and blessing it, more than two thousand years before it entered into the statute law of Israel. It cannot, therefore, be a church ordinance.

Will it be said, that the Sabbath, though not altogether a church ordinance, is nevertheless so in part? If this can be established, then certainly so much of it as partook of this character must necessarily have been abolished by the death of Christ, and that part only remains which had no such character. But I ask, what part of the Sabbath law can claim to be a church or-

But is it true, that the Sabbath is not sanctioned by the New Testament? What means our Savior's course in regulating the manner of its observance, in vindicating it from Pharisaic austerities, determining what is lawful to be done, &c., Matt. xii. 1—13. It can mean nothing else than sanctioning it, as a precept of the moral law, as we have already shown in our remarks upon this text, p. 10. But even if this express sanction were wholly wanting, inasmuch as it is a part of the moral law, as we have clearly proved, it stands firm, unaltered, and unalterable, receiving, from the very nature of the case, all the sanction of the New Covenant. It is impossible for the New Covenant to affect it in any other way than to strengthen and uphold it.

Section III.

RELATION OF THE SABBATH TO POSITIVE INSTITUTIONS

Is there then no difference between the law of the Sabbath and the other precepts of the decalogue? We do not mean to say there is no difference whatever. There is something in it which partakes of the nature of a *positive institution*, as theologians are

dinance, peculiar to the old dispensation. It will be said that the particular day of the week set apart for observance, was such. This, as all the world confesses, was the seventh in distinction from every other. But the same rule which determines every other part of the Sabbath law to be something else than a church ordinance, determines the same thing with regard to the seventh day of the week. If the Sabbath was not a church ordinance, but obligatory upon all men indiscriminately, long before any church existed, the same is true of the seventh day of the week. One part of the law was not brought into existence without the other, nor one part before the other. We conclude, therefore, that the particular day which was consecrated, partook no more of the nature of a church ordinance, than all the rest of the law did.

pleased to term it. Positive institutions are generally considered to be such as are not discoverable by the light of nature, their obligation resting upon the mere will of the Lawgiver. While on the other hand, moral precepts are supposed to be ascertained by the light of nature, and to be binding independently of any appointment of the Lawgiver.

We are free to admit the positive nature of the Sabbatic institution, so far as it respects the particular day to be observed, and the proportion of time; also as it respects the great reason on which the law is founded. For it is not a dictate of nature, that one seventh part of time is more holy, or has any more demand upon us in a religious way, than one tenth, or one fifth, or any other proportion. Nor is it a dictate of nature, that God created the world in six days, and rested on the seventh, blessing and sanctifying *it*. The light of nature, it is true, teaches that the world was created by eternal Power; but it gives no information of the time occupied in it, nor of the fact of his resting on the seventh day, after it was finished. Therefore, so far as the mere light of nature is concerned, we are left in the dark respecting what constitutes the very foundation of the institution.

But after all, we very much doubt the propriety of classing all those precepts which we cannot discover by the mere light of nature, under the sweeping name of positive institutions, as if they were on the same level with the passover, circumcision, the ordinance of the red heifer, &c. Indeed, we utterly protest against it, if the intention is to underrate their importance, or to depreciate them as "*non-essential*," according to the cant term of the day. For what in such case would become of the whole system of Christianity itself? We mean the system of appointing a Mediator, and the redemption of the world through him. It is a positive institution, that is, purely a matter of revelation, and wholly undiscoverable by the light of nature. But shall we therefore call it a non-essential? Shall we regard it as something of minor importance in comparison with the religion of nature? Does it not devolve upon us with obligations just as strong and overwhelming as the moral law? Most certainly it does; not only because it is enjoined by the same authority, but also because it is the only means of promoting a conformity to the moral law. The same may be said of all positive institutions: they are designed to promote a conformity first to that dispensation to which they are peculiar, and second, to the moral law.

Whoever attempts a close investigation of the nature of positive institutions, will find that the line of separation between them and moral duties, is not always so easy to be drawn as might at first be imagined. We say, indeed, that the former are not discoverable by the light of nature. The reason of that, however, may be, not because they do not in reality originate in the nature of things, but merely because our powers of discovery are so feeble. Were these powers expanded, and the range of our intellectual vision widened, we might possibly see that those very institutions we call positive, grow naturally and necessarily out of the relation between God and us. Not only might we see the reasons of positive institutions in general, (which indeed is already sufficiently obvious,) but with such enlarged capacities, we might see the reason why such particular ones are pitched upon rather than others. The real difference between moral and positive duties may, after all, be nothing more than this, that the former we can readily discover for ourselves, narrow as the range of our vision is—while the latter, we are so short-sighted, we cannot discover, and are therefore wholly dependent on revelation for them. Hence we suppose it is assuming more than can be proved, when it is argued that positive appointments are altogether arbitrary, and have no real foundation in the nature and fitness of things.*

Now when we admit that the Sabbath is a positive institution, we mean that it is not discoverable by the light of nature, but is purely a matter of revelation; and this is all we mean. It still possesses the main attributes of a moral precept. For as we have already shown, any duty which has its origin in the natural relation of creature to Creator, must be of a moral nature, whether we can discover it for our-

* "The reason of positive institutions in general, is very obvious; though we should not see the reason why such particular ones are pitched upon, rather than others. Whoever, therefore, instead of caviling at words, will attend to the thing itself, may clearly see, that positive institutions in general, as distinguished from this or that particular one, have the nature of moral commands, since the reasons of them appear. Thus, for instance, the *external* worship of God is a moral duty, though no particular mode of it be so. Care then is to be taken, when a comparison is made between moral and positive duties, that they be compared no farther than as they are different—no farther than as the former are positive, or arise out of mere external command, the reasons of which we are not acquainted with; and as the latter are moral, or arise out of the apparent reason of the case, without such external command. Unless this caution be observed, we shall run into endless confusion."—*Butler's Analogy of Religion to Nature. Part II. Chap.* 1.

It is very commonly said, that positive institutions are changeable, and therefore are unlike moral precepts, which are unchangeable and eternal in their nature. But we deny that positive precepts are changeable, so long as the relation subsists in which they originate. Such positive institutions as originated in the peculiar relation which God sustained towards the Jews, by reason of the Sinaitic covenant, remained unchanged and unchangeable so long as that relation subsisted. Such as originate in the relation He sustains towards man as his Redeemer through Jesus Christ, also remain unchangeable so long as such relation remains. On the same principle, such as originate in the natural relation He bears to man as his Creator, remain just as long as this relation exists; which is forever.

selves, or whether by reason of our short-sightedness, we are altogether dependent on revelation for it. That such is the origin of the Sabbath law, is plain from the most casual inspection of it. It grew out of God's creating the world in six days, and resting on the seventh, and is a constant memorial of it. Besides, it provides for the performance of the worship of God, which is confessedly a moral duty; while the satisfaction it yields to the conscience of every man, is a sufficient indication of its parity with other moral precepts.*

But to dismiss all further argument concerning the distinction between moral and positive duties, let it be admitted that the Sabbath is a positive institution in the very strictest sense; let it be admitted to be nothing more than an arbitrary appointment, having no foundation in the natural and primary relation of man to his Creator—it must nevertheless remain in force so long as that dispensation lasts to which it is peculiar. Hence it must still be in force; for the dispensation to which it belongs, is the dispensation of nature itself. While the dispensation of nature lasts, the day which God the Creator originally "blessed and sanctified," will continue to be sacred. It is utterly impossible that it should be otherwise; and therefore all speculations about its changeable nature

* President Dwight observes, [Sermon 185,] "The distinction between *moral* and *positive commands*, has been less clearly made by moral writers than most other distinctions." He says the law of the Sabbath is entirely of a moral nature, as to the whole end to which it aims, so far as man is concerned; that "it makes no difference here, whether we could have known it without information from God, that one day in seven would be the best time and furnish the best performance of these [religious] things, or no. It is sufficient that we know them."

"The decalogue exhibits *a perfect standard of morality*; and a standard of morality not providing for the public acknowledgement and stated worship of God as the Creator, would be *essentially defective.*'—*Parkinson's Letters to Elder W. B. Maxson.*

resulting from its being a positive appointment, are vain. Changeable and positive as were the carnal ordinances of the old economy, they were not changeable while that economy lasted, but were sacred throughout the whole of it. Changeable and positive as are the ordinances of Baptism and the Lord's Supper, they are not changeable while the dispensation to which they belong continues, but are sacredly binding until the dispensation ends. So of the Sabbath; yes, even of the very day originally appointed.

Customary as it is with writers to draw the broad line of distinction between what they call the *moral* and *positive* parts of the institution, and whatever advantage it may have in *theory*, so far as *practice* is concerned, nothing is gained by it. Indeed, with those who pretend to be guided by divine revelation, rather than by the unaided deductions of their own minds, it is always an unnecessary distinction. He whose heart is subdued to the will of God, will not be studious to inquire which of his commands are of a moral, and which of a positive nature. His inquiry will be simply this: "Lord, what wilt thou have me to do?" If God command, he will obey, let the nature of the command be what it will. Were man left to deduce the knowledge of his duty from the nature and fitness of things, without the aid of any light from above, God would not blame him if he should wholly neglect to practice those duties, which are commonly called positive. All that would be required of him in such case, would be the practice of those duties which are most obviously of the moral kind. But with the statute book of Almighty God in his hand, he stands on very different ground. He is thus brought under obligation—yea, under *moral* obligation, to esteem ALL the divine precepts concerning ***all things***, to be right. Psalm cxix. 128

Section IV.

THE IMPORTANCE AND NECESSITY OF THE SABBATIC INSTITUTION.

There are very few bearing the Christian name—perhaps none except such as are a scandal to the profession—who do not feel the importance of a weekly day of rest, which shall be dedicated to the service of the Most High God. Whatever may be their scruples in regard to the application of the term *Sabbath* to such a day, and though they may suppose that it is not to be observed according to the rigorous exactness of the ancient law, they nevertheless feel that it would be sapping the foundation of religion, morality, and good order, to abolish all distinction of days, leaving none for religious and moral improvement. Nay, even those who, in theory, maintain that under the gospel all days are alike, still feel—though it is difficult for them to account for it—that their theory and their experience will not harmonize together. Their very nature calls for a day of repose, while the wants of their souls are so clamorous as to drive them to some moral and religious improvement of it. If they heed not these monitions, they do but feel some aching void, some uneasy distress, wholly unlike those peaceful feelings which result from a due improvement of the season. Whatever be a man's *theory*, he *feels* better when he sanctifies one day in seven to the Lord: his body feels better—his soul feels better. This feeling is not one which grows out of the airy visions of a distempered brain; but it is one which is capable of being resolved into solid arguments.

Without a Sabbath, it would be utterly impossible to promote the interests of religion. Were there no set time for suspending the business of the world, the church of God would soon lose its visibility, and hell obtain complete triumph over the fallen soul of man. Ministers might preach, embodying in their discourses the most powerful reasoning, and garnishing the whole with the sweetest flowers of rhetoric; but, to whom would they preach? A few, of exalted piety, who rejoice in the sacred testimonies more than in all riches, and who feel that "a day in the courts of the Lord is better than a thousand," Psalm lxxxiv. 10, would perhaps be there. But the mass—the throng—the great multitude—would be elsewhere. They would be immersed in the service of the world, their souls perishing for lack of knowledge. It would be impossible, utterly impossible to bring the word of God to bear upon their minds. How then could they be saved? For faith cometh by hearing, and hearing by the word of God, Rom. x. 17. And if men are not brought to believe the gospel, what becomes of the church? Its visibility is gone—the gates of hell have prevailed against it. But God has sworn that the church shall stand; nay, that all nations shall flow unto it, Isa. ii. 2. Wherefore, He who said "the gates of hell shall not prevail against it," Matt. xvi. 18, is also Lord of the Sabbath for the benefit of the church. As Lord of the Sabbath, he will forever perpetuate an institution so necessary to the interests of his kingdom.

This object—the promotion of Zion's welfare—could not be accomplished, unless the day were strictly a Sabbath; that is, a day of rest from all sorts of work. It is not sufficient that the day be merely an honorable day—a notable season, or a day for holding religious meetings. If men are not obliged to intermit their worldly business, and that too by the express authority of God, they will give themselves but little trouble to repair to a place of worship. Or even should they go, their minds would be so filled with the world, that the instructions from the desk would be as seed cast upon the way side. Even with regard to the Christian himself, how could the life of God be maintained in his soul, by an attention to religious duties just barely for the short space allotted to the public assembly? It would be impossible. His soul would be eaten up by the world. Public opportunities must be followed up by secret prayer, and close meditation in the sacred word. For this, one entire day in seven is little enough. The experience of all devoted Christians—let their theory about the Sabbath be what it may—has taught them, that nothing less will suffice to keep their souls in prosperity and health.

It appears, then, that we need just such a Sabbath as the fourth commandment enjoins; one, the law of which is, "in it thou shalt not do any work, thou, nor thy son, nor thy daughter, nor thy man-servant, nor thy maid-servant, nor thy cattle, nor thy stranger that is within thy gates." If the great object of evangelizing men, and bringing them to the knowledge and worship of Jehovah cannot be accomplished with any thing less than one entire day in seven, sanctified for the purpose, then unquestionably we need a Sabbath. It is therefore fair to presume, that the Sabbath of the Decalogue was given with special reference to man's necessities, and was not a mere *shadow* to be annulled for the weakness and unprofitableness thereof.

The Sabbath is necessary to promote the growth and strength of the moral principle. A man may render obedience to all the other precepts of the moral law; we may suppose them to be written on his heart; we may even suppose them to be so perfectly wrought into the temper and texture of his soul, that there is no deviation whatever. By his obedience he gives evidence of being in possession of the great principle of holiness. But this principle lives not by its own inherent vitality; it must be nourished and fed continually, or it withers and dies. However holy, however perfect the creature may be, he possesses no self-replenishing, self-renovating principle,—he must constantly resort to the great uncreated source for new supplies. The contrary supposition makes him independent of his Maker. Now the Sabbath is the season set apart and sanctified by God Almighty for this very purpose. It is the means of grace for keeping alive the great moral principle—the season when the creature goes right up to the Great Fountain, and drinks of its invigorating streams, whereby he comes forth rejoicing as a strong man to run a race. Hence we find that even when man was innocent; when he was in possession of the moral principle to perfection, still he was not left without a Sabbath season for the replenishing of his spiritual powers. If he needed a Sabbath then, much more does he need it now. For though he has been created anew in Christ Jesus,—the principle of holiness being thus re-implanted—yet has he a harder task to live holy to the Lord, inasmuch as there is "a law in his members warring against the law of his mind," "the flesh lusting against the spirit." Therefore he needs all the aid the Sabbath can bring to his soul. He needs "the restoring, the awakening day—the day of recovery and reformation—the day that brings him back to recollection, to seriousness, to penitence, to prayer." And when the last traces of sin shall have become obliterated, and man put in possession of all that perfection which pertains to the glorified state; still that perfection, we believe, will not be sustained by its own vitality, but will be preserved by means having a similarity to those employed on earth. For it is an everlasting Sabbath there, Heb. vi. 9. Yes,

> "——there's a nobler rest above,
> To which our lab'ring souls aspire,
> With ardent pangs of strong desire."

But that the great importance of the Sabbatic Institution may be more distinctly felt, let it be blotted out from existence. Not only let the day which God himself "sanctified and blessed," be disregarded; but let there be no day whatever devoted as a season of rest and religious improvement. Let every thing which has the least semblance of the Sabbatic rest be annihilated. What now is the state of morals? What kind of order prevails in society? Why, men are not ashamed when they commit abomination, neither can they blush. They can glory in their shame, and hell seems to be let loose. What is true of communities, is also true of individuals. Such as have disregarded all seasons and opportunities for instruction in those principles which serve as restraints upon the heart, have proceeded from bad to worse; have become perfect pests of society, the ringleaders of all wickedness, at the head of every miscreant gang, foaming out their own shame, and ending their career in a prison or on the gallows. Witness the poor criminal, as he stands on the dividing line between time and eternity, and his long-slumbering conscience wakes up, and begins to speak out its thunders. What does he say in that dread moment, when he feels that the eye of God is directly upon him? What!—Why, that in the beginning of his career, all the powers of his nature called him to a day of rest, and warned him not to trample upon seasons devoted to moral and religious improvement;—that he disregarded these monitions, until at length the voice of conscience was hushed in silence, and the work of death was easy. Therefore, says he, I am a ruined man. Reader, when you contemplate such facts, can you say that a Sabbath is not necessary? Do you not see that the obliteration of it is the brand upon the forehead of morality?

Need we, in this little essay, pause to consider the bearing of the Sabbath upon the temporal welfare of man? It is a matter so obvious, that we are almost ashamed to make it the subject of a separate paragraph. It is a fact well attested by experience, that the human frame sinks under uninterrupted toil. The utmost productive labor of man is in the proportion of six days exertion to one of repose. So that the Sabbath, instead of being an interruption to our necessary business, is really a help to it. The utmost prolongation of human life also, is in the like alternation of toil and rest. While the poor beast of burden, if doomed to continued service, drags out a miserable existence, and at length sinks under the premature exhaustion of his powers. What lustre, then, does the Sabbath cast upon the benevolence of its Author. What mercy, what God-breathed humanity appear in this holy Institution. Let those who dwell in the habitations of cruelty, be its enemies.

Section V.

MANNER OF OBSERVING THE SABBATH.

Notwithstanding God has given the Sabbath for the spiritual and temporal benefit of man, it is manifest that we may suffer a woful loss of all the good it proposes, if we neglect to make a proper improvement of it. Like all the other means of grace, it may prove a savor of death unto death to those who abuse it. It therefore becomes a momentous inquiry, How shall this holy day be observed?

This great institution is to be regarded as a weekly testimony of our allegiance to Him who created us. It thus becomes the mark of distinction between the worshipers of Jehovah and heathens. This being the case, it becomes a matter of thrilling importance that the testimony of our allegiance be sincere, characterized by nothing of hypocrisy or formality. If, in all our acts of worship, we must be careful to worship "in spirit and in truth," surely it is of the highest importance to do so on this solemn occasion, when the Great King comes down to test our loyalty Let it be remembered, too, that in this business there can properly be no uninterested spectators. It is not for a few to go through with the solemn act of dedicating themselves, while the rest make it a mere holiday, in which they look on, as boys witness the manouverings of soldiers on parade day. But *all* the sons and daughters of Adam—for all are alike the workmanship of the Divine Being—are equally bound to direct their eyes and their hearts to Him who made them, and to say, "Come, let us join ourselves to the Lord in a perpetual covenant that shall not be for gotten."

On this day we should by no means omit to celebrate the praise of creation. To be a memorial of this great work of the Almighty, the Sabbath was originally instituted. Shall we then lose sight of the original design of the institution, or even throw it into the shade as a matter of secondary importance? Is not the soundness of that system of theology to be suspected, which would teach us to do so? Some, it is true, teach us that the work of Redemption being much more stupendous than that of creation, is therefore to be made the chief object of our praise. But however plausible this sentiment may seem, it is a sufficient answer to say it is not contained in the Scriptures. How much more vast the work of Redemption is than that of creation, we pretend not to say, as we are not able to measure the extent of either. To say which work makes the most powerful impression upon our minds, and fills us with more sublime ideas, is more easy. But that is no criterian by which to judge of their relative magnitude. Let it even be conceded that Redemption exceeds in glory the work of creation, still, whence do we *derive* those powers by which we estimate its glory? Whence did we obtain those faculties by which we contemplate the great scheme of Redemption, and know that it is glorious? Is it not to the wisdom and goodness of God as displayed in creation, that we are indebted for all these? And what are the *objects* upon which Redemption is accomplished? Are they not *created* objects? And what is the *effect* which redemption has upon them? Is it not that of putting an end to the disorders which sin has introduced, and bringing them to their original glory? Is not the final result of redemption to be that of bringing man back to that state of holiness and rectitude which the work of creation originally bestowed upon him? How then can the praise of Redemption be celebrated, without celebrating the praise of creation also? The one certainly leads directly to the other. So that if Redemption accomplish its proper fruits upon us, it will lead us to be still more devout in observing the proper memorial of the Creator's works.

But let it not be thought, because the work of creation holds so prominent a place in our Sabbath meditations, that redemption is therefore cast into the shade. It is rather the contrary. For as those powers by which we contemplate the work of creation, and become acquainted with its grandeur and with its author, are impaired by sin, so it is impossible for us to enter into the subject profitably, except by the aid which Redemption affords. If we attempt to bring our mental powers to act upon the works of creation, and to "look through nature up to Nature's God," we shall find them slow and lifeless to perform their duty, until first purified and invigorated by the influence of the great Atonement. Much, therefore, as it is our duty to celebrate the praise of creation, we cannot do so to the glory of God, without recognizing at the same time the redemption that is in Christ Jesus, as the means by which we do it. From which it appears, that the praises of creation and of redemption go hand in hand in this matter. There is no clashing, —no contrariety,—nor even such an elevation of one above the other in respect to glory, that they cannot be celebrated together, and upon the very day which most fitly serves as the memorial of the former; which memorial cannot be transferred to another day without manifest incongruity.

It is manifest from the slightest consideration of the nature and design of the Sabbatic institution, that Redemption cannot be excluded from our meditations on this holy day, but must hold a very prominent place. For one great design of the Sabbath is, to promote our conformity to holiness. But man partakes of no holiness except through the gospel. The mediation of Christ is the only channel through which it is communicated to him, and this always in connection with the most vigorous action of his mind on the subject.

Another very important thing among the duties of the Sabbath, is the cultivation of a right spirit with reference to it. We should "*count it a delight*," Isa. lviii. 13 Can that man be called a Christian, who counts it an irksome season? Is he spiritually minded to whom it is an unwelcome interruption of his worldly business, who in the avariciousness of his heart says "when will the Sabbath be gone that we may set forth wheat?" Amos. viii. 5. Surely not. His temper is any thing but in accordance with the sacredness of the Sabbath season. His thoughts, his feelings are a direct violation of that law which says, "Remember the Sabbath-day to keep it holy." To a real Christian, however, the Sabbath is the most delightful season he enjoys on earth. It is something like a heaven below; for the things of God and Christ come then into direct contact with his holy soul. He is as eager for the approach of this holy season, as a child is for his holiday. Instead of it being too long for him, it is too short; and with joy does he look forward to a Sabbath which shall never end, that which remaineth for the people of God, Heb. iv. 9. Such a spirit ought ever to be cultivated. In no other way can the Sabbath become a means of grace to the soul. What will mere abstinence from labor do? It will only contribute to the renovation of the corporeal system; which, it is true, is one design of the institution. But this is a small part. Shall we take care of the body, and not of the soul! Yet the soul suffers unto death, if there be no care to cherish a right spirit with reference to the day which is "the holy of the Lord." Our very thoughts must be put under restraint, and the greatest care taken that nothing of a worldly nature intrude into the mind.

This leads us to observe, that our conversation should have no reference to worldly things, but should be upon such subjects as are spiritual and tend to the furtherance of the soul in the divine life. "Not speaking thine own words," Isa. lviii. 13. But, alas! we shall enter the dwellings of some, and when the Sabbath approaches, we shall not know it by any difference that we can discover in their conversation. It is still upon subjects that have not the remotest connection with the glory of God. Follow them to the place of public worship, and up to the very threshhold of the door, their speech still savors of this world. Follow them through the whole of the day —the state of their crops, the currency of the country, the political aspect of things, banks, bonds, mortgages; these are the themes upon which they expatiate. These render them animated, and even eloquent. "Out of the abundance of the heart the mouth speaketh." Reader, thinkest thou that such persons can say in truth, "O how I love thy law." That law says, Remember the Sabbath-day to keep it holy. Thinkest thou that the love of God reigns in their hearts? This is the love of God, that we keep his commandments. John. v. 3.

All visiting for pleasure is inconsistent with a right observance of the Sabbath. Express and plain is the word of God—"Not finding thine own pleasure." Isa. lxviii. 13. Visiting the sick for the purpose of alleviating their sufferings, and rendering what help we can, either as it regards their bodies or their souls, is not only allowable, but is a Sabbath duty. But even this is liable to abuse. Multitudes take the Sabbath to visit the sick, merely because they are not willing to take time on any other day; and it is to be feared that if there were no Sabbath, the sick would be sadly neglected by them. Others go merely because the rigid improvement of the day at home is irksome to them. They watch the occasion, and convert it as much as possible into a visit for their own pleasure, while they quiet their consciences by the reflection that they have been visiting the sick. Reader! be careful how you seek to evade the restraints of Heaven's law. Every attempt on your part to convert the season of holy rest into a day of pleasure, evinces a heart that counts the commandments of God grievous. Is this a *renewed* heart? Impossible. Remember, too, that while you visit others for your own pleasure, you drive them to a violation of the Sabbath, as well as yourself. You take them from their closet, their reading, their meditations.

All traveling, for business or for pleasure, is also forbidden by the Sabbath law. Such traveling as may be necessary in order to promote the due sanctification of the day, is of course not included. Harnessing our horses and riding to our accustomed places of worship, may be necessary to promote the sanctification of the Sabbath, and is, therefore, no breach of of it. It stands on the same level with the labor performed by the priests of the Old Economy in the temple, for which they were "blameless." Matt. xii. 5. Yet traveling one half the distance for pleasure, is a profanation of the day, inasmuch as the word of God says, "not finding thine own pleasure." For the same reason, and because there are six days in which men ought to work, journeying for business on the Sabbath, is a violation of it. Take the following case: Brother A. is out on a journey The Sabbath comes, and instead of putting up and resting until the sacred season is past, he keeps right forward just as he had done every other day of the week. True, he professes to regret the necessity of traveling on this day, but pleads in excuse that he cannot afford to stop at a public house during the time. He is too poor; or, he says, the tavern is a noisy, bustling place, and unfavorable to his religious enjoyment, and, therefore, he concludes it will be no greater violation of the Sabbath to proceed quietly on his journey than it would be to spend it in such a situation. But, brother, let me talk with you about this. How much would it cost you to stop at the public house? A dollar, or two dollars; or it may be, if your family is with you, five dollars. Well, will you barter away the sanctity of the Sabbath for five dollars! Poor as you are, will you make sale of the ordinance of God for money? For this is what you do in reality. Turn it and turn it whichever way you will, it comes at last to this. Pause, then, and consider whether, under such circumstances, and actuated by such principles, you can class yourself with those who "esteem the law of God better to them than thousands of gold and silver." Ps. cxix. 72. The true Christian would rather impoverish himself to the last farthing than violate one of God's precepts. "But the tavern was noisy and bustling." How came you to put up at such a tavern? Those who *remember* the Sabbath, and are anxious to spend it to the glory of God, will carefully look out and make their inquiries beforehand, and in most cases will not have much difficulty in lodging themselves at a quiet place. But if through circumstances beyond their own control, they are lodged in a place of different character, their duty is to submit to it, and do the best they can. Your enjoyment may not be so great; but what of that? Your spiritual prosperity does not always depend on your enjoyment; nor does God's glory depend upon it. God's glory depends upon your obedience to his law, and so does your prosperity. It is a mistaken notion that Christians are never in the way of duty but when they are in the way of enjoyment. Besides, dare you prescribe terms to the Almighty, and say you will obey him, provided he will grant you such enjoyments and privileges as you want, otherwise you will not? How daring the impiety! What if God lodged you at such a wicked place on purpose that you might, by your conduct and your words, be a reproof to the ungodly sinners that frequented there. Will you be ashamed of your duty, and shrink from the trial? "He that is ashamed of me and of my words, of him shall the Son of Man be ashamed." Luke ix. 26. Remember, my brother, God's law says, "Remember the Sabbath to keep it holy." The exceptions which you make, God has not made.

After what has been offered, it seems almost needless to add, that Sabbath-keeping includes abstinence from labor. The Divine law enjoins us "to keep it holy." The plain meaning of which is, that it is a day peculiarly sacred to the Lord. For the word *holy*, when applied to things inanimate, or to portions of time, denotes them to be set apart exclusively for religious purposes. If, then, the day in question, according to the divine mandate, is to be kept holy, it is manifestly a sin to devote it, or any part of it, to secular pursuits. Wherefore the law is express—"in it thou shalt not do any work." All that work which on other days is perfectly lawful, is on the holy Sabbath to be laid aside, except such as may be absolutely necessary for the prevention of distress, or the relief of objects of mercy. But alas! what kind of commentary upon this law is the conduct of many who call themselves by the name of our Lord Jesus Christ. Let us see.—Neighbor B. has a large grass farm, and milks daily from thirty to fifty cows. The product of his dairy is cheese, of which he makes one or perhaps two each day during the proper season. The Sabbath comes, and the cows must be milked. Well, that is right and necessary for the prevention of distress. But then the milk must be subjected to the same operation as on other days, and the accustomed cheese must be made, because otherwise it would be lost. Lost!—well, suppose it should be, how much is it worth? Why, five dollars, more or less. And so he barters away the sanctity of the Sabbath for *five dollars!* Well, Judas sold his master for thirty pieces of silver, and how much better is your conduct than his? Or what better is your conduct than mine would be in the following case? I have a valuable horse, which I will sell for one hundred dollars. A traveler passes my door on Sabbath day, and offers me my price. Now the times are hard, and by closing the bargain it will be a profit to me of twenty or twenty-five dollars. By refusing to do so, I lose the chance of selling him, and he remains on my hands. Rather than lose so good an opportunity, I strike the bargain, Sabbath though it be. Thus have I sold the sanctity of the Sabbath for twenty dollars! Neighbor B., who makes his cheese on the Sabbath, is horror-struck, and comes over to admonish me. But, "*Physician heal thyself.*"

We might multiply cases to illustrate our argument, but it is needless. Every instance of departure from God's law, we believe, will be found to have originated in selfishness. But that manner of keeping the day which looks at our own interest, rather than the honor of God, can in no way be called "keeping it holy." For if it is holy, it is consecrated to the Lord, not to ourselves. But in all the foregoing instances, it is manifest, the individual looks first to himself. Such selfishness is idolatry, and is the very spirit that governs the carnal mind. But God, in the just retributions of his providence, sometimes defeats the very end proposed to be obtained by it. For instance, the cheese, which is the product of Sabbath labor, spoils on the dairyman's hands; or if that does not take place, he fails of getting his pay for it. The farmer who was in haste to gather in his hay or his grain on the Sabbath for fear of a shower, has no sooner secured it than the storm begins, and a single flash of lightning consumes the whole. Or, it may be, when winter comes, he takes it to market, trusts it out, and finally gets nothing for it. The man who could not afford the expense of stopping at the hotel over Sabbath while on his journey, gets home, and finds perhaps that on the very day he was profaning God's holy institution, some person's cattle broke into his grain-field and destroyed enough to pay for his lodging at the hotel half a dozen times. What then did he gain by it? That such retributions overtake those who violate the law of God, is not merely imaginary. On the contrary, it is believed, that were men more close observers of the dealings of Providence, they would be sensible that such things take place often. But, alas! "God speaketh once, yea, twice, and man perceiveth it not."

It seems almost superfluous to say any thing about public worship, as an important part of Sabbath exercises. If it were necessary to their spiritual prosperity that Jews should meet together in "holy convocation," Lev. xxii. 3, and be instructed in the testimonies concerning a Messiah to come, it cannot be less important that Christians should now assemble and celebrate the fulfilment of those testimonies, and "the grace and truth which came by Jesus Christ." Our Lord has ordained public worship to be a means of promoting the growth of his people in holiness; and if the Sabbath is a means to the same end, they ought both to go together, unless our situation render it impossible. If on the holy Sabbath we cannot say, "How amiable are thy tabernacles, O Lord of hosts," when can we? If on this holy day we cannot say, "I had rather be a door-keeper in the house of my God, than to dwell in the tents of wickedness," when will it ever be the language of our hearts?

But we cannot enlarge. Our essay has already exceeded the limits we had designed. We submit the subject to your consideration, as being one of incalculable importance. Reader, what course will you take? God Almighty has separated one day in particular from all others, and pronounced it holy. Will you then say that all days are alike? Or will you assume to yourself the prerogative of setting apart whatever portion of time you choose, in open disregard of that particular portion which God "sanctified and blessed," saying, "it is the Sabbath of the Lord thy God?" Will you suffer your convenience or your selfishness to come into conflict with the claims of your Maker? Who is it that said, "If any man will come after me, let him DENY himself?" Pause then, before you suffer yourself to be lulled into indifference on this matter. A vain sophistry insinuates that it is a subject of minor importance—a *non-essential.* But be not deceived. God has magnified its importance throughout his holy oracles. It is God the Lord that speaks, will you obey or will you turn again to folly?

THE SIXTH-DAY NIGHT.

"Sweet to the soul the parting ray,
  Which ushers placid evening in,
When with the still expiring day,
  The Sabbath's peaceful hours begin;
How grateful to the anxious breast,
The sacred hours of holy rest!

I love the blush of vernal bloom,
  When morning gilds night's sullen tear:
And dear to me the mournful gloom
  Of Autumn—Sabbath of the year;
But purer pleasures, joys sublime,
Await the dawn of holy time.

Hushed is the tumult of the day,
  And worldly cares, and business cease,
While soft the vesper breezes play
  To hymn the glad return of peace;
O season blest! O moments given,
To turn the vagrant thoughts to Heaven.

What though involved in lurid sight,
  The loveliest forms in nature fade,
Yet mid the gloom shall heavenly light
  With joy the contrite heart pervade;
O thou, great source of light divine,
With beams etherial gladden mine.

Oft as this hallowed hour shall come,
  O raise my thoughts from earthly things,
And bear them to my heavenly home,
  On living faith's immortal wings—
Till the last gleam of life decay
In one eternal Sabbath Day!"

No. 3.

THE SABBATH:

AUTHORITY FOR THE CHANGE OF THE DAY.

It being clear from the Scriptures, that the seventh day was instituted by divine authority for a weekly Sabbath, and religiously regarded throughout the times of the Old Testament, those who now relinquish its observance, and keep the first day of the week, take the ground that the Sabbath was either abrogated and a new institution introduced in its room, or that the time of its observance was changed from the seventh to the first day of the week, in commemoration of the resurrection of our Lord Jesus Christ. To be consistent with themselves, therefore, they are bound to evince one or the other of these positions The burden of proof evidently lies on their part For unless it can be shown, that the fourth command ment, which requires the sanctification of the seventh day, has been abolished, or amended by the substitution of the first for the seventh day of the week, it is clear that the original appointment remains obligatory and is now binding on the entire human family. And to substantiate either of these points, the proof must be clear and decisive. It will not do to rest upon doubtful deductions. We have an unquestionable right to demand that divine warrant, in either case, which pertained to the institution as originally delivered.

We will therefore first examine the proofs adduced in favor of the abrogation of the former weekly Sabbath and the introduction of a new institution.

To sustain this position, the broad ground is taken by some, that the Decalogue itself, in which the law of the Sabbath is contained, was abrogated; and that, under the new dispensation, no part of it is binding but what is newly enjoined or expressly recognized, either by Christ or his Apostles.

The perpetual obligation of the Decalogue implies, of course, the perpetual obligation of the Sabbath as enjoined in the fourth commandment. But if *that* was abrogated, the Sabbath which it enjoined was also abrogated; and, consequently, it ceases to be binding, unless renewed under the new economy. What, then, is the proof here relied upon? One of the principal passages in which this proof is supposed to be contained is 2 Corinthians 3 : 7, 8, 13. "But if the ministration of death, written and engraven in stones, was glorious, so that the children of Israel could not steadfastly behold the face of Moses for the glory of his countenance, which glory was to be done away, how shall not the ministration of the Spirit be rather glorious? . . . . And not as Moses, which put a veil over his face, that the children of Israel could not steadfastly look to the end of that which is abolished." It is argued from this passage, that the clauses "which glory was to be done away," and "to the end of that which is abolished," refer to the whole law, *moral* as well as *ritual*, because mention is made of "that which was written and engraven in stones," which is an evident allusion to the Decalogue. But, on careful examination, it will be found that "that which was to be done away," was not the *Decalogue itself*, but "the *ministration* of it," which was then appointed—the same being emblematically illustrated by the glory of Moses' countenance, which was merely temporary. This clause refers expressly to the glory of his countenance, and not to the glory of the law itself. So also the clause "that which is abolished," does not refer to the Decalogue, but to the ministration of Moses, including the appended rites and usages, the priesthood and its sacrifices, which were useful merely for the time being. It cannot be supposed that the Decalogue was abolished, without expressly contradicting Christ's testimony, Matt. 5 : 17—19, as well as many other representations of the Scriptures. The abolishment spoken of, therefore, evidently respected no other than what the Apostle calls in another place "the law of commandments contained in ordinances," inclusive of the entire ministration of Moses. There is unquestionably a reference in this chapter to the Decalogue, but not as abolished. It was merely the ministration of it, or the then instituted manner of teaching, illustrating, and enforcing it, which was abolished, to be succeeded by a new ministration of the same law by the Spirit. For it is written, "I will put my law" —(the very law of the ten commandments)—"in their inward parts, and write it in their hearts." Again, "We are not without law to God, but under the law to Christ." What law but the Decalogue is here referred to ? Evidently none. For surely we are not under the Mosaic ritual. Again, "Do we make void the law through faith ? . . Yea, we establish the law." The same, no doubt, which was contained in the Decalogue. Hence, the Apostle James says, "If ye fulfil the royal law according to the Scripture, Thou shalt love thy neighbor as thyself, ye shall do well." Here the title "the royal law" is given by way of eminence to the Decalogue ; and its permanent obligation is manifestly recognized ; for the precept alluded to is a summary of the last six commandments of this code, and the allusion is so made as to imply the continued obligation of the first four, which are summed up in supreme love to God. Again, the Apostle John testifies, "Hereby do we know that we know him, if we keep his commandments." And again, "Blessed are they that do his commandments, that they may have right to the tree of life, and may enter in through the gates into the city." In both these passages reference is evidently had to the precepts of the Decalogue, as the essential and permanent rule of obedience for Christians. The doing away or abolishment, therefore, spoken of in the above passage, cannot refer to the Decalogue or the moral law *itself*, but to the Mosaic dispensation or ritual.

Another of the proofs alledged for the abrogation of the Decalogue, and consequently of the Sabbath, is Colossians 2 : 14—17. "Blotting out the hand-writing of ordinances that was against us, which was contrary to us, and took it out of the way, nailing it to his cross ; and, having spoiled principalities and powers, he made a show of them openly, triumphing over them in it. Let no man therefore judge you in meat, or in drink, or in respect of an holy day, or of the new moon, or of the sabbath days, which are a shadow of things to come ; but the body is of Christ."

By "the hand-writing of ordinances," is most evidently meant the ceremonial law—not the Decalogue, or the moral law. This is never characterized as "the hand-writing of ordinances." Therefore, the "blotting out," "taking away," and "nailing to the cross," spoken of, have no reference to this law, but to the Mosaic ritual. This is particularly distinguished from the Decalogue, and fitly described as "the law of commandments contained in ordinances." It was this, and this only, which was "blotted out" and "nailed to the cross." As, therefore, the reference made by the Apostle is expressly to this law, it follows, by a fair inference, that "the sabbath days" alluded to, or, strictly rendered, "sabbaths," are those which were contained in this law, or among these "ordinances," and do not include the Sabbath of the fourth commandment. There were, besides the weekly Sabbath, various other sabbaths appointed, which belonged to that ritual, and not to the Decalogue. Accordingly, these were expressly included in "the hand-writing of ordinances," and like the rest were "a shadow of things to come," and ceased to be obligatory at the death of Christ. There is evidently no authority in this passage for including any sabbaths but what properly belonged to the Mosaic ritual. This view of the matter is corroborated by a more literal rendering of the 17th verse, viz: "Let no one therefore judge you in meat, or in drink, or in a part or division of a festival, or of a new moon, or of sabbaths." The sabbaths alluded to are obviously those which are found in the same place with meats and drinks, festivals and new moons, and which were of the same general character. The weekly Sabbath, therefore, is not affected at all by their abrogation, but remains in full force, as does every other precept of the Decalogue.

We find the same distinction as to the law which was abolished, in Ephesians 2: 14, 15. "For he is our peace, who hath made both one, and hath broken down the middle wall of partition between us, having abolished in his flesh the enmity, even the law of commandments contained in ordinances, for to make in himself of twain one new man, so making peace." Here the middle wall of partition between Jews and Gentiles, called "the enmity," is expressly defined, as before, to be "the law of commandments contained in ordinances." This, and this only, therefore, was abolished, leaving the Decalogue, or the moral law, in its original character and obligation. This is the language of the whole Bible. There is no proof in any of these passages, that the law of the ten commandments was abolished, or that the Sabbath enjoined therein was done away.

Nor is there such proof in Romans 14: 5, 6. "One man esteemeth one day above another; another esteemeth every day alike. Let every man be fully persuaded in his own mind. He that regardeth the day, regardeth it to the Lord ; and he that regardeth not the day, to the Lord he doth not regard it. He that eateth, eateth to the Lord, for he giveth God thanks : and he that eateth not, to the Lord he eateth not, and giveth God thanks." This passage is frequently adduced as proof that the obligation to keep the ancient Sabbath has ceased, and that under the Gospel dispensation there is no divinely authorized distinction in the days of the week ; that there is no one constituted *holy* in distinction from the *rest ;* and consequently that every one is left at his own liberty to keep a Sabbath or not. It will be easily perceived, that if this argument has any weight in reference to the *seventh* day as the Sabbath, it operates equally against the obligation to keep the *first* day, either as a substitute for the seventh, or as a memorial of the resurrection, seeing it places all distinctions whatever as to days on the same ground with the confessedly obsolete rites of the Mosaic ritual. According to this view of the passage, we have under the Gospel dispensation *no Sabbath at all*—not so much as an *authorized* memorial of the resurrection. He who claims the least authority for the observance of the *first* day of the week for *any* purpose, takes a course which completely overthrows the argument based upon this passage. But, in reality, this text has nothing more to do with the subject before us, than either of those which have been examined. It respects merely the distinctions which formerly existed in regard to the six working days of the week—some of them being appointed in the Mosaic ritual as sabbaths, others as days of atonement and purification, and others as festivals. Some of the early Christians thought these distinctions still binding, as also the distinctions in regard to meats and drinks ; others thought they were not. Hence the exhortation which is sub joined to mutual forbearance. That the distinctions referred to as to days, were those noted in the Mosaic ritual, and did not include the one contained in the fourth commandment, is manifest from the whole scope of the chapter. There is particular reference made to one's freely eating all things, while another would eat only herbs; and accordingly the following rule, to be respectively observed, is laid down: "Let not him that eateth, despise him that eateth not; and let not him that eateth not, judge him that eateth; for God hath received him." This quotation clearly evinces that the Apostle was treating of *ritual* distinctions, and not of *that* distinction of days which was constituted by the ancient law of the Sabbath.

Again, the abrogation of the Decalogue is supposed to be taught in Romans 7: 4, 5, 6. "Wherefore, my brethren, ye also are become dead to the law by the body of Christ, that ye should be married to another, even to him who is raised from the dead, that we should bring forth fruit unto God. For when we were in the flesh, the motions of sin which were by the law, did work in our members, to bring forth fruit unto death. But now we are delivered from the law, that being dead wherein we were held; that we should serve in newness of spirit, and not in the oldness of the letter." But if the term law here includes the *moral* as well as the *ceremonial* law, it is manifest that believers are not said to be delivered from it, considered in any other light than as *a covenant of works*. Certainly they are not delivered from it as *a rule of obedience*. To suppose this, is inconsistent with Christ's sermon on the mount, before alluded to, and many other decisive proofs of the perpetual obligation of the Decalogue. It is probable the Apostle had special reference to the deliverance of believers from the *curse* of the moral law. This is reasonably inferred from the clause, "that being dead wherein we were held." If any thing more pertaining to this law be intended, it must be its original character when given to Adam as a covenant of works or of life. For surely we are not and cannot be delivered from it as a rule of obedience, so long as God is what he is, and we are what we are. Seeing that as long as the relation constituted by his character as Supreme Ruler, and by ours as moral subjects, exists, we shall be bound to love him supremely, and our neighbor as ourselves, which is the fulfilling of this law. And to suppose that this law, as a rule of obedience, was actually annulled, and that those precepts only are now to be considered obligatory, which are enacted or published anew under the Gospel, is to suppose that God, at a certain time, actually rescinded the rule requiring supreme love to him, and to our neighbor as ourselves, which is palpably inconsistent, and contrary both to the current of Scripture and the nature of things. It would be maintaining that to be changed which is manifestly unchangeable. It would imply that, for the time being, the obligation recognized by the law did not exist; that the tie by which God and moral beings are united, was sundered, not by rebellion on the part of his subjects, but by his own act of abrogation. Can this be admitted?

But if it *were* admissible, and if no part of this law is binding on Christians but what is newly enacted or particularly recognized under the Gospel dispensation, the Sabbath of the fourth commandment could not in this way be set aside; because its continued obligation is plainly taught in the New Testament. It is altogether a mistake, that we have no express recognition of this precept under the Christian dispensation. It is plainly recognized by the Savior in Matthew 5: 17—19, where he says, that he "came not to destroy the law, but to fulfill;" that "one jot or one tittle shall in no wise pass from the law, till all be fulfilled ;" and that " whosoever shall break one of these least commandments, and shall teach men so, shall be called the least in the kingdom of heaven ; but whosoever shall do and teach them, shall be called great in the kingdom of heaven." If any commandment of this law is binding, the fourth is binding of course, even if it should be called the least. It is also recognized in the following declaration of Christ, Mark 2 : 27—" The Sabbath was made for man, and not man for the Sabbath." The word *man* is here obviously used for the entire race—not for a part—not for the Jews in distinction from the Gentiles—not for those who lived under the Old Testament dispensation, or till the time of Christ's death ; but for man in his protracted existence during all future periods of time, i. e. *for mankind in general.* This is the plain import of the declaration. And if we render the original with the article, it is still more evident that the entire race is included. " The Sabbath was made for *the man*," i. e. for Adam, the original parent of man, including, of course, his posterity. But, according to either rendering, the entire human race is manifestly included in the term. The Sabbath, then, was as truly made for the Gentiles as for the Jews ; and for those who should live after the crucifixion, as for those who lived before ; which is an explicit recognition of its perpetual obligation.

The same recognition also appears from its continued observance under the ministry of the Apostles, and there being not the least hint or stir in reference to its abrogation, or to the substitution of another day in its room. The weekly Sabbath is frequently mentioned in the Apostolic records, as a part of practical duty, and it was unquestionably the seventh day. Thus we have the continued obligation of the Sabbath sanctioned by Apostolic example. If, therefore, a new edition, or an express recognition of the Sabbath of the fourth commandment be considered necessary, to bind the consciences of men under the new dispensation, the foregoing considerations will show that we have such an edition or recognition, as truly as we have of the other precepts of the Decalogue. So that nothing is gained in regard to setting aside the seventh day of the week, by attempting to show the abrogation of the Decalogue. If those precepts of that law which require that we should have no other gods before the Lord—that we should not kill, nor commit adultery, nor steal—are newly enjoined or expressly recognized under the present dispensation, and, consequently, universally binding, the same is true of the fourth commandment, which requires the keeping of the seventh day.

Again, an attempt is made to prove the abrogation of the original Sabbath, by showing that the entire Decalogue was peculiar to the Jewish nation, constituting a national covenant, which, at the coming of Christ, was annulled, and a new covenant introduced. But admitting that it was delivered immediately to them, in the form of a national covenant, this does not in the least imply that it was not equally binding, as a rule of obedience, upon other portions of the human family. We might as well argue that the New Testament belonged merely to the primitive Christians, because it was delivered directly to them, and constituted the rule of their conduct and the basis of their hopes. Yea, we might as well suppose that no nation except the Jews were bound not to have any other gods before the Lord, not to kill, not to commit adultery, not to steal, not to bear false witness, as to suppose that the Decalogue was purely of a national character, and binding merely on that people during their continuance as a national church. And, as the Decalogue was not merely national *as a whole*, so there was nothing national in the fourth commandment. It belonged, equally with the other nine, to the entire family of man, inasmuch as the essential reasons of all and of either of the commandments, were of universal obligation.

Again, that the original Sabbath was peculiar to the Jews, and consequently abrogated by the introduction of the new dispensation, is argued from its being specially urged upon them by the consideration of their deliverance from Egypt. But this argument is of no force, because the same reason is urged in the preface to the entire Decalogue.

For the same purpose, also, an argument is founded upon the fact that the fourth commandment was enforced with a deadly penalty. But this argument also fails; because a similar penalty was annexed to the breach of the other precepts of this law. The truth of the case is, that these penalties belonged not to the Decalogue itself as first promulgated, any more than they belong to it now under the milder dispensation of the Gospel. They were added in the Mosaic ritual, and constituted a part of the political arrangements for the time being. Their abrogation, therefore, affects not the original law. Though there be no civil power now given to the church to enforce obedience to this precept by temporal punishments, as formerly, the sacredness and obligation of the institution are not thereby at all affected. The sin of disobedience will be visited in God's own time.

Again, some have inferred the abrogation of the former Sabbath, or at least its change, from our Lord's vindication of the act of the disciples, in plucking the ears of corn, and rubbing them in their hands, as they passed through the corn-fields on the Sabbath day, and from his saying, that "the Son of Man is Lord also of the Sabbath day," Mark 2: 23--28. But there is evidently nothing in this narrative, or in this declaration, to justify such an inference. It must be admitted on all hands, that the fourth commandment was obligatory, as originally given, till the death of Christ, if no further ; and therefore Christ, who "was made under the law," was bound to obey it in its original strictness. Admitting that he possessed the right, in a given instance, to intermit its obligation, it is not consistent to maintain that he did it ; because he came to render perfect and universal obedience. Hence he affirmed, that one jot or one tittle should in no wise pass from the law "till all be fulfilled." His whole life was a perfect comment on the requirements of the law. Had he failed in the least particular, he would have been inadequate to the great purposes of our salvation. It is obvious, therefore, that the transaction alluded to was not, under the circumstances, a breach of the fourth commandment, but in perfect accordance with its prescriptions—the labor implied by the act of the disciples being a matter of urgent necessity. "It is lawful," said he, "to do well on the Sabbath day." Neither does the declaration, that "the Son of Man is Lord also of the Sabbath day," imply that he abrogated or changed it, but rather that he was bound and engaged to protect it as a divine institution, and to enforce an enlightened and strict obedience to its requirements.

The foregoing being the principal proofs adduced for the abrogation of the Decalogue, and the original Sabbath, it is evident that this view of the subject cannot be sustained. It is not sanctioned by any plain scriptural evidence. It is, therefore, palpably absurd to rest so important a matter upon so slender a basis. It is laying violent hands on a code of moral and immutable precepts, given by God, and promulgated under peculiar and terrible signs of purity and majesty, to vindicate a practice which was introduced long after the commencement of the Christian era.

Another portion of the observers of the first day, seeing the absurdity of holding to the abrogation of the Decalogue, and, consequently, of the Sabbath of the fourth commandment, readily admit its perpetual obligation, but alledge that the Sabbath is changed, under the new dispensation, from the *seventh* to the *first* day of the week—thus transferring the authority for keeping the seventh day to the first. It is not pretended that we have an explicit warrant from God, pointing out and authorizing the change in question, but that we have what is tantamount to such a warrant. We will examine the principal arguments for this supposed change.

In the first place, this change is inferred from the resurrection of Christ on the first day of the week, which is supposed to be an event of such magnitude as to constitute an *equal* and even *greater* reason for observing the first day of the week as the weekly Sabbath under the new dispensation, than that which existed for observing the seventh under the old. But what does this argument amount to? It is not perfectly clear that the resurrection occurred on the first day of the week. Very plausible reasons may be assigned for the opinion, that it occurred on the evening of the seventh day, although it was not publicly declared till the morning of the first. But admitting that it occurred on the morning of the first day, how does this prove that it was substituted for the seventh day as the Sabbath? Is the inference absolutely necessary? Is there any designation of the first day for a sabbatic purpose? If another than the seventh day was in any wise admissible, as according better with the Christian dispensation and the work of redemption, why should we fix upon the day of Christ's resurrection, rather than the day of his birth, or of his crucifixion, or of his ascension? Will it be alledged, as a reason for the preference, that he finished the work of redemption on the day of his resurrection? This reason might be offered with equal if not superior propriety, for commemorating the day of his crucifixion; because, when he bowed his head and gave up the ghost, he said, "*It is finished,*" which is more than is said in reference to the day of his resurrection. If a day were to be selected as a weekly Sabbath, which was "validly the day of redemption," it seems most proper to select the day of his death, which was the end of his temptation and conflict with the powers of darkness, and the severest test of his obedience; or the day of his final ascension, when he emphatically entered into his rest, and was crowned King in Zion. If, therefore, a day were to be selected, under the new economy, for the appropriate commemoration of the work of redemption, as the seventh day was for the commemoration of the work of creation, it is by no means clear that it should be the day of the resurrection. It might with equal, perhaps greater propriety, be some other day of the week. And hence, the different preferences of Christians might clash, and by that means counteract in a great measure the design of a Sabbath. But, in truth, the argument from the resurrection in favor of the first day of the week, rests upon the wisdom of man and not upon the appointment of God. It seems to men befitting the ends of a weekly Sabbath, under the Christian dispensation, to observe the first rather than the seventh day, and hence a change is inferred, without any express authority from God to that effect; as though it were lawful to change a divine institution when it *appears to us* that greater reasons exist for a change, than for its unamended continuance—a principle which would justify all the innovations and extravagancies of Popery. But no such power is given unto men. However many and important the reasons which exist in human view for the change in the Sabbath contended for, it is invading God's prerogative to make a change without his express warrant. So long, therefore, as there is no divine enactment which goes to authorize this change, but the permanent and unvaried nature of the entire Decalogue expressly forbids it, as does the continued practice of the primitive church, it is grossly erroneous and presumptuous to make it. This argument for the supposed change is surely without any validity.

In the next place, it is alledged that Christ's appearance to the disciples, after his resurrection, on the first day of the week, marks this as the Christian Sabbath. This argument is adopted both by those who hold to the abrogation of the former institution, and those who contend for its change. But, in reality, it is as devoid of solid weight as the one previously examined. It is easy to account for his appearing in the course of the day of his resurrection, or of the first declaration of it, because the earliest information of this great event was of the utmost importance to the afflicted and desponding disciples. It was important, also, as a testimony to the truth of the Savior's prediction that he would rise on the third day. There is nothing in his several appearances during that day, which seems intended for any other purpose than giving the necessary proof of his resurrection, and the light and consolation which the circumstances of the disciples required. There is nothing in either of them which favors the idea of a new Sabbath. But the circumstance of his appearing to the two disciples who were on a journey to Emmaus, and traveling a while with them, which was a distance much too long for a Sabbath day's journey, expressly forbids it, as it shows that it was regarded as a day for labor. And as to his appearance the following evening, there is nothing in that circumstance which savors of a newly appointed Sabbath. The disciples were not assembled together to keep a Sabbath, but "for fear of the Jews" Besides, according to the Jewish method of reckoning time, this evening actually belonged to the second day of the week. So that all which is said concerning his appearances on this day and evening, is perfectly devoid of proof of a change of the Sabbath.

As to the next appearance recorded, there is no evidence that it occurred on the first day of the week. The record states, that "After eight days, again his disciples were within, and Thomas with them. Then came Jesus, the doors being shut, and stood in the midst, and said, Peace be unto you." Surely the phrase, "and after eight days," cannot be fairly construed to mean a week. Who can tell but that he appeared on the *ninth* day after his first appearance? But even if it could be so interpreted as to mean precisely a week, and hence to show that his second appearance took place on the first day, as before, it would be no proof of the point in question, because the subject of the Sabbath was not introduced in any form.

The next instance of his appearing is very far from corroborating the opinion that he sanctioned the first day as the New Testament Sabbath by appearing on it; for the disciples, or some of them, were fishing at the sea of Tiberias, and consequently were not observing the first day as a Sabbath. Indeed, this appearance must have taken place as late as the second day of the week, if not later; for they had been engaged in fishing, as the record will show, the day before he appeared to them. And they could not have been so engaged on the *seventh* day, because it would have been contrary to the universal and unbroken practice of their nation. Hence it could not have been on the first day of the week that Christ appeared to them. It must have been on the second or some later day of the week. The argument, therefore, from the several appearances of Christ, amounts to nothing.

The next, and the principal argument for the change of the Sabbath, is the supposed Apostolic practice of meeting on the first day of the week for public worship and the breaking of bread. It is often confidently affirmed, that the keeping of the first day instead of the seventh is sanctioned by Apostolic usage. The proof of this position rests mainly on two passages. Let us examine them.

The first is Acts 20 : 7. "And upon the first day of the week, when the disciples came together to break bread, Paul preached unto them, ready to depart on the morrow, and continued his speech until midnight." But is there any thing in this transaction, or the attendant circumstances, which clearly and undeniably proves an Apostolic example in favor of a new Sabbath, or of keeping the first day of the week, in any manner, as a substitute for the former institution? Surely there is not. The passage does not so much as prove that the practice of meeting for worship on the first day of the week was then common and general. But if it did, it would not determine the change contended for. There is nothing said in the narrative, which characterizes it as a Sabbath. Assembling for public worship is proper on any day of the week; and so is the breaking of bread. The Supper was first administered on one of the six working days; and there is nothing in the Scriptures which restricts its subsequent administration to a particular day—not even to the authorized Sabbath. Besides, in this case, the breaking of bread was deferred till after midnight. Of course, according to the Jewish reckoning of time, it was attended actually on the second day; and this must have been the case, also, according to the prevailing custom among observers of the first day, of commencing the day at midnight. It seems, therefore, that the Apostle and his brerhren were not very precise in regard to its being done on the first day. Let the most be made of this passage, and it lacks a divine designation of the first day as the Christian Sabbath; and hence it is entirely wanting as to the requisite evidence of a change in the sabbatic law. Surely, if there had been such a change, and this, with one more instance of meeting on the first day of the week, were to contain the evidence for all after generations, we should have been informed of the fact. Something would have been said to determine that the first day of the week was regarded as a Sabbath, and that it had taken the place of the seventh. But there is nothing of this. The record is perfectly silent in regard to either point. Besides, it is evident that the original Sabbath continued to be observed, as already noticed, throughout the entire period of New Testament history. This is so plain a fact, that no one whc gives the subject a candid examination will deny it. This shows the opinion of a new Sabbath—observed, as it must have been, in connection with the Sabbath of the fourth commandment, and without a word being said on the subject, or the least objection, stir, query, or excitement whatever being raised—to be perfectly preposterous. Such is the result of this reasoning from a supposed Apostolic example, giving the passage its widest possible scope, as implying a common practice of meeting for public worship on the first day of the week. But in reality there is nothing in this text which proves or implies that such a practice was common at that period. For aught appears, it might have been an occasional meeting, appointed merely in consequence of Paul's being about to depart on the morrow. Therefore, to adopt a practice so important as the one in question, upon such vague, uncertain, and inadequate testimony—especially when, in order thereto, we must dispose of a plain and positive command of God respecting the observance of the seventh day, and of a usage as old as the completion of the creation—is unreasonable in the extreme.

Another passage quoted in proof of an Apostolic example of keeping the first day of the week, and, consequently, in support of the opinion that the Sabbath is changed, is 1 Corinthians 16 : 2. "Upon the first day of the week let every one of you lay by him in store, as God hath prospered him, that there be no gatherings when I come." This passage, like the others, does not imply that the first day was then commonly and generally regarded as a day for public worship. Indeed, it does not necessarily imply a public meeting of any kind. The direction for "every one to lay by him in store," for the benefit of the poor saints at Jerusalem, "on the first day of the week," necessarily amounts to no more than an appointment of this day to make up their bounty *at home*, so that it might be sure to be ready when the Apostle should come—a very judicious arrangement, as the time of his coming for it was uncertain, and he would not know how to wait. But if it be understood to imply any thing more, it is simply that they should bring their donations together publicly on the first day of the week, so as to be prepared in the fullest sense for the Apostle's visit. Therefore, according to this view of the case, it proves no more than an occasional meeting on this day for the purpose of a public contribution for an important object of benevolence. But even if it could be so construed as clearly to imply that it was then a common and general practice to meet for public worship and instruction on this day, it would not thereby be pointed out to us as the Christian Sabbath, and a substitute for the seventh day, seeing that it contains no information to that effect, and that no divine warrant appears on any part of the New Testament records for the supposed change. Meetings for public worship, taking up of collections, and even breaking of bread, do not constitute a Sabbath, though they are proper exercises for such a day. *To sabbatize* is to rest from our own secular labors, and keep a season holy to God. These proofs for a change of the Sabbath, therefore, which are unquestionably the best that can be produced, are utterly deficient, and the argument therefrom, as generally presented, is deceptive, and unworthy of confidence.

Another of the proofs adduced for the supposed change of the Sabbath, is the following prediction. Psalm 118: 22—24. "The stone which the builders refused is become the head stone of the corner. This is the Lord's doing; it is marvelous in our eyes. This is the day which the Lord hath made; we will rejoice and be glad in it." But this, like all the previous quotations, wants solidity. The main points in the argument are *assumed*. First, it is assumed, that Christ's becoming the head of the corner refers to the day of his resurrection; whereas there is no conclusive evidence that it refers to this rather than to the day of his birth, or of his entrance on his public ministry, or of his final ascension into heaven. Next, it is assumed that the day spoken of is a natural day of twenty-four hours; whereas this word is often used to designate an indefinite period of time—particularly the Gospel era (John 8: 56)—and may very probably be so used here. Again, it is assumed, that the day mentioned is the first day of the week; whereas there is nothing which designates this rather than some other in the course of his mediatorial work, allowing a natural day to be referred to. And even if the resurrection day be intended, it is not certain that this occurred on the first day of the week. It is further assumed, that the emphasis which is laid on the day alluded to as "the day which the Lord hath made," and in which the church would "rejoice and be glad," determines it to be the New Testament Sabbath in distinction from the Sabbath of the fourth commandment; whereas there is nothing in these circumstances which necessarily intimates any such change, while there are various important considerations by which this opinion is absolutely precluded. The entire argument, therefore, fails.

Another argument for the change of the Sabbath is based upon the supposition that the day of Pentecost occurred on the first day of the week, which was a remarkable season of the outpouring of the Spirit, and of Christ's triumph as the risen and exalted Savior. But this will appear, on a very little examination, to be wholly inconclusive. In the first place, it is far from being conclusively proved that this event occurred on the first day of the week. It is much more likely to have occurred either on the *fifth* or the *seventh*. Indeed, it is quite manifest from the best calculations that can be made, from the time of eating the passover supper, the first paschal sabbath, the crucifixion and the resurrection, that it occurred on one or the other of these days. Secondly, if the feast of Pentecost had actually occurred on the first day of the week, this would furnish no proof of its being the New Testament Sabbath, in the absence of a divine warrant to that effect.

There is one other argument for the change in question, founded on the supposed application of the title "the Lord's day," to the first day of the week. The only passage referred to for the purpose of sustaining it, is Revelations 1: 10. "I was in the spirit on the Lord's day." But that the day here called the Lord's day, is the first day of the week, is merely assumed, and hence is not to be considered as proved. It is not, in fact, *probable* that this is the day referred to. It is much more likely that the expression here used refers to the day of Christ's reign; and that St. John meant to declare that in spirit he had a view of the scenes of that period. This use of the term *day* is sanctioned by the Savior's declaration, "Abraham rejoiced to see my day," (John 8: 56,) as well as by the Psalmist's, who, when speaking of the glories of Christ's kingdom, says, "This is the day which the Lord hath made; we will rejoice and be glad in it," (Psalm 118: 23.) The nature of the visions afterwards described also corroborates this view of the passage, and warrants the opinion that the expression "Lord's day," (or, as some translate it, *lordly* day,) here used, does not refer to a natural day, but to a longer period of time. If, however, these words be understood to refer to a natural day, it is more likely to be the seventh day, which God had blessed and sanctified for his special service, than the first day. The seventh day is called by Him "*my holy day*," and "*the holy of the Lord*"—phrases very similar to the one in this passage. This was also the Sabbath which was made for man, and of which Christ says he is Lord. And since it was observed up to the close of the New Testament history, it would be perfectly natural for John to speak of it as "the Lord's day." Further, there is no evidence that the first day of the week was denominated the Lord's day, at so early a period. Only one writer mentions the expression till towards the close of the second century; and the reputed author of this passage, when speaking, in his Gospel, (which was written some years later than the Apocalypse,) of the resurrection of Christ, and the first day of the week, never intimates that the day should be called by any other name. The learned Morer, though an advocate for the first day, in mentioning the different days to which this phrase may be applied, acknowledges the entire uncertainty as to what day is intended, and says, " It is very likely that the more solemn and public use of the words was not observed until about the time of Sylvester II., when, by Constantine's command, it became an injunction." It is evident, therefore, that this passage cannot justly be used as proof that the Sabbath had been transferred to the first day of the week.

We have now examined the proofs commonly adduced for the abrogation or change of the original Sabbath, and have found them utterly insufficient and deceptive. Hence the claims of the Sabbath of the fourth commandment, without alteration, are fully sustained. The advocates for the first day are aware that if an abrogation or change of the original Sabbath law cannot be made out, the seventh day is still the true Sabbath. Dr. Dwight, for instance, makes the following admission : " If we cannot find in the Scriptures plain and ample proof of the abrogation of the original day, or the substitution of a new one, the seventh day undoubtedly remains in full force and obligation, and is now to be celebrated by all the race of Adam." Here, then, the laboring oar is confessedly put into the hands of the advocates of the first day ; and with what success they have used it, the foregoing examination will show. We ask, is it not a total failure ? Has such "plain and ample proof" been produced from the Scriptures for the supposed abrogation or change ? Indeed, it is evident that neither one nor the other of these things is *practicable*. An *abrogation* is not practicable ; for the Decalogue, in which the law of the Sabbath is contained, is unchangeable. " Not one jot or one tittle shall in any wise pass from the law, till all be fulfilled ;" which implies its continued obligation, as long as moral beings exist. And the *change* contended for is not practicable; because the substitution of another day for the seventh would annul the institution. It contains no warrant to keep the first day of the week as a Sabbath, but the seventh only. Its authority is limited to the seventh day, and cannot be transferred. The reason given for its institution, likewise, is limited to this day. It is obvious that it will not apply to another. The Sabbath law, therefore, contains no warrant whatever for the observance of the first day of the week. If the day is changed, the institution is annulled; and another institution, in some respects similar, but not in all, is introduced, in the total absence of *divine* authority, and hence rests altogether upon that which is *human*. This consideration, of itself, shows the absurdity of holding to the change of the original day, while the validity of the entire Decalogue is admitted.

From what has been here presented, it is evident that the Scriptures do not authorize the abrogation or change of the original Sabbath, but enforce its observance by precept and example. The opposite view is supported wholly by tradition and human authority, as an impartial examination of the history of the change will show. Have we not a right to expect, then, that when the great body of professing Christians shall become enlightened on this subject, and have sufficient grace and fortitude to act up to their convictions, the result will be, a general return to the faithful keeping of the Sabbath of the fourth commandment?

Published by the American Sabbath Tract Society,
No. 9 Spruce Street, N. Y.

[No. 4.]

THE

SABBATH AND LORD'S DAY;

A

HISTORY OF THEIR OBSERVANCE

IN

THE CHRISTIAN CHURCH.

NEW YORK:
PUBLISHED BY THE AMERICAN SABBATH TRACT SOCIETY,
No. 9 Spruce-Street.
1852.

HISTORY OF THE SABBATH.

In the preceding numbers of this series of Tracts, we have given an account of the institution of the Sabbath, and the reasons for believing it to be moral and perpetually binding, together with an examination of the authority for a change of the day. As the result of this examination, we have been driven to the conclusion, that the Sabbath was given to man in Paradise; that the fourth commandment was but a reënforcement of it; that the Scriptures do not authorize a change of the day of the Sabbath; and that, therefore, *the seventh day of the week ought now to be observed by all men.* But there are many persons who admit the early institution of the Sabbath, and the absence of any authority from the Scriptures for a change, yet suppose that the example of the early Christians, and the sayings of "the Fathers," warrant them in observing the first day of the week, to the neglect of the seventh. For the benefit of such, we now come to consider the history of the Sabbath since the establishment of the Christian Church. By consenting to do this, it is not meant to admit, that if a regard for the first day of the week can be traced to near the time of the Apostles, it is necessarily of apostolic authority; for it is affirmed by St. Paul, that even in his time "the mystery of iniquity had begun to work." We believe that "the Holy Scripture containeth all things necessary to salvation, so that whatsoever is not read therein, nor may be proved thereby, is not to be required of any man;" and we cannot admit, therefore, that the early existence of the practice is sufficient to give it divine authority, unless sanctioned by the inspired writings. In order to establish the claims of the first day of the week to be the Sabbath, two things are indispensable: 1. To prove from the Scriptures that the seventh day (which all acknowledge to have been originally the Sabbath) has been abrogated. 2. To show from the same source that the first day has been appointed in the place of the seventh. It is not sufficient to prove that a religious regard was early paid to the first day. There is an important distinction between *the Sabbath* and a *religious festival;* the former requiring abstinence from all ordinary labor, and devotion of a whole day to the public and private duties of religion; the latter requiring only the commemoration of some important event, and allowing the time not occupied in the public celebration of it to be devoted to labor or amusement. That this distinction was understood to exist between the regard for the seventh day and that for the first day, seems evident from the fact that in the early history of the church no Christians are charged with abandoning the Sabbath, while we are assured that after the meetings on the first day of the week they went about their ordinary labor. This apparently innocent regard for the day on which Christ first appeared to his disciples after his resurrection, it is believed, has given rise to the whole apostacy from the Sabbath. The following pages are designed to show the steps by which it was brought about.

The Sabbath in the Apostolic Church.

Before entering upon the history of the Sabbath, as it is derived from uninspired records, it is proper to inquire how it was regarded by Jesus Christ and his Apostles.

That Jesus Christ embraced the observance of the Sabbath among other duties enjoined in the Decalogue, is evident from Matt. 5 : 17 :—" Think not that I am come to destroy the law or the prophets ; I am not come to destroy, but to fulfill ; for verily I say unto you, till heaven and earth pass, one jot or one tittle shall in no wise pass from the law, till all be fulfilled." He here declared the precepts of this law, without distinction, to be permanent and unchangeable. Had he commanded his disciples to keep the Sabbath, by enacting a new precept, it would have been equivalent to saying that he considered it in the light of a ceremonial and expiring institution, which, in truth, it was not. He therefore most wisely enforced all those precepts as inseparable, unchangeable, and unrepealable. And he plainly said, in the connection referred to, that no person is worthy of a place in his church, who will break any one of these commandments, or teach others to do so. In all his subsequent allusions to this subject, he speaks of the Sabbath as an ancient and well-established ordinance, founded in the nature and fitness of things, made for and adapted to the uses of mankind. (Mark 2 : 27.) His *example* was in strict conformity with his teachings on this subject. His "*custom*" was to go to places of public worship, and to preach the Gospel on the Sabbath. His *disciples*, being educated in the observance of the Sabbath, could have entertained no doubts as to its perpetuity, nor have reasons to suppose that Christianity relaxed their obligation to observe it. It is very certain, that during the whole time that our Lord was with his disciples before his death, he gave no intimation to them that the duty of keeping the Sabbath was to be in any wise affected by his death; and we find that after this event, the disciples "rested the Sabbath day, according to the commandment." (Luke 23 : 56.) Further, our Saviour himself, when speaking of the destruction of Jerusalem, an event not to take place until forty years after his death, tells his disciples to pray that their flight might not be on the Sabbath day. It is difficult to conceive why this day should be spoken of at so late a period, unless it was to continue.

The same views respecting the sacredness of the Sabbath seem to have been entertained by the Apostles, after the resurrection of Christ, that they held before his death; and they appear to have occupied that day as they had formerly done, in attending places of public worship, and preaching the Gospel. See Acts 13 : 14, 42, 44, where it is said, "They came to Antioch, in Pisidia, and went into the synagogue on the Sabbath day." After Paul had preached Christ as the true Messiah, "and when the Jews were gone out of the synagogue, the Gentiles besought that these words might be preached to them the next Sabbath." "And the next Sabbath day came almost the whole city together to hear the word of God." Or, see Acts 16 : 13, where, "on the Sabbath we went out of the city, by a river side, where prayer was wont to be made." Or Acts 15 : 21—"For Moses, of old time, hath in every city them that preach him, being read in the synagogue every Sabbath day." This last passage is given by St. James as a reason why they should write to the Gentile converts only that "they abstain from things offered to idols," &c. From this it is apparent that the custom was common, both to hold meetings on the Sabbath day, and for the Gentile Christians to attend those meetings. If it was not common, the reading of Moses would not benefit them. If it was common, then they kept the Sabbath.

St. Paul, in 1 Thess. 2 : 14, says to the Thessalonians, "For ye, brethren, became followers (imitators) of the churches of God, which in Judea are in Christ Jesus." And as these Gentile Christians were followers of the churches in Judea, so they were ensamples, or patterns, to all the believers in Macedonia and Achaia. (Ch. 1 : 7.) As to the character of the churches in Judea touching the Sabbath, we need only to consult Acts 21 : 20. It is there asserted, that there were many thousands of the Jews who believed, and that they were all zealous of the law. And the context shows that they were zealous of even the ceremonies of the Jewish ritual. Hence we infer, that there was uniformity with the Jewish and Gentile Christians, in the observance of the Sabbath, and that the whole apostolic church religiously kept it.

Notwithstanding the Sabbath continued to be observed until the sacred canon was closed, it has been quite common, since the Reformation, to refer to certain passages of Scripture as indicating that the first day had been, or was to be, substituted for the seventh. It is said that Christ's meeting with his disciples on the evening of his resurrection day indicates that it was to be religiously regarded thereafter. Those who make such use of this circumstance seem to overlook, what it is very important to remember, that two of the disciples traveled from Jerusalem to Emmaus and back on that day, a distance of fifteen miles, and a part of this in company with the Saviour. This fact alone shows that it could not have been regarded as a Sabbath. Nor is there any thing in the circumstances of the meeting to indicate it. The disciples were not all present, and those who were present had assembled for other reasons, without any expectation of seeing the Master.

The meeting *"after eight days"* affords no help. Who can say positively that this expression means a week? Or, granting that it does mean a week, what does the passage make for the religious character of the first day? Jesus met his disciples on one occasion when fishing, and was seen of them forty days. Now, if his meeting with them proves the day of that meeting to be a Sabbath, a fishing day would be such, and the whole forty.

In regard to those two places, (Acts 20 : 7, and 1 Cor. 16 : 2,) where the expression *"first day of the week"* occurs, they make nothing for the sanctification of the day, since there is no hint of any such thing. The meetings there spoken of were for special purposes, and nothing was done at either which might not with perfect propriety have been done on any day. It is not quite certain that the passage, "They came together to break bread," refers to the Lord's Supper. Indeed, both St. Chrysostom among the ancients, and Calvin among the moderns, deny that it was to celebrate the Supper, and refer it to a friendly meal.

The text, Rev. 1 : 10, where St. John was *"in the spirit on the Lord's day,"* is likewise not a good proof text. That reference is there had to the first day of the week, is by no means certain. There are some who refer it to a much longer period—to the gospel era; while others, among whom is Bede, refer it to the day of judgment. The fact that none of those who early mention the Lord's day refer to this passage, is much against it. In these circumstances, it would not be safe to draw conclusions in regard to practice therefrom. Indeed, none of the earliest writers found the observance of the Lord's day upon the Scriptures.

Observance of the Sabbath from the time of the Apostles to Constantine.

Thus far we have been guided by the inspired Scriptures, and we think they prove beyond dispute, that the Christians of the apostolic age had received no new doctrine concerning the Sabbath, but continued without any change to devote the seventh day of the week to the duties of religion. But we now enter a period in which the history of the Sabbath must be derived from other sources. It may be difficult to trace exactly every step which has been taken, as the histories of the early ages are very defective on many subjects. They have come to us, to a considerable extent, through the church of Rome; and since she claims to have changed the day of the Sabbath, it is not to be expected that testimony against herself would be very faithfully preserved. In pursuing our sketch, we shall follow the best lights we have to guide us.

After the period described in the Acts of the Apostles, Christianity soon became widely spread in the Roman empire, which, at that time, extended over most of the civilized world. But as it receded from the time of the Apostles, and the number of its professors increased, the church became gradually less spiritual, and more disposed to deck the simple religion of Jesus with mysteries and superstitious formalities; and the bishops or pastors became ambitious of their authority over the churches. Those churches, even in Gentile cities, appear to have been composed, at first, principally of converted Jews, who not only observed the weekly Sabbath, but also the feast of the Passover, adapted particularly to Christian worship; respecting which, there was much contention. In the mean time, converts were greatly multiplied from among the Gentiles and were united with those from the Jews, who, [illegible]ithout reason, considered themselves entitled to some distinction as the original founders of the gospel church, and as being better informed in the writings of Moses and the prophets, having been in the habit of reading them every Sabbath in the synagogues.

About three years after the martyrdom of Peter and Paul, according to the common account, Judea was invaded by the Roman armies, and Jerusalem was besieged and destroyed, as our Lord had predicted. By this awful calamity, it is supposed that most of the churches in Judea were scattered; for they fled their country at the approach of their enemies, as they were taught by Jesus Christ to do. (Matt. 24 : 16.) This war resulted not only in the breaking up of the nation, and the destruction of a great portion of the people, but also in bringing a general odium upon the Jews wherever they were found; so that even the Christians of Judea suffered what our Saviour taught them to expect, (Matt. 24 : 9,) "And ye shall be hated of all nations for my name's sake." These circumstances, added to the enmity which formerly existed between the Gentiles and the Jews, produced a prejudice which had its influence in the church in bringing into disrepute, and in fixing a stigma upon, whatever was regarded as Judaism. "The doctrines of our Saviour and the church, flourishing from day to day, continued to receive constant accessions," says *Eusebius*, "but the calamities of the Jews also continued to grow with one accumulation of evil upon another." The insurrectionary disposition of the conquered Jews in the reign of *Trajan*, in the early part of the second century, and the calamities that followed them, seemed to confirm the opinion that the Jews were given over by the Almighty to entire destruction. But their calamities increased in the reign of *Adrian*, who succeeded *Trajan*, in whose reign the revolt of the Jews again proceeded to many and great excesses, and *Rufus*, the lieutenant governor of Judea, using their madness as a pretext, destroyed myriads of men, women and children, in crowds; and by the laws of war, he reduced their country to a state of absolute subjection, and the degraded race to the condition of slaves." The transformation of the church in Jerusalem is thus described by *Eusebius:* "The city of the Jews being thus reduced to a state of abandonment for them, and totally stripped of its ancient inhabitants, and also inhabited by strangers; the Roman city which subsequently arose changing its name, was called *Ælia*, in honor of the emperor Ælias Adrian; and when the church was collected there of the Gentiles, the first bishop after those of the circumcision was *Marcus*." Thus was extinguished the Hebrew church in Jerusalem, having had a succession of fifteen pastors; "all which," says *Eusebius*, "they say, were Hebrews from the first. At that time the whole church under them," he adds, "consisted of faithful Hebrews, who continued from the time of the Apostles to the siege that then took place."

This church, which heretofore held the first rank in regard to its influence, being now composed entirely of Gentiles, and stripped of its apostolic character and influence, could no longer successfully oppose the growing ambition and influence of the bishops of the church in the metropolis of the empire.

Up to this period, and for some time after, there does not appear to have been any change in the sentiments or practice of the church, in any place, relative to the Sabbath; but from what is related by subsequent writers, which will be noticed in its place, it is certain that it was observed by the churches universally. This fact is so generally acknowledged by those acquainted with the history of the matter, that we need refer to only a few passages in proof.

The learned *Grotius* says, in his Explication of the Decalogue, "Therefore the Christians also, who believed Christ would restore all things to their primitive practice, as Tertullian teacheth in *Monogamia*, kept holy the Sabbath, and had their assemblies on that day, in which the law was read to them, as appears in Acts 15 : 21, which custom remained till the time of the council of Laodicea, about A. D. 365, who then thought meet that the gospels also should be read on that day."

Edward Brerewood, Professor in Gresham College, London, in a Treatise on the Sabbath, 1630, says: "It is commonly believed that the Jewish Sabbath was changed into the Lord's day by Christian emperors, and they know little who do not know, that *the ancient Sabbath did remain and was observed by the eastern churches three hundred years after our Saviour's passion.*"

At what time the first day of the week came into notice as a festival in the church, it is not easy to determine. The first intimation we have of this, in any ancient writer of acknowledged integrity, is from Justin Martyr's Apology for the Christians, about A. D. 140. He is cited as saying, "that the Christians in the city and in the country assembled on the day called Sunday, and after certain religious devotions, all returned home to their labors;" and he assigns as reasons for this, that God made the world on the first day, and that Christ first showed himself to his disciples on that day after his resurrection. These were the best, and probably all the reasons that could then be offered for the practice. He also speaks of Sunday only as a festival, on which they performed labor, when not engaged in devotions, and not as a substitute for the Sabbath. From this author we can learn nothing as to the extent of the practice; for though he says this was done by those "in the city and in the country," he may have intended only the city of Rome and its suburbs, since *Justin*, although a native of Palestine in Syria, is stated by *Eusebius* to have made his residence in Rome. Nor can we determine from this, that he intended any thing more than that they did thus on the Sunday in which the church of Rome, a short time after this, is known to have closed the paschal feast, which was observed annually.

It is contended, however, that mention is made of keeping the first day previous to *Justin*. The first intimation of this kind, it is believed, is from an apocryphal writing, styled the *Epistle of Barnabas;* but to this epistle it is objected, that there is no evidence of its genuineness. *Eusebius*, who lived near the time when it was written, mentions it as a spurious writing, entitled to no credit. *Dr. Milnor* says it is an injury to St. Barnabas to ascribe this epistle to him. *Mosheim* says it is the work of some superstitious Jew of mean abilities. And we think it has but little to recommend it besides its antiquity. Barnabas' theory for observing the first day, rests upon the tradition that the seventh day was typical of the seventh millennium of the age of the world, which would be purely a holy age, and that the Sabbath was not to be kept until that time arrived; and he says, "We keep the eighth day with gladness, in which Jesus rose from the dead."

The citations from *Ignatius*, are as little to the purpose. In the passage of which most use has been made, he did not say that himself or any one else kept the Lord's day, as is often asserted. His own words are, that "the prophets who lived before Christ

2

came to a newness of hope, not by keeping Sabbaths, but by living according to a lordly or most excellent life." In this passage, Ignatius was speaking of altogether a different thing from Sabbath-keeping. There is another quotation from him, however, in which he brings out more clearly his view of the relation existing between the Sabbath and Lord's day. It is as follows: "Let us not keep the Sabbath in a Jewish manner, in sloth and idleness; but let us keep it after a spiritual manner, not in bodily ease, but in the study of the law, and in the contemplation of the works of God." "And *after* we have kept the Sabbath, let every one that loveth Christ keep the Lord's day *festival*." From this it seems that he would have the Sabbath kept first, *as such*, and in a manner satisfactory to the strictest Sabbatarian, after which the Lord's day, not as a Sabbath, but as a festival. Indeed, with this distinction between the *Sabbath* and a *festival* before us, it is easy to explain all those passages from early historians which refer to the first day. We shall find them to be either immediately connected with instructions about such seasons as *Good Friday* and *Holy Thursday*, or in the writings of those who have recommended the observance of these festival days.

It is also said that *Pliny*, Governor of Bithynia, A. D. 102, in a letter to *Trajan*, states that the Christians met on the first day of the week for worship; but by no fair interpretation of his words can he be so understood. He says, in writing about those of his own province, "that they were accustomed to assemble on a *stated day*." This might be referred to the first day, if there were credible testimony that this day was alone regarded at that time; but as there is no evidence of this, and as the Sabbath is known to have been the stated day of religious assembling a long time after this, it seems more proper to refer it to the Sabbath.

We will mention but one more of these misinterpreted citations, and this is from *Dionysius*, bishop of Corinth, who lived a little after *Justin*. His letter to *Soter*, bishop of Rome, is cited as saying, "This day we celebrated the holy Dominical day, in which we have read your epistle." As given by *Eusebius*, it is thus: "To-day we have *passed the Lord's holy day*," &c. The only ground upon which this phrase can be referred to the first day, is, that this day was at that time known by the same title that God has given to the Sabbath, (see Isaiah 48 : 13,) of which there is no proof. Therefore it is not just to cite this passage as evidence of the observance of the first day at that time.

It is, indeed, a well-known fact, that the first day has come into very extensive use among the great body of Christians, as the only day of weekly rest and worship. The origin of this practice does not appear, however, to be as ancient, by some centuries, as many suppose; nor was its adoption secured at once, but by slow and gradual advances it obtained general notice in Christian countries. This is frankly admitted by *Morer*, an English Episcopalian, in his *Dialogues on the Lord's day*, p. 236. He says, "In *St. Jerome's* time, (that is, in the fifth century,) Christianity had got into the throne as well as into the empire. Yet for all this, the entire sanctification of the Lord's day proceeded slowly; and that it was the work of time to bring it to perfection, appears from the several steps the church made in her constitution, and from the decrees of emperors and other princes, wherein the prohibitions from servile and civil business advanced by degrees from one species to another, till the day got a considerable figure in the world." The same author says, on the same page: "If the Christians in St. Jerome's time, after divine service on the Lord's day, followed their daily employments, it should be remembered, that this was not done till the worship was quite over, when they might with innocency enough resume them, because the length of time and the number of hours assigned for piety were not then so well explained as in after ages."

It is probable that no other day could have obtained the same notice in ancient times as the first day of the week did; for there were circumstances, aside from the resurrection, that had an influence in promoting its observance. It was at first a celebration of the same character as the fourth and sixth days of the week, and the annual festivals of saints and martyrs. These celebrations were comparatively unobjectionable, when not permitted to interfere with a divine appointment; but when they were made to supersede or cause a neglect of the Sabbath, they were criminal. In respect to these days of weekly celebration, *Mosheim*, when remarking upon this early period, and the regard then paid to the seventh and first days, says, "Many also observed the fourth day, in which Christ was betrayed, and the sixth day, in which he was crucified." He adds, "The time of assembling was generally in the evening after sunset, or in the morning before the dawn."

The respect which the Gentiles had for the first day, or Sunday, *while they were Pagans*, contributed much to render its introduction easy, and its weekly celebration popular, among such materials as composed the body of the church of Rome in the second, third, and fourth centuries. The observance of the first day of the week as a festival of the Sun, was very general in those nations from which the Gentile church received her converts. That an idolatrous worship was paid to the Sun and other heavenly bodies by the Gentiles, the Old Testament abundantly testifies; and this kind of adoration paid to the Sun in later times, is as plainly a matter of historical record. *Thomas Bampfield*, an English writer of the seventeenth century, quoting *Verstegan's* Antiquities, p. 68, says: "Our ancestors in England, before the light of the Gospel came among them, went very far in this idolatry, and dedicated the first day of the week to the adoration of the idol of the Sun, and gave it the name of Sunday. This idol they placed in a temple, and there sacrificed to it." He further states, that from his historical reading, he finds that a great part of the world, and particularly those parts of it which have since embraced Christianity, did anciently adore the Sun upon Sunday. It is also stated by *Dr. Chambers*, in his Cyclopedia, that "Sunday was so called by our idolatrous ancestors, because set apart for the worship of the Sun." The Greeks and the Latins also gave the same name to the first day of the week. *Dr. Brownlee*, as quoted by *Kingsbury*, on the Sabbath, p. 223, also says, "When the descendants of Adam apostatized from the worship of the true God, they substituted in his place the Sun, that luminary which, more than all others, strikes the minds of savage people with religious awe; and which, therefore, all heathens worship." Attachment to particular days of religious celebration, from habit merely, is well known, even in our own day, to be very strong, and powerful convictions of duty are often required to produce a change. This was no doubt well understood by the teachers of Christianity in those times. *Dr. Mosheim*, when treating on that age, says, "that the leaders imagined that the nations would the more readily receive Christianity when they saw the rites and ceremonies to which they had been accustomed established in the churches, and the same worship paid to Jesus Christ and his martyrs which they had formerly offered to their idol deities. Hence it happened, that in those times, the religion of the Greeks and Romans differed but little in its external appearance from that of Christians."

Prejudice against the Jews, was another influence against the Sabbath, and in favor of the first day. This was very strong, and directly calculated to lead the Gentile Christians to fix a stigma upon every religious custom of the Jews, and to brand as *Judaism* whatever they supposed had any connection with the Mosaic religion. Hence it was that in those times, as often occurs in our own, to produce disaffection and disgust to the seventh day as the Sabbath, they spoke of it and reproached its observance as Judaizing. This feeling in relation to Judaism led *Athanasius*, bishop of Alexandria, in Egypt, in the fourth century, who with his people then observed the Sabbath, to say, in his *Interpretation of the Psalms*, "We assemble on Saturday, not that we are infected with Judaism, but to worship Jesus the Lord of the Sabbath." In a community of Christians whose religion was formal, and whose celebrations were designed more to act upon their passions and senses than to improve their hearts or to conform them to divine requirements, a more powerful argument could scarcely be used against the Sabbath day, or one that would more effectually promote the observance of the first day, which was raised up as its rival. *Dr. Neander* says distinctly, "Opposition to Judaism introduced the particular festival of Sunday very early."

The observance of the Passover, or Easter, by the early Christians, aided the introduction of the first day as a religious festival in the church, if it was not indeed the direct cause of it. This feast was held by the Asiatic Christians, who began it at the same time the Jews began their Passover, and ended it in like manner, without regard to the particular day of the week. The church of Rome does not appear to have observed it until the latter part of the second century, when, in the time of *Victor*, bishop of Rome, it seems that it was observed by the Roman and western churches. *Victor* insisted upon the fast being closed on the first day of the week, on whatever day it might commence; and he claimed the right, as bishop of Rome, to control all the churches in this matter. "Hence," says *Eusebius*, "there were synods and convocations of the bishops on this question, and all (i. e. the western bishops) unanimously drew up an ecclesiastical decree, which they communicated to all the churches in all places, that the mystery of our Lord's resurrection should be celebrated on no other day than the Lord's day, and that on this day alone we should observe the close of the paschal feasts." The bishops of Asia, however, persisted for a considerable time in observing the custom handed down to them by apostolic tradition, until, either by the threats of excommunication which were made, or by a desire for peace, they were induced partially to adopt the custom of the western churches. This change was made, as we are told, "partly in honor of the day, and partly to express some difference between Jews and Christians." But the question does not appear to have been fully settled; for we find *Constantine*, in an epistle to the churches, urging them to uniformity in the day of the celebration, wherein, after a strong invective against the practice of the Jews, he says, "For we have learned another way from our Saviour, which we may follow. It is indeed most absurd that they should have occasion of insolent boasting on account of our not being able to observe these things in any manner unless by the aid of their instruction." "Wherefore, let us have nothing in common with that most odious brood of the Jews." By this contest an important point was gained for the first day, although it was but an annual celebration. The Sabbath, however, does not appear to have been laid aside in any place, but continued to be the principal day of religious worship throughout the whole Christian church.

At what time the first day began to be observed weekly, we have no particular account; but from the favor it received from the bishops of Rome, and some of the Christian fathers, at the close of the third and beginning of the fourth century, we suppose it had then become a practice in Rome and some of the western churches.

This brings us to near the close of the third century. And here it ought to be noted, that Lord's day, or Sunday, was not the only holy-day of the Church during these three centuries. *Origen* (as quoted by Dr. Peter Heylyn in his History of the Sabbath) names the *Good Friday* as we call it now, the *Parasceve* as he calls it there; the feasts of *Easter* and of *Pentecost.* And anciently, not only the day which is now called *Whitsunday* or *Pentecost,* but all the fifty days from Easter forward, were accounted holy, and solemnized with no less observance than the Sundays were. Of the day of the *Ascension,* or *Holy Thursday,* it may likewise be said, that soon after, it came to be more highly esteemed of than all the rest. Such was the estimation in which the Lord's day was held. It was on a level with those other holy days which are now disregarded by the body of the Protestant Church. It is to be remembered, farther, that the term Sabbath was applied exclusively to the seventh day of the week, or Saturday. Indeed, wherever, for a thousand years and upwards, we meet the word *Sabbatum* in any writer, of what name soever, it must be understood of no day but Saturday.

The Sabbath from the time of Constantine to the Reformation.

We have seen how the matter stood until the commencement of Constantine's career. The Sabbath was generally observed, while the Lord's day was regarded as a festival of no greater importance or authority than Good Friday or Holy Thursday. No text of Scripture, or edict of emperor, or decree of council, could be produced in its favor. But from this time forth may be found emperors and councils combining to give importance to the Lord's day and to oppose the Sabbath.

An important change in the regard paid to the first day was produced soon after the accession of *Constantine*, the first Christian emperor, in the early part of the fourth century. When he became master of Rome, he soon gave himself up to the guidance of the Christian clergy. According to Jones' Church History, "He built places of public worship; he encouraged the meeting of synods and bishops; honored them with his presence, and employed himself continually in aggrandizing the church. He was scrupulously attentive to the religious rites and ceremonies which were prescribed to him by the clergy. He fasted, observed the feasts in commemoration of the martyrs, and devoutly watched the whole night on the vigils of the saints," and showed great anxiety for uniformity in the doctrines and observances of religion in the church. He was, therefore, exactly suited to the wishes of the Roman bishop and clergy, in establishing, by his imperial authority, what they had no Scripture to support, and what their influence had hitherto been insufficient to effect, viz. a uniformity in the celebration of Easter and the first day. In 321, *Constantine* first published his edicts enjoining upon his subjects these superstitious celebrations.

Eusebius, in his Life of Constantine, says: "He appointed as a suitable time for prayers the Dominical day, which then was an especial day, and now is undoubtedly the very first. His body guard observed the day, and offered on it prayers written by the Emperor. The happy prince endeavored to persuade all to do this, and by degrees to lead all to the worship of God; wherefore he determined that those obeying Roman power should abstain from every work upon the days named after the Saviour, that they should venerate also the day before the Sabbath, in memory, as seems to me, of the events occurring on those days to our common Saviour." He says again, "An edict also, by the will and pleasure of the Emperor, was transmitted to the Prefects of the provinces, that they thenceforth should venerate the Dominical day; that they should honor the days consecrated to the martyrs, and should celebrate the solemnities of the festivals in the churches, all which was done according to the will of the Emperor." And, as quoted by *Lucius*, he says, that he admonished his subjects likewise that those days which were *Sabbaths* should be honored or worshiped.

Sozomen, in his Ecclesiastical History, b. 1, c. 8, says, "He (Constantine) also made a law that on the Dominical day, which the Hebrews call the first day of the week, the Greeks the day of the Sun, and also on the day of Venus, (i. e. Friday,) judgments should not be given, or other business transacted, but that all should worship God with prayer and supplications, and venerate the Dominical day, as on it Christ rose from the dead, and the day of Venus, as the day on which he was fixed to the cross."

Dr. Chambers says, "It was Constantine the Great who first made a law for the observance of Sunday, and who, according to Eusebius, appointed that it should be regularly celebrated throughout the Roman empire. Before him, and even in his time, they observed the Jewish Sabbath as well as Sunday, both to satisfy the law of Moses, and to imitate the Apostles, who used to meet together on the first day." He adds, "Indeed, some are of opinion that the Lord's day mentioned in the Apocalypse is our Sunday, which they will have to have been so early instituted." "By Constantine's laws, made in 321, it was decreed that for the future the Sunday should be kept a day of rest in all cities and towns; but he allowed the country people to follow their work. In 538, the Council of Orleans prohibited this country labor.

To give the more solemnity to the first day of the week, (as we learn from Lucius' Ecclesiastical History,) *Sylvester*, who was bishop of Rome while Constantine was Emperor, changed the name of Sunday, giving it the more imposing title of *Lord's day*.

It cannot be doubted, that the laws of *Constantine* did much to make the first day conspicuous throughout the empire, as all public business was forbidden upon it. They changed its character from a special day, in which, as a weekly festival, all kinds of business and labor were performed in city and country, to be, as *Eusebius* says, *the very first*. This imperial favor for the first day operated against all who conscientiously regarded the Sabbath from respect to the fourth commandment, in obedience to which the seventh day had always been observed; and if it had produced a general abandonment of its observance, it would not have been very surprising, considering the influence of court example, and the general ignorance and darkness of the age. This, however, does not appear to have been the case. The Sabbath was still extensively observed; and to counteract it the Council of *Laodicea*, about A. D. 350, passed a decree saying, "It is not proper for Christians to Judaize, and to cease from labor on the Sabbath, but they ought to work on that day, and put especial honor upon the Lord's day, as Christians. If any be found Judaizing, let him be anathematized."

But this did not produce any material change, for *Socrates*, a writer of the fifth century, who resided at Constantinople, makes the following remarks upon the celebration of the Sabbath at the time he wrote, A. D. 440. He says, "There are various customs concerning assembling; for though all the churches throughout the whole world celebrate the sacred mysteries on the Sabbath day, yet the Alexandrians and the Romans, from an ancient tradition, refuse to do this; but the Egyptians who are in the neighborhood of Alexandria, and those inhabiting Thebais, indeed have assemblies on the Sabbath, but do not participate in the mysteries, as is the custom of the Christians. At Cæsarea, Cappadocia, and in Cyprus, on the Sabbath and Dominical day, at twilight, with lighted lamps, the presbyters and bishops interpret the Scriptures. At Rome they fast every Sabbath."

This account of the manner of celebrating the Sabbath in the fifth century, is corroborated by *Sozomen*, in his Ecclesiastical History, b. 7, c. 9. He says, "At Constantinople, and almost among all, the Christians assembled upon the Sabbath, and also upon the first day of the week, excepting at Rome and Alexandria; the ecclesiastical assemblies at Rome were not upon the Sabbath, as in almost all other churches of the rest of the world; and in many cities and villages in Egypt, they used to commune in the evening of the Sabbath, on which day there were public assemblies."

In regard to fasting on the Sabbath at Rome, referred to by Socrates, it ought to be said, that from the earliest times to the fourth century, the practice had been to observe the Sabbath as a holiday. But the Church of Rome, in its opposition to the Jews, made it a fast day, that the separation might be marked and strong. In the eastern churches they never fasted upon the Sabbath, excepting one Sabbath in the year, which was the day before the Passover. But in the western churches they celebrated a fast every week. It was in reference to this that *Ambrose* said, "When I come to Rome, I fast upon the Sabbath; when I am here, I do not fast." *Augustine* also said concerning this, "If they say it is sinful to fast on the Sabbath, then they would condemn the Roman Church, and many places near to and far from it. And if they should think it a sin not to fast on the Sabbath, then they would blame many eastern churches, and the far greater part of the world." This Sabbath fasting was opposed by the eastern church; and in the sixth general council, held at Constantinople, it was commanded that the Sabbath and Dominical days be kept as festivals, and that no one fast or mourn upon them. The practice of fasting, therefore, was chiefly in the western churches, about Rome.

It is perhaps difficult to determine exactly the relative importance attached to the seventh and first days of the week at this time. Sufficient may be found, however, to assure us, that the Sabbath was observed, and that no one regarded Sunday as having taken its place. This is shown by the provision of the Council of Laodicea, A. D. 365, that the Gospels should be read on that day. It is shown by the action of a Council in 517, (mentioned in *Robinson's History of Baptism*,) which regulated and enforced the observance of the Sabbath. It is shown by the expostulation of *Gregory of Nyssa*, "How can you look upon the Lord's day, if you neglect the Sabbath? Do you not know that they are sisters, and that in despising the one you affront the other?" And as sisters we find them hand in hand in the ecclesiastical canons. Penalties were inflicted by the councils both of Laodicea and Trullo, on clergymen who did not observe both days as festivals.

How the first day of the week, or Lord's day, was observed in the early part of the fifth century, we may learn from the words of *St. Jerome.* In a funeral oration for the Lady *Paula,* he says: "She, with all her virgins and widows who lived at Bethlehem in a cloister with her, upon the Lord's day, repaired duly to the church, or house of God, which was nigh to her cell; and after her return from thence to her own lodgings, she herself and all her company *fell to work,* and they all performed their task, which was the making of clothes and garments for themselves and for others, as they were appointed."

St. Chrysostom, patriarch of Constantinople, "recommended to his audience, after impressing upon themselves and their families what they had heard on the Lord's day, to return to their daily employments and trades."

Dr. Francis White, Lord Bishop of Ely, speaking of this matter, says, "The Catholic Church, for more than six hundred years after Christ, permitted labor, and gave license to many Christian people to work upon the Lord's day, at such hours as they were not commanded to be present at the public service by the precepts of the church."

In the sixth century efforts were made to prevent this labor. The following promulgation of a synod held by command of King *Junthran,* of Burgundy, will show the condition of things, and the means used to improve it: "We see the Christian people, in an unadvised manner, deliver to contempt the Dominical day, and, as in other days, indulge on continual labor."

Therefore they determined to teach the people subject to them to keep the Dominical day, which, if not observed by the lawyer, he should irreparably lose his cause, and if a countryman or servant did not keep it, he should be beaten with heavier blows of cudgels. The council of Orleans, held 538, prohibited the country labor on Sunday which Constantine by his laws permitted. According to Chambers, this council also declared, "that to hold it unlawful to travel with horses, cattle, and carriages, to prepare food, or to do any thing necessary to the cleanliness and decency of houses or persons, savors more of Judaism than Christianity." According to Lucius, in another council held in Narbonne, in France, in the seventh century, they also forbid this country work.

Early in the seventh century, in the time of Pope *Gregory I.*, the subject of the Sabbath attracted considerable attention. There was one class of persons who declared, "that it was not lawful to do any manner of work upon the Saturday, or the old Sabbath; another, that no man ought to bathe himself on the Lord's day, or their new Sabbath." Against both of these doctrines Pope *Gregory* wrote a letter to the Roman citizens. *Baronius*, in his Councils, says, "This year (603) at Rome, St. Gregory, the Pope, corrected that error which some preached, by Jewish superstition, or the Grecian custom, that it was a duty to worship on the Sabbath, as likewise upon the Dominical day;" and he calls such preachers the preachers of Antichrist.

Nearly the same doctrine was preached again in the time of *Gregory VII.*, A. D. 1074, about five hundred years after what we are now speaking of. This is sufficient to show that the Sabbath was kept until those times of decline which introduced so many errors in faith and practice. Indeed, it is sufficient to show, that wherever the subject has been under discussion, the Sabbath has found its advocates, both in *theory* and in *practice.*

According to *Lucius*, Pope *Urban II.*, in the eleventh century, dedicated the Sabbath to the Virgin Mary, with a mass. *Binius* says, "Pope *Innocent I.* constituted a fast on the Sabbath day, which seems to be the first constitution of that fast; but dedicating the Sabbath to the Virgin Mary was by *Urban II.*, in the latter part of the eleventh century." About this time we find *Esychius* teaching the doctrine that the precept for the observance of the Sabbath is not one of the commandments, because it is not at all times to be observed according to the letter; and *Thomas Aquinas*, another Romish ecclesiastic, saying, "that it seems to be inconvenient that the precept for observing the Sabbath should be put among the precepts of the Decalogue, if it do not at all belong to it; that the precept, '*Thou shalt not make a graven image,*' and the precept for *observing the Sabbath*, are ceremonial."

The observance of the first day was not so early in England and in Scotland as in most other parts of the Roman Empire. According to *Heylyn*, there were Christian societies established in Scotland as early as A. D. 435; and it is supposed that the gospel was preached in England in the first century by St. Paul. For many ages after Christianity was received in those kingdoms, they paid no respect to the first day. *Binius*, a Catholic writer, in the second volume of his works, gives some account of the bringing into use of the Dominical day [Sunday] in Scotland, as late as A. D. 1203. "This year," he says, "a council was held in Scotland concerning the introduction of the Lord's day, which council was held in 1203, in the time of Pope *Innocent III.*," and he quotes as his authority Roger

Hoveden, Matth. Paris, and Lucius' Eccl. Hist. He says, "By this council it was enacted that it should be holy time from the twelfth hour on Saturday noon until Monday."

Boethus (de Scottis, p. 344) says, "In 1203, *William*, king of Scotland, called a council of the principal of his kingdom, by which it was decreed, that Saturday, from the twelfth hour at noon, should be holy, that they should do no profane work, and this they should observe until Monday."

Binius says that in 1201 *Eustachius*, Abbot of Flay, came to England, and therein preached from city to city, and from place to place. He prohibited using markets on Dominical days; and for this he professed to have a special command from heaven. The history of this singular document, entitled, *A holy Command of the Dominical Day*, the pious Abbot stated to be this: "It came from Heaven to Jerusalem, and was found on St. Simeon's tomb in Golgotha. And the Lord commanded this epistle, which for three days and three nights men looked upon, and falling to the earth, prayed for God's mercy. And after the third hour, the patriarch stood up; and Akarias the archbishop stretched out his mitre, and they took the holy epistle of God and found it thus written."

[We give some extracts from this epistle, partly as a matter of curiosity, and partly to show the credulity of our ancestors, and the means by which they were awed into what was to them a new religious observance.]

"I, the Lord, who commanded you that ye should observe the Dominical day, and ye have not kept it, and ye have not repented of your sins, as I said by my gospel, heaven and earth shall pass away, but my word shall not pass away; I have caused repentance unto life to be preached unto you, and ye have not believed; I sent pagans against you, who shed your blood, yet ye believed not; and because ye kept not the Dominical day, for a few days ye had famine; but I soon gave you plenty, and afterwards ye did worse; I will again, that none from the ninth hour of the Sabbath until the rising of the sun on Monday, do work any thing unless what is good, which if any do, let him amend by repentance; and if ye be not obedient to this command, amen, I say unto you, and I swear unto you by my seat, and throne, and cherubim, who keep my holy seat, because I will not change any thing by another epistle; but I will open the heavens, and for rain I will rain upon you stones, and logs of wood, and hot water by night, and none may be able to prevent, but that I may destroy all wicked men. This I say unto you, ye shall die the death, because of the Dominical holy day and other festivals of my saints which ye have not kept. I will send unto you beasts having the heads of lions, the hair of women, and tails of camels; and they shall be so hunger-starved that they shall devour your flesh, and ye shall desire to flee to the sepulchres of the dead, and hide you for fear of the beasts; and I will take away the light of the sun from your eyes; and I will send upon you darkness, that without seeing ye may kill one another; and I will take away my face from you, and will not show you mercy; for I will burn the bodies and hearts of all who keep not the Dominical holy day. Hear my voice, lest ye perish in the land because of the Dominical holy day. Now know ye, that ye are safe by the prayers of my most holy mother Mary, and of my holy angels who daily pray for you. I gave you the law from Mount Sinai, which ye have not kept. For you I was born into the world, and my festivals ye have not known; the Dominical day of my resurrection ye have not kept; I swear to you by my right hand, unless ye keep the Dominical day and the festivals of my saints, I will send pagans to kill you."

Provided with this new command from heaven, "*Eustachius* preached in various parts of England against the desecration of the Dominical day, and other festivals; and gave the people absolution upon condition that they hereafter reverence the Dominical day, and the festivals of the saints." And the people vowed to God, that thereafter they would neither buy nor sell any thing but food on Sunday.

"Then," says *Binius*, "the enemy of man, envying the admonitions of this holy man, put it into the heart of the king and nobility of England, to command that all who should keep the aforesaid traditions, and chiefly all who had cast down the markets for things vendible upon the Dominical day, should be brought to the king's court to make satisfaction about observing the Dominical day."

Binius relates many miraculous things that occurred on the Sabbath to those that labored after the ninth hour (i. e. after three o'clock in the afternoon) of the seventh day, or Saturday. He says, that upon a certain Sabbath, after the ninth hour, a carpenter, for making a wooden pin, was struck with the palsy; and a woman, for knitting on the Sabbath, after the ninth hour, was also struck with the palsy. A man baked bread, and when he broke it to eat, blood came out. Another, grinding corn, blood came in a great stream instead of meal, while the wheel of his mill stood still against a vehement impulse of water. Heated ovens refused to bake bread, if heated after the ninth hour of the Sabbath; and dough, left unbaked out of respect to Eustachius' new doctrine, was found on Monday morning well baked without the aid of fire. These fables were industriously propagated throughout the kingdom; "yet the people," says Binius, "fearing kingly and human power more than divine, returned as a dog to his own vomit, to keep markets of saleable things upon the Dominical day."

Mr. Bampfield, in his Enquiry, p. 3, says, "The king and princes of England, in 1203, would not agree to change the Sabbath, and keep the first day, by this authority. This was in the time of *King John*, against whom the popish clergy had a great pique for not honoring their prelacy and the monks, by one of whom he was finally poisoned."

Binius (Councils, cent. 13) states that King John of England, in 1208, in the tenth year of his reign, for not submitting to popish impositions upon his prerogatives, was excommunicated by the Pope, and his kingdom interdicted, which occasioned so much trouble at home and abroad, that it forced him at last to lay down his crown at the feet of Mandulphus, the Pope's agent. After he was thus humbled by that excommunication and interdiction, the king, in the fifteenth year of his reign, by writ, removed the market of the city of Exon from Sunday, on which it was held, to Monday. The market of Lanceston was removed from the first to the fifth day of the week. In the second and third years of Henry III. many other markets were removed from the first to other days of the week, which the King at first would not permit. He also issued a writ which permitted the removal of markets from the first day to other days without special license.

The Parliament of England met on Sundays until the time of Richard II., who adjourned it from that to the following day.

In 1203, according to *Boethus*, "a council was held in Scotland to inaugurate the king, and concerning the feast of the Sabbath; and there came also a legate from the Pope, with a sword and purple hat, and indulgences and privileges to the young king. It was also there decreed, that Saturday, from the twelfth hour at noon, should be holy." The *Magdeburgenses* say that this Council was about the observance of the Dominical day *newly brought in*, and that they ordained that it should be holy from the twelfth hour of Saturday even till Monday.

Binius says, "A synod was held in Oxford, A. D. 1223, by *Stephen*, Archbishop of Canterbury, where they determined that the Dominical day be kept with all veneration, and a fast upon the Sabbath."

According to Bampfield, the first law of England made for the keeping of Sunday, was in the time of Edward VI., about 1470. "Parliament then passed an act, by which Sunday and many holy days, the feasts of all Saints and of holy Innocents, were established as festivals by law. This provided also, that it should be lawful for husbandmen, laborers, fishermen, and all others in harvest, or at any other time of the year when necessity should require, to labor, ride, fish, or do any other kind of work, at their own free will and pleasure, upon any of the said days."

By such means as these, the observance of the first day was gradually forced upon the people wherever they owned allegiance to the Pope as head of the church, and the Sabbath was as gradually brought into contempt and disuse.

The process by which the change was effected appears to be this: By first obtaining an annual celebration of the first day at the close of the Passover, in honor of the resurrection; then a partial observance of the day weekly, it being generally so observed among the heathen; then obtaining for it the support of civil laws, ecclesiastical canons and penalties, and by giving it the title of Lord's day; then by requiring the consecration of the entire day. To abate and ultimately eradicate all respect for the Sabbath, it was first turned into a fast; then it was dedicated to the Virgin Mary, resting upon it was stigmatized as Judaism and heresy, and the preaching of it was called Antichrist; and finally the fourth commandment was pronounced ceremonial, and was effectually abstracted from the Decalogue. And thus, so far as the Roman church was concerned, the point was gained; and thus, probably, she performed her part in the fulfillment of the prophecy of Daniel, (7 : 25,) "He shall think to change TIMES and LAWS; and they shall be given into his hand until a time and times and the dividing of time."

The cause of the Sabbath must also have been seriously affected by the rise of the Ottoman Empire in the seventh century, and the success of the Mahometans in conquering the eastern division of the church. Mahomet formed the plan of establishing a new religion, or, as he expressed it, of replanting the only true and ancient one professed by Adam, Noah, Abraham, Moses, Jesus, and the prophets; by destroying idolatry, and weeding out the corruptions which the later Jews and Christians had, as he supposed, introduced. He was equally opposed to both Jews and Christians. To distinguish his disciples from each, he selected as their day of weekly celebration the sixth day, or Friday. And thus, as a writer of the seventeenth century remarks, "they and the Romanists crucified the Sabbath, as the Jews and the Romans did the Lord of the Sabbath, between two thieves, the sixth and the first day of the week."

We have thus traced the history of the Sabbath in the Roman church down to the thirteenth century; and we see that through the whole of this period, the seventh day every where retained the honor of being called the Sabbath, and that no other day had ever borne that title; that not until the remarkable letter found on St. Simeon's tomb, had it been asserted by any one, that the observance of the *first day, Lord's day,* or *Sunday,* was enjoined by the authority of Jesus or his apostles, nor was any example of theirs plead in its favor. Even then it was not pretended that the Scriptures required its observance.

There are some traces of the Sabbath among those Christians who separated from the Catholic communion, or were never embraced in it. The Greek church separated from them about the middle of the eleventh century, and had a larger extent of empire than the papists. According to *Brerewood's Enquiries,* p. 128, this church solemnized Saturday festivals, and forbade as unlawful to fast on any Saturday except in Lent, retaining the custom followed before their separation. The same author states that the Syrian Christians, who composed a numerous body in the East, celebrated divine worship solemnly on both the Sabbath and first day, continuing the custom of the Roman church at the time they separated from that community. *Sandy's Travels,* p. 173, speak of a Christian empire in Ethiopia that celebrate both Saturday and Sunday, "that they have divers errors and many ancient truths." The Abyssinian Christians, another numerous body, are represented as being similar in some respects to the

Papists; and *Purchase* speaks of them as "subject to Peter and Paul, and especially to Christ," and as observing the Saturday Sabbath. They are also mentioned by *Brerewood. Mosheim* mentions a sect of Christians in the twelfth century, in Lombardy, called *Pasaginians,* charged with circumcising their followers, and keeping the Jewish Sabbath. *Mr. Benedict* considers the account of their practicing the bloody rite a slander charged on them on account of their keeping the Jewish Sabbath. *Binius* says that in 1555 there were Christians in Rome who kept the Sabbath, and were therefore called *Sabbatarii,* and they are represented as differing in other respects from the Romanists. Many of the Armenian Christians are believed to observe the ancient Sabbath. *Dr. Buchanan,* in his Researches, when speaking of those of them who are settled in the East Indies, says, "Their doctrines are, as far as the author knows, the doctrines of the Bible. Besides this, they maintain the solemn observation of Christian worship throughout our empire on the seventh day."

Probably there has not existed a class of Christians since the times of the Apostles, who could more justly claim to be Apostolic than the *Waldenses,* formerly a numerous people living in the valleys of Piedmont; whither they retired, says Burnside, on the promulgation of Constantine's laws for the observance of the first day, in the fourth century; and where they remained, according to Scaliger and Brerewood, in the time of Elizabeth of England, in the latter part of the sixteenth century. They adhered firmly to the apostolic faith, and suffered severe persecutions from the Catholics. *Robinson,* in his *History of Baptism,* says, "They were called *Sabbati* and *Sabbatati,* so named from the Hebrew word *Sabbath,* because they kept the *Saturday* for the Lord's day." They were also called *Insabbatati*, because they rejected all the festivals, or Sabbaths, in the low Latin sense of the word. The account the Papists gave of their sentiments in 1250, was briefly this: That they declared themselves to be the apostolic successors, and to have apostolic authority; that they held the church of Rome to be the 'whore of Babylon;' that none of the ordinances of the church which have been introduced since Christ's ascension ought to be observed; that baptism is of no advantage to infants, because they cannot actually believe. They reject the sacrament of confirmation, but instead of that their teachers lay their hands upon their disciples. *Jones*, in his Church History, says that because they would not observe *saints' days*, they were falsely supposed to neglect the Sabbath also. Another of their enemies, an Inquisitor of Rome, charged them with despising all the feasts of Christ and his saints. Another, a Commissioner of Charles XII. of France, reported to him, "that he found among them none of the ceremonies, images, or signs of the Romish church, much less the crimes with which they were charged; on the contrary, they kept the Sabbath day, observed the ordinance of baptism according to the primitive church, and instructed their children in the articles of the Christian faith and commandments of God."

The Sabbath since the Reformation.

With the commencement of the Reformation, a new spirit of religious inquiry was awakened. Nearly every item of Christian practice was brought under review, and not dismissed until either approved or rejected. Among the subjects for discussion we find the Sabbath early introduced and thoroughly examined. There were three leading views then maintained by different classes of Reformers, which deserve particular notice.

1. One class of Reformers there was, who, dwelling alone on the sufficiency of faith, and the freeness of the Gospel, trembled at the thought of imposing rules upon men, and seemed to fear the term *law*. These declared, that the law of the Sabbath was abolished; that Sunday was no Sabbath, only a festival of the church, which had been appointed and might be altered at her pleasure. That we may not be thought in error here, as well as to give a full understanding of the opinions of that time, we will present the assertions of some of these men.

Bishop Cranmer's Catechism, A. D. 1548, says: "The Jews were commanded in the Old Testament to keep the Sabbath-day, and they observed it every seventh day, called the Sabbath, or Saturday; but we Christian men are not bound to such commandments in Moses' law, and therefore we now keep no more the Sabbath, or Saturday, as the Jews did, but we observe the Sunday, and some other days, *as the magistrates do judge convenient*."

William Tindal says, in his answer to More, chap. 25: "We be lords over the Sabbath, and may change it into Monday, or any other day, as we see need; or may make every tenth day holy-day, only if we see cause why; we may make two every week, if it were expedient, and one not enough to teach the people. Neither was there any cause to change it from the Saturday, other than to *put a difference between us and the Jews*, and lest we should become servants to the day after their superstition."

Bullinger, on Rev. 1: 10, says: "Christian churches entertained the Lord's day, not upon any commandment from God, but according to their free choice."

Melancthon says: "The Lord's day, from the Apostles' age, hath been a solemn day; notwithstanding, we find not the same commanded by any apostolic law; but it is collected from hence that the observance thereof was free, because Epiphanius and St. Augustine testify that on the fourth and the sixth days of the week church assemblies were held, as well as upon the Lord's day."

The Augustan Confession, drawn up by Melancthon, and approved by Luther, says: "We teach that traditions are not to be condemned which have a religious end, ... namely, traditions concerning holy-days, the Lord's day, the feast of the nativity, easter, &c."

These passages distinctly do away with the Sabbath, and place the observance of the Lord's day on the ground of human authority. In the books of some early authors who adopted these views, may be found frequent references to a difficulty which drove them to deny the perpetuity of the Sabbath. Bishop *White*, in 1635, says: "If the fourth commandment, concerning the keeping of the seventh day, is moral and perpetual, then it is not such in respect to the first and eighth day; for this precept requireth the observance of that one day only which it specifieth in that commandment." In speaking of the Lord's day, he says: "Every day of the week and of the year is the Lord's; and the Sunday is no more the Lord's by the law of the fourth commandment, than the Friday, for the Lord's day of that fourth commandment is the Saturday."

From each of these quotations, it appears to have been felt to be inconsistent to admit the perpetuity of the Sabbath, without keeping the seventh day. But to come back to this ancient day, and keep it in company with Jews, seemed too great a change. Hence the abrogation of the institution was asserted, as the easiest way of escaping from the dilemma. John Milton, speaking of this difficulty, says: "If we under the Gospel are to regulate the time of our public worship by the prescriptions of the Decalogue, it will surely be far safer to observe *the seventh day*, according to the express command of God, than, on the authority of mere human conjecture, to adopt the *first*."

Another influence which led to the rejection of the Sabbath by these men, was the view of it which was held by the Romish Church. When the leaders of the Reformation separated from that church, it was claimed that all her festival days, including Sundays, were holier than other days, not only in relation to the use made of them, but to a natural and *inherent holiness* wherewith they thought them to be invested. In addition to this, many and hurtful restraints had been imposed upon the consciences of God's people, until these were days of *punishment*, rather than of holy pleasure and profit. Seeing these days perverted from their real design, and made the means of strengthening papal power, it is not surprising that they were discarded together. Anxious to escape one error, they fell into another equally dangerous.

2. But another class of Reformers, (probably somewhat fearful of the consequences of those lax notions to which we have just referred,) considering that the Sabbath was given in Paradise, rehearsed at Sinai, and placed among the precepts of the Decalogue, declared that it must be moral in its nature, and perpetually binding. But having admitted its perpetuity, and having rested its claims upon the fourth commandment, the way of explaining and enforcing the change of the day presented an obstacle to the spread of this view. How this was treated, let their own words answer. *Dr. Bound*, in 1595, says, "The fourth commandment is simply and perpetually moral, and not ceremonial in whole or in part." *Richard Byfield*, 1630, says, "The fourth commandment is part of the law of nature, and thus part of the image of God, and is no more capable of a ceremony to be in it than God is."

Afterwards he says, "The institution of the Lord's day is clearly in the work of Christ's resurrection, as the institution of the seventh day was in the work of finishing the creation." "The resurrection applieth and determineth the Sabbath of the fourth commandment to the Lord's day." Such was the course of reasoning adopted by this class of persons. Having established the morality and perpetuity of the Sabbath by means of Scripture, and brought the sanctions of the Word of God to sustain them, they apply all this to the support of an institution, the existence and time of keeping which is inferred from Christ's resurrection. It is easy to see what must have been the consequence.

3. There was another class among the disputants about the Sabbath, who endeavored, by strict adherence to the Scriptures, to escape the difficulties and inconsistencies into which others had been led. They contended for the early institution of the Sabbath, for its morality and perpetuity as inferred from its being placed in the Decalogue, and for *the seventh day of the week* as an essential and necessary part of the commandment. *Theophilus Brabourne*, in 1628, says: "1. The fourth commandment of the Decalogue is a divine precept, simply and entirely moral, containing nothing legally ceremonial, in whole or in part, and therefore the weekly observation thereof ought to be perpetual, and to continue in full force and virtue to the world's end. 2. The Saturday, or seventh day of the week, ought to be an everlasting holyday in the Christian church, and the religious observation of this day obligeth Christians under the Gospel, as it did the Jews before the coming of Christ. 3. The Sunday, or Lord's day, is an ordinary working day; and it is superstition and will-worship to make the same the Sabbath of the fourth command-

ment." These opinions were vindicated by Brabourne in two volumes which appeared, one in 1628, and the other in 1632. They have never been answered to the satisfaction of many candid mind. It is true, an answer has been attempted. But this answer, laboring as it did mainly to prove that such doctrine "is repugnant to the public sentence of the Church of England, and to the sentence of divines who lived at the beginning of the Reformation," could not satisfy one who believed the Scriptures to be a sufficient rule of faith and practice. To these volumes might be added others, which appeared soon after, and to the results of which, living witnesses have testified from that day to this.

It was while the discussion just referred to was yet in progress, that King James, in 1618, published his Book of Sports for Sunday, in which is set forth, that "by the preciseness of some magistrates and ministers in several places in this kingdom, in hindering people from their recreations on the Sunday, the papists in this realm being thereby persuaded that no honest mirth or recreation was tolerable in our religion," wherefore, it pleased his majesty to set out his declaration, "that for his good people's lawful recreation, his pleasure was, that after the end of divine service, they should not be disturbed, letted, or discouraged, from any lawful recreation, such as dancing, either men or women, archery for men, leaping, vaulting, or any other such harmless recreations; nor from having of May-games, Whitsun-ales, or Morrice-dances, and setting up of May-poles, or other sports therewith used; so as the same be had in due and convenient time, without impediment or let of divine service." This book was designed to counteract what was then called the Puritan notion, and may be regarded as expressing the opinion of the English Church at that time in regard to the sacredness of the day. It was re-published in 1636, by Charles, with how much real effect upon the practices of his subjects it is not easy to determine.

It is evident that a reäction in favor of the sabbatic institution had already commenced; and the earnestness of Puritanism on this subject, joined to the influence of Sabbatarianism, affected almost the whole body of the English Church. To Puritanism and Sabbatarianism belong the credit of having preserved to that country a regard for the day of rest, which raises it indefinitely above many other Protestant countries. Had Scriptural ground been taken, who can estimate the results which would have followed?

In Germany, according to Ross' "Picture of all Religions," observers of the seventh-day as the Sabbath were common in the sixteenth century, their numbers being such as to lead to organization, and attract attention. A number of these formed a church, and emigrated to America in the early settlement of the country. There were Sabbath-keepers in Transylvania, about the same time, among whom was *Francis Davidis,* first chaplain to the Court of Sigismund, the prince of that kingdom, and afterwards superintendent of all the Transylvanian churches. In France, also, there were Christians of this class, among whom was *M. de la Roque,* who wrote in defense of the Sabbath, against Bossuet, the Catholic Bishop of Meaux. But it is difficult to determine to what extent this day was observed in those countries.

In England we find Sabbath-keepers very early. *Dr. Chambers* says, "They arose in England in the sixteenth century;" from which we understand that they then became a distinct denomination in that kingdom. They increased considerably in the seventeenth century; and we find that towards the close of that century there were eleven flourishing churches in different parts of that country. Among those who held this view were some men of distinction. Theophilus Brabourne was called before the Court of High Commission, in 1632, for having written and published books vindicating the claims of the seventh day. One Traske was about the same time examined in the Starr Chamber, where a long discussion on the subject seems to have been held. Nearly thirty years after this, John James, preacher to a Sabbath-keeping congregation in the east of London, was executed in a barbarous manner, upon a variety of charges, among which was his keeping of the Sabbath. Twenty years later still, Francis Bampfield died in Newgate, a martyr to non-conformity—especially as one who could not conform in the matter of the Sabbath. It is needless to mention more names, or to speak particularly of Edward, Joseph, Dr. Joseph, and Dr. Samuel Stennett, John Maulden, Robert Cornthwaite, and others, who have written and suffered in proof of their attachment to this truth.

But the Sabbath met with great opposition in England being assailed, both from the pulpit and the press, by those who were attached to the established church. Many men of learning and talent engaged in the discussion, on both sides of the question. It is evident that the opposers of reform felt the difficulty of defending themselves against the strength of talent and scripture brought to bear in favor of the seventh day. The civil powers attempted to check the progress of all Dissenters by means of the famous *Conventicle Act*. By that law, passed in 1664, it was provided, that if any person, above sixteen years of age, was present at any meeting of worship different from the Church of England, where there were five persons more than the household, for the first offense he should be imprisoned three months, or pay five pounds; for the second, the penalty was doubled; and for the third he should be banished to America, or pay one hundred pounds sterling. This act was renewed in 1669, and, in addition to the former penalties, made the person preaching liable to pay a fine of twenty pounds; and the same penalty was imposed upon any person suffering a meeting to be held in his house. Justices of the Peace were empowered to enter such houses, and seize such persons; and they were fined one hundred pounds if they neglected doing so. These acts were exceedingly harrassing to those who observed the Sabbath. Many of their distinguished ministers were taken from their flocks and confined in prison, some of whom sunk under their sufferings. These persecutions not only prevented those who kept the Sabbath from assembling, but deterred some who embraced their opinions from uniting with them, and discouraged others from investigating the subject. At present the Sabbath is not as extensively observed in England as formerly. But the extent of Sabbath-keeping cannot be determined by the number and magnitude of the churches, either there or in other countries. For many persons live in the observance of the seventh day and remain members of churches which assemble on the first day; and a still greater number acknowledge its correctness, who conform to the more popular custom of keeping the first day.

At what time the Sabbath became the subject of attention in America, we cannot definitely say. The intolerance of the first settlers of New England was unfavorable to the Sabbath. The poor Christian who may have been banished to this country for its observance could find no refuge among the *Pilgrim Fathers.* The laws of Rhode Island were more tolerant than those of some other States, and observers of the Sabbath first made their appearance at Newport in 1671. The cause of the Sabbath has gradually gained ground in this country from that period; but it has found much to oppose its progress, even in Rhode Island. It was in opposition to the general practice of Christians, on which account an odium was put upon it, and those who have kept the Sabbath have been reproached with Judaizing, and classed with Jews. Besides this, they have ever been subjected to great inconvenience in their occupations, especially in cities and towns.

At no time does there appear to have been in this country any general excitement on the subject. The observers of Sunday have avoided as far as possible its discussion; so that those who have observed the Sabbath have had but little encouragement, as they have supposed, to try to extend their sentiments. But the propagation of their opinicns has not depended exclusively on their efforts. The common English version of the Bible has been found in many instances a sufficient means of converting men to the truth. Churches observing the Sabbath have been formed in Rhode Island, Connecticut, New York, New Jersey, Pennsylvania, Virginia, South Carolina, Georgia, and in most of the Western States, embracing, as is supposed, a population of forty or fifty thousand.

Conclusion.

From the foregoing historical sketch, it appears that through the apostolic age, and for a long time after, the Sabbath was religiously observed by the church of Christ; and that not until the latter part of the second century was the first day introduced to religious notice as a festival of the resurrection; and then, probably, as an annual celebration at the close of the Passover only. It also appears, that it was a work of some hundreds of years to establish the weekly celebration of this day, even in the Romish church; and that this was not done without the aid of ecclesiastical and civil laws and penalties—the same instrumentalities used to bring the Sabbath into disrepute in the popular branches of the church. Thus it appears that the Romish clergy, and the princes under their control, have been the principal actors in bringing about the change from the Sabbath to the first day of the week.

For a long time before the Reformation the popular branches of the Christian church were literally without a Sabbath. Until after that period, it is not known that a single passage of Scripture was ever cited as authority for the celebration of the first day, even as a festival; the notion that the apostles observed it as a memorial of the resurrection, being of comparatively modern origin. When, however, the Reformers threw off the yoke of the Romish church, and protested against her corruptions, some of them could no longer be satisfied to let the observance of the first day rest upon her authority. They saw that they must either give it up as a human invention, or find some Scripture to support it. Hence the numerous theories which have been invented to justify its observance—theories which necessarily conflict with each other, as well as with Scripture, and are altogether unsatisfactory to inquiring minds.

The history of this matter shows us, that neither the adoption of the first day, nor the abandonment of the seventh, took place until the corruptions of the Catholic church in other respects had become so numerous and flagrant, as to drive from her communion many of her most conscientious and apostolic members, who still retained the observance of the Sabbath. The case of those sects in different ages of the church who have kept the Sabbath in connection with the first day, and practiced other things peculiar to the Romish church, furnishes additional evidence that the observance of the first day was adopted while the Sabbath was retained, and consequently that the first day was not adopted as a substitute for the Sabbath, which it ultimately displaced. The permitting of labor on the first day in the earlier ages of the church, and the canons of Councils and Synods and the edicts of Princes to bring about a general conformity in this respect, together with the slow progress made, even in Catholic countries, evince in the strongest manner that it was viewed in no other light, even by its warmest advocates, than that of a human institution, and one that could be enforced by human authority only. As such it was looked upon by enlightened and conscientious Christians in every age, who would not make void a commandment of God through a tradition of men.

In the light of these facts, we are led to the conclusion of Dr. Neander, set forth in his Church History, that "the festival of Sunday was always only a human ordinance, and it was far from the intention of the Apostles to establish a divine command in this respect, far from them, and from the early apostolic church, to transfer the laws of the Sabbath to Sunday." As a "*human ordinance*," the observance of Sunday has long been and is now considered by many. While they consider it in this light, it is not to be expected that they will render it that sacred regard which the Sabbath claims, and must have in order to our safety and its usefulness.

What, then, shall be done? Shall we allow an institution of so much importance to rest upon mere human authority? To such a proposition every friend of the institution ought to say, No. To set it adrift, or to attempt to enforce it upon such authority, would be to withdraw from it the high sanction which it once had, and expose it to certain contempt and neglect. There is but one course dictated by wisdom and prudence. If we would save the Sabbath from threatened destruction, we must come back to the law as it was originally given, place the institution under the care of the Lawgiver, and enforce its claims by his authority. We must join the commandment, "Remember the Sabbath day to keep it holy," with the explanation of it, "The seventh day is the Sabbath of the Lord thy God," and united they shall stand. Let this be done, and we need not fear. The Lord of the Sabbath is pledged for its safety; and he will cause those who "call the Sabbath a delight, holy of the Lord, honorable," to rejoice in Him, and ride upon the high places of the earth.

No. 5.

A CHRISTIAN CAVEAT

TO THE

OLD AND NEW SABBATARIANS.

BY EDWARD FISHER, ESQ.

The following article is taken from the fifth edition of a work with the above title, printed in London, 1653. The book was written in defence of the ' orthodoxal doctrine of the Church of England," respecting festivals, against the " Sabbatarian novelties," as they were called, of the Puritans. While it demolishes the claims set up on behalf of *Sunday* or *Lord's Day*, it fully establishes the claims of the *Sabbath* or *Seventh Day*. And it is worthy of note here, that it is not possible to refute any of the erroneous views in regard to the Sabbath and Lord's Day, without taking positions which necessarily lead to the observation of *the Seventh Day*. How much easier it would be to fasten the claims of the Sabbatic institution upon the consciences of men, if we were satisfied to take the fourth commandment *as it reads*, and enforce it by " *Thus saith the Lord.*"

" The third opinion is, of the new Sabbatarians, who dream of a middle way betwixt a Jew and a Christian; and this they usually lay down in two propositions. The first is, *That the Lord's Day, or first day of the week, namely* Sunday, *may be called* the Sabbath: the next is, *That the observation of the Lord's Day is a moral duty, enjoined by God himself, and declared both by the doctrine and practice of Christ and his apostles.* The first appearance of this kind of teachers was in the year of our Lord 1595, near the end of the reign of Queen Elizabeth: and because they are neither able to produce direct Scripture, nor solid reason for what they say, they labor to support their conceits by fallacies, falsities and wrestings of God's holy word, as upon scanning their proofs will be manifest to the meanest capacity.

"For their first proposition, they alledge two reasons why the *Lord's Day* may be called *the Sabbath.* One is, because the Sabbath signifies *a rest;* and therefore the Lord's Day being a *rest*, may be called the Sabbath. But to this we answer, it is false that *the Sabbath* signifies *a rest;* for when by custom of speech a common name is restrained to a particular place, thing, or person, it then becomes a proper name, and so losing its community, does signify that only particular, unto which by custom of speech it is applied; as for instance, *the temple* is a common name, signifying *the Church;* yet in London, where by custom of speech this name, *The Temple*, is restrained to an Inns of Court, it is false and absurd to say you were at *the Temple*, and mean *the Church of St. Giles.* In like manner *the Sabbath* is a common name, signifying *the rest;* yet in the Christian Church, where by custom of speech, according to God's holy phrase throughout the Old and New Testament, this name, *the Sabbath*, is restrained to the Jewish weekly festival, it is false and absurd to speak of *the Sabbath*, and mean *the Lord's Day.* Their other reason why the Lord's Day may be called *the Sabbath*, is, because the Lord's Day succeeded in the room of the Sabbath. But if this argument be good, then may *baptism* be called *circumcision*, the *Lord's Supper* the *Passover*, and King *James* Queen *Elizabeth.*

"As for the second proposition, wherein they assert the *morality and divine institution of the Lord's Day*, we shall here notice only three of their reasons. The first is, because Adam, according to God's command, kept the Sabbath in the state of innocency. . . . . . But what is the sanctification of the Sabbath spoken of by Moses in the second chapter of Genesis, to our observing the Lord's Day? That was appointed to be kept on *the seventh* and *last* day of the week; this is kept on *the first* day of the week: that was the day in which God *rested* from his work of creation; this is the day in which God *began* to create the heavens and the earth: that was our *Saturday;* this is our *Sunday.* Their second proof for the morality of the Lord's Day, is from the fourth commandment, where they seek to corrupt the very text, and would persuade us that for *the* seventh day, we must read *a* seventh day; as if God did not there set apart a certain day of the week, but left it to man to keep which of the seven he pleased. Unto which we answer, that this conceit is not only against the letter of all our translations, but even repugnant to the sense of the commandment; for the words are express that God blessed and hallowed the Sabbath day; that Sabbath day was *the seventh* day; that seventh day was *the day in which God rested from his six days' work of creation.* Nay, grant it were true (as these men would have) that this special precept does exactly oblige us, and that no particular day of the seven was by God appointed to be kept holy, then may we set apart Monday, or Tuesday, or any other day to God's service, as well as Sunday; and so, by their own argument, the Lord's Day is no more moral than any other day of the week. Their third proof is from the title or name, *Lord's Day,* which (say they) cannot be for any other reason, but because it is of the Lord's institution. We answer, this is false; for the Lord's Day was not so called because it was *instituted by the Lord,* but be cause it was *dedicated to the Lord;* as we commonly say, Saint Mary's Church, or Saint Peter's Church; which no man did ever imagine were built or founded by Saint Mary or Saint Peter."

Near the close of his book, after having examined each of the positions here referred to, he comes directly to his design, and says:—

"In vain, therefore, it is, and most absurd, for you our opponents to charge us with *befooling and misleading the people.* Your own *practice,* your own *doctrines,* shall bear witness betwixt us.

"You who say one while, that God did not appoint *the* seventh day, the day on which he rested, to be kept holy, but *a* seventh day, and so one day in seven be observed, no matter which of them; another while, that by this commandment God enjoins us to keep holy *the first day of the week* on which he *began* his work of creation—Do you not *befool and mislead the people?*

"You who (forgetting your own doctrine of the fourth commandment) do teach, that the keeping holy the first day of the week, or Lord's Day, was appointed and practised by Christ and his apostles, yet cannot produce so much as one *example* for it, much less a *precept*—Do you not *befool and mislead the people?*

"You who infer, because St. Paul, and the disciples at Troas, spent the whole night of the first day of the week in praying, preaching, and heavenly conference, in regard he was to leave them and depart on the morrow; *therefore,* St. Paul and the disciples at Troas met *that night* to keep holy *the day past; therefore* the disciples at Troas met *every first day of the week*, to keep that day holy; *therefore* the Church at *Philippi*, the Church in *Cilicia*, and *all* Christian Churches, did then keep holy the first day of the week; *therefore all the apostles* did constantly keep holy that day; *therefore* Christ and his apostles *appointed the first day of the week* to be for ever celebrated, instead of the Sabbath—Is not this pitiful logic? Do you not *befool and mislead the people*?

"You who tell stories of an *old* Sabbath and a *new* Sabbath, a *Jewish* Sabbath and a *Christian* Sabbath, a Sabbath of the *seventh* day and a Sabbath of the *first* day of the week; that so you may slily fix the name *Sabbath* on *the Lord's Day*, and then persuade the simple and ignorant that all those texts of Scripture wherein mention is made of *the Sabbath day*, are intended of *the Lord's Day;* when indeed to call the Lord's Day *the Sabbath*, is as senseless as to call Sunday *Saturday*, or the *first* day *the last day* of the week, when throughout the Old and New Testament we have not the least intimation of any other weekly Sabbath, save the old, Jewish, seventh day Sabbath; when you yourselves confess that the name Lord's Day, is more proper and particular, and less obvious to exception, than the name Sabbath; and that the name Sabbath is in dignity inferior to both Lord's Day and Sunday—Do you not *befool and mislead the people*?

You that condemn the yearly observance of Christ's birth-day as heathenish, yet acknowledge this feast to be a constitution of the ancient primitive Church—Do you not *befool and mislead the people*?

"Take ye heed; these are not small matters; consider well with yourselves what it is to stand guilty before God of belying Christ and his apostles, and wilfully wresting the Holy Scriptures. Be advised; take time while time is to repent of those notorious slanders wherewith you have aspersed the ancient approved ways of God's worship; and let the sincerity of your repentance appear by the speedy abandoning of your unchristian practices and principles; lest the heavy judgment of seducers, *to wax worse and worse*, fall upon you, and God in the end *deliver you up* to such *strong delusions*, that you *should believe your own lies*."

Published by the American Sabbath Tract Society,
No. 9 Spruce Street, N. Y.

No. 6.

TWENTY REASONS

FOR KEEPING HOLY IN EACH WEEK,

THE SEVENTH DAY INSTEAD OF THE FIRST DAY.

1. Because the Seventh Day was blessed and sanctified for a Sabbath, by God, immediately after the creation of the world, as a perpetual memorial of that wonderful work, and of His own resting from it; and because there is now as much need for man to remember God's creative work, and to enjoy a weekly rest, as ever there was.

2. Because there is evidence that the Seventh Day was observed from Adam to Moses, by Noah, Jacob, Joseph, and Job. (See Gen. vii. 4, 10; viii. 10, 12; xxix. 27, 28; l. 10; Job. ii. 3.)

3. Because the Seventh Day is a necessary part of the fourth commandment, given at Mount Sinai, graven on stone by the finger of God, and incorporated with the other nine precepts of the Decalogue, which are admitted to be moral in their nature, and perpetually binding. "Remember the Sabbath Day to keep it holy." "The Seventh Day is the Sabbath of the Lord thy God." "For in six days the Lord made heaven and earth, the sea, and all that in them is, and rested the *Seventh Day ; wherefore* the Lord blessed the Sabbath Day and hallowed it."

4. Because the Old Testament abounds with declarations of God's blessing upon those who keep holy the Seventh Day, and of his vengeance upon those who profane it.

5. Because our Lord Jesus Christ enforced the claims of the law to the fullest extent, saying in regard to the code to which the Seventh Day belonged, "Till heaven and earth pass, one jot or one tittle shall in no

wise pass from the law, till all be fulfilled;" and because He always kept holy the Seventh Day, in this doubtless "leaving us an example that we should follow in His steps."

6. Because the holy women who had attended Jesus Christ at his death and burial, are expressly said to have "rested the SABBATH DAY *according to the commandment*," (Luke xxiii. 56;) and because, though the narrative proceeds immediately to record the appearance of Jesus Christ, on the morning of the *first day of the week*, neither there nor elsewhere is one word said about a change of the Sabbath, or about the sabbatic observance of the First Day of the Week.

7. Because the Apostles of our Lord constantly kept the Seventh Day, of which there is abundant evidence in the Acts of the Apostles, and it is declared o, Paul, that, "*as his manner was*," he went into the synagogue frequently on the Sabbath Day. (Compare Luke iv. 16 with Acts xvii. 2; see also Acts xiii. 14, 42, 44, and xvi. 13.)

8. Because Jesus Christ, foretelling the destruction of Jerusalem, warned his disciples to pray that their flight might not happen "on the Sabbath Day;" and as that event was to take place almost forty years after the resurrection of our Lord, it appears that the same Sabbath was to be then observed by his disciples.

9. Because there is no other day of the week called by the name of "Sabbath," in all the Holy Scriptures, but the Seventh Day alone; and because, when "the First Day of the Week" is mentioned in the New Testament, it is always clearly distinguished from "the Sabbath."

10 Because not one of those passages which speak of the "First Day of the Week," records an event or transaction peculiar to the Sabbath.

11. Because when God had so carefully committed his Law to writing, had repeated his precepts throughout the prophetic books, and had left so many testimonies and examples of the Seventh Day Sabbath on His sacred records, it is most unreasonable to suppose that He would have repealed or changed one single article thereof, without recording it among the words of our Lord Jesus or His Apostles, in the writings of the New Testament.

12. Because the observance of the Moral Law, without any exception from it,) is constantly enjoined, in the writings of the Apostles; and one of them says that "Whosoever shall keep the whole law, and yet offend in one point, he is guilty of all," quoting at the same time the sixth and seventh commandments. (See Rom. xiii. 9; Gal. v. 14; Eph. vi. 2, 3; and James ii. 8–11.)

13. Because the religious observance of the *Seventh Day* of the Week *as the Sabbath,* was constantly practised by the primitive Christians, for three or four hundred years at least; and because, though it gradually fell into disuse, the neglect of the Sabbath was caused only by those corruptions of Christianity, which at length grew up into the grossest idolatry; so that the second commandment was in fact, and the fourth was in effect, abolished by an ignorant, superstitious, and tyrannical priesthood.

14. Because it was only through the superstitious observance of the anniversaries of saints and martyrs, and a multitude of other fasts and feasts, with which the simplicity of revealed religion was encumbered and overwhelmed, that the sabbatic observance of the Seventh Day went out of use; and not (in fact) by any real or pretended command of Christ or His apostles, nor at first by the express authority of any Pope or Council: for it was kept *as a strict fast,* for ages after it lost every other token of a holy day.

15. Because the leaders of the Reformation never claimed for the First Day the name of the Sabbath, and never enforced the observance of that day by any other authority than that of the Church.

16. Because it is obviously absurd—(*and it is an objection often made by irreligious people*)—that the observance of the First Day of the Week as the Sabbath, should be grounded on a divine precept which commands the observance, not of the *First*, but of the *Seventh* Day.

17. Because, if the fundamental principle of Protestantism be right and true, that "the Bible alone is the religion of Protestants," then the Seventh Day must be the true and only *Sabbath of Protestants*; for, unless that day of the week be kept, they have no *scriptural* Sabbath at all.

18. Because the pertinacious observance of the First Day of the Week, in the stead of the Seventh, has actually given occasion of great scandal to the Protestant faith; it has caused the Papists to declare that Protestants admit the *authority of human tradition* in matters of religion; and it has led to intolerance and persecution.

19. Because the observance of the First Day, and neglect of the Seventh, having been adopted partly in contempt of the Jews, has always laid a burden upon them, and presented an obstacle to their receiving Christianity, which ought to be removed.

20. Because the observance of the Seventh Day obeys God, honors the Protestant Principle, rebukes Papacy, removes stumbling-blocks, and secures for us the presence and blessing of "the Lord of the Sabbath."

Published by the American Sabbath Tract Society,
No. 9 Spruce Street. N. Y.

No. 7.

PLAIN QUESTIONS.

Reader! be pleased to give a plain answer to each of these plain questions, without equivocation or mental reservation.

1. Did God, after he had finished the work of creation, "bless and sanctify" THE *seventh day of the week;* or simply the *seventh part of time*, without reference to any *particular day* of the seven?

2. Did He not sanctify THE *very day in which he rested* from his work? Was not that *the last day* of the seven? Did He sanctify any other?

3. WHY did He "bless and sanctify" *the* seventh day? Was it not because he *rested* on that day? Will this reason apply to *any other day* of the seven? Did he not *work* on EVERY other day? (See Gen. 2: 2, 3.)

4. Is not God's example of resting on the seventh day enjoined upon us for imitation? (Ex. 20: 8—11.) Do we imitate him, when we rest upon some other day than the one in which He rested?

5. Is it the special *appointment of God* which renders a day holy, or is it *our own act?* Is the day holy because we *count* it so, or because God has made it so?

6. When God enjoins us to count the Sabbath, "the holy of the Lord," (Isa. 58: 13,) is it not equivalent to telling us that He himself has *previously* constituted it a holy day by blessing and sanctifying it? Is it any thing more than requiring us to reckon the day to possess that dignity which He *has already* conferred upon it?

7. If God's blessing does not rest upon one particularly specified day, to the exclusion of all others, and we are

nevertheless required to keep a day holy, are we not re- required to do what *is impossible?* For how can we count a day to be holy, which God has not previously made so? (Compare Quest. 5.)

8. If God's blessing did not rest upon one particularly specified day, could he challenge to himself any propriety in one day more than in another? Yet in the Sabbath day he claims a special propriety; "MY *holy day.*" (Isa. 58: 13.)

9. Are we not commanded to refrain from labor in *that very day* which God once "blessed and sanctified," and thereby made holy time? "In IT thou shalt not do any work," &c. Do we obey this command when we work all of that day, and make it the busiest day of all the seven?

10. If it be downright disobedience to set about our work on the seventh day, when God says, "in *it* thou shalt NOT do any work," can we think to make amends for this act of disobedience by ceasing from work on another day? Even the performance of a required duty will not make amends for another one neglected. How much less, then, the performance of something which is not required! "Who hath required this at your hand?"

11. Has God ever *taken away* the blessing which he once put upon the seventh day, and made that day a common or secular day?

12. Does not the *reason* of the blessing (See Quest. 3,) possess all the cogency now that it ever did? Has it lost force by the lapse of time? And while the reason of an institution remains, does not the institution itself remain?

13. Was the reason of the blessing which God originally put upon the seventh day, founded upon any need that men then had of a Redeemer? Was it therefore to receive its accomplishment and fulfillment by the actual

coming of the Redeemer? In what possible sense can it be said, that Jesus Christ fulfilled and made an end of this reason?

14. Has God ever said of the first day of the week, In *it* thou shalt not do any work? Has Christ ever said so? Have the apostles?

15. Is there any scriptural proof that Christ, or his apostles, or the Christian churches in the days of the apostles, *refrained from labor* on the first day of the week?

16. As there is no transgression where there is no law, (Rom. 4 : 15; John 3 : 4,) what sin is committed by working on the first day of the week?

17. Does not the Sabbatic Institution RESULT from the blessing and sanctifying of *a particular day*? Is not this *the very thing in which it consists?* How then is the institution *separable* from the day thus "blessed and sanctified"? How can it be separated from that upon which its very existence depends?

18. If the very life and soul of the institution consist in the blessing which was once put upon a particular day, is it not idle to talk of the *transfer* of the institution to another day? If another day has been sanctified and blessed, then it is an *entirely new* institution, and not a transfer of the old.

19. Does not the law of the Sabbath require the weekly commemoration of *that* rest which God entered into after he had finished the work of creation? By what principle of law or logic, then, can that law be made to *require* the commemoration of the work of redemption?

20. If it be necessary that the work of redemption be commemorated weekly by a positive institution, must not the obligation so to commemorate it arise from some law which directly and specifically requires it? But when, instead of this, the attempt is made to derive the obligation from the Sabbath law, is it not a tacit acknowledgment

that there is no law requiring the weekly commemoration of the work of redemption?

21. Does the Scripture ever apply the name, *Sabbath*, to the first day of the week? Even in the *New* Testament, where the term is used, is not the reference always o the *seventh* day?

22. If Luke, who wrote the Acts of the Apostles ful thirty years after the death of Christ, under the inspiration of the Holy Spirit, still calls the seventh day of the week the Sabbath, can it be wrong in us to do so? (See Acts 13 14, 42, 44; 16: 1, 3; 17: 1, 2; 18: 4.) If this be the *inspired* application of the term so many years after all the ceremonial institutions were nailed to the cross, is it not our duty to make the same use of the term now?

23. Is it not a manifest perversion of the scriptural use of terms, to take away the sacred name from the seventh day of the week, and give it to the first day?

24. When the first day of the week is so generally called the Sabbath, are not the common people thereby led to suppose that the Bible calls it so? Are they not thus grossly deceived?

25. If the name *Sabbath* were no longer applied to this day, and it should simply be called first day of the week, as in the Bible, is it not probable that it would soon lose its sacredness in the eyes of the people?

26. Is it possible, then, that God has not given the day a name sufficiently sacred to secure for it a religious regard, nor even guarded it with a law sufficient to prevent its desecration?

27. *What then?* HAS GOD LEFT HIS WORK FOR MAN TO MEND! IS IT NOT SAFE TO LEAVE THE DAY AS GOD HAS LEFT IT! "Who hath directed the Spirit of the Lord, or being his counsellor hath taught him?" (Isa. 11: 13.)

[No. 7.]

28. Are you very sure that by the Lord's day, (Rev : 10,) is meant the first day of the week? Have you any *Scripture* proof of it? Have you any other proof of it than the testimony of those who are called the early Fathers?

29. If the testimony of the early Fathers is to be relied on, that the Lord's day means the first day of the week, ought not their testimony to be just as much relied on, as to the manner in which the primitive Christians observed the day?

20. If it were even certain that by the Lord's day the writer of the book of Revelations meant to designate the first day of the week, would it thence follow that it is a day *sacred* by *divine* appointment, any more than that the "*Sabbath day's journey*," (Acts 1: 12,) was a distance limited and prescribed by *divine* authority? If Luke could select the latter expression from the vocabulary of *human tradition*, without intending to sanction it as being of divine origin, could not John do the same with regard to the former expression?

31. Do the Fathers, or any one of them, inform us that the Lord's day was observed by *abstinence from labor?*—that it was observed as the Sabbath? Mark the question. It is not, was the day *observed*, simply; but, was it observed *as the Sabbath*?

32. Is there not an important distinction between the *Sabbath* and a *religious festival?* Does not the word Sabbath mean *rest?* Can any day, therefore, be called a Sabbath day, which is not a day of rest from ordinary labor?

33. Does a religious *festival* require any thing more than the commemoration of some important event, allow

ing the time not occupied in the public celebration of it to be spent in labor or amusement? Is not this precisely the manner in which the first day of the week was observed, according to the testimony of the ancient Fathers?

34. Though the observance of the first day of the week as a religious festival be in itself innocent, (Rom. 14: 5,) so long as it is not made a pretext for dispensing with an express law of God, (Matt. 15: 6,) yet do you find it any where in the word of God *commanded* as a *duty?*

35. Do you believe that a Sabbath, in the true and proper sense of the term; namely, a day of rest from all ordinary labor, is necessary and indispensable to the well-being of mankind? If so, do you honestly suppose that God would set it aside, and have its place supplied by nothing more than a religious festival?

36. Is it not wicked to uphold a course which makes the commandment of God of none effect? (Matt. 15: 1—9; Mark 7: 1—13.

Reader! carefully ponder the foregoing questions, together with the Scripture references. Answer them as you would if you stood at the gates of death. Do not trifle with the Holy Spirit of God, by forcibly wresting his word from its obvious meaning. Let conscience be unfettered; and act, as fully realizing that "THOU, GOD, SEEST ME."

Published by the American Sabbath Tract Society,
No. 9 Spruce Street, N. Y.

DIALOGUE,

Between a Minister of the Gospel and a Sabbatarian

Sabbatarian. Did Jehovah ever sanctify one day above another?

Minister. He did.

S. And what day was that?

M. The seventh.

S. When?

M. When he finished his creative work.

S. Where?

M. In Eden.

S. On whom was it obligatory?

M. On our first parents, and all their posterity.

S. Did he ever unsanctify that day?

M. No.

S. Did he ever sanctify the first, or any other day than the seventh, as a day of rest?

M. Not that I know of.

S Then do not those who neglect the seventh day, take away something from the word of God? And do not those who keep the first day add to that word? Read the threatnings of the Lord against such:—"If any man shall add unto these things, God shall add unto him the plagues that are written in this book: and if any man shall take away from the words of the book of this prophecy, God shall take away his part out of the book of life, and out of the holy city, and from the things which are written in this book."

COUNTERFEIT COIN.

Being the substance of a recent Conversation between an eminent Counsellor at Law and a Sabbatarian.

The Lawyer contended that although the first day of the week had no divine authority for its sanctity or observance as a Sabbath, yet if it be kept as scrupulously and conscientiously as the seventh day demanded, *it could not but be* as acceptable to God

In answer to such sophistry, the Sabbatarian submitted the following legal case to him:—

"I am told that I can purchase, in the State of Connecticut, *one hundred* copper cents, bearing the impress and superscription of the United States Mint, and equal in every respect in value to the mint coin, for *sixty-five* cents, payable in gold or silver. But I admit them to be counterfeit. I admit, also, that I circulate this spurious coin. Now, will you undertake, for a fee of $10,000, to defend my cause against a prosecution for passing such false coin, and exonerate me from conviction in the United States' Courts."

The honest lawyer's answer unhesitatingly was, "I cannot argue your cause in the very teeth of so unquestionable a law as appears to exist on the Statute Books."*

The Sabbatarian replied:—"Then, as you admit *your first day Sabbath a counterfeit*, allow me to answer you as the celebrated Mr. Whiston did Chancellor King of England upon a similar question: 'If God Almighty should be as consistent, as just, and as jealous of his laws in the Court of Heaven, as my Lord Chancellor is in his. *where are we then?*'"

The Inference.—If, then, I cannot obtain an advocate on earth, (for no one of repute would undertake it,) to plead my cause with the offer of a fee of $10,000, for the violation of a law of man's making, what ground have I to expect that the only advocate to be obtained in the Court of Heaven, i. e. *the Lord Jesus Christ*, will defend my cause against a breach of that law which his father ever made punishable with DEATH, temporal and eternal? —and who himself, when on earth, in his comment on that law, averred that not one *jot* or *tittle* could in any wise pass from it? (Matt. 5: 18, 19.)

* If any person shall falsely make or counterfeit any copper coin of the United States, or pass or publish the same, he shall be subjected to a fine of $1000, and suffer imprisonment to hard labor for a term not exceeding three years.—Gordon's Digest, p. 922.

Published by the American Sabbath Tract Society,
No. 9 Spruce Street, N. Y.

No. 8.

SABBATH CONTROVERSY.

THE TRUE ISSUE.

ONE of the greatest difficulties which we who observe the seventh day have ever found in the Sabbath controversy, is to make our opponents understand what is the real question at issue. So long have their thoughts, feelings and habits, been moulded under one particular view of the subject, that it seems almost a miracle if one is found who can disregard all foreign matter, and look at the precise point in debate long enough to come to any certain and intelligent conclusion about it. But it is evident, that if an opponent is suffered to raise false issues, or to be continually striking off into the discussion of some point which does not affect the final question, we may prolong the controversy *ad infinitum.*

Let us then endeavor to state distinctly what is, and what is not, the issue between us and the observers of the first day of the week.

1. The issue is not whether the first day of the week was observed at a very early period by Christians. We admit that it was. We admit that its observance may be traced up to very near the borders of the apostolic age. What more can a generous, conscientious opponent, who scorns any other aid than what the truth will give him, ask? He knows in his own soul that this is the very utmost that can be produced from any of his histories. Let him ransack his old musty volumes all the way backward, till he fancies he can almost talk to the "beloved disciple" face to face, and what more can he find? Verily, nothing.

But when you have got this admission from us, then we have another question to ask. *How*—don't dodge the question—HOW was the day observed by the early Christians? We admit the observance of it; but that is not the issue. The issue respects the *manner* of observing it. You, if you are consistent, will say that the early Christians observed it not only by public worship, but by *abstaining from labor.* We, on the other hand, deny that they abstained from labor. We admit that they held public worship; but—we repeat it—*we deny that they abstained from labor.* We deny that they regarded it as a *Sabbath,* "resting according to the commandment." Now with the issue thus fairly stated, we put the laboring oar into your hands, and challenge you to prove your position. Bring proof, if you can, that the early Christians regarded the first day of the week as any thing else than a *religious festival;* between which and a *Sabbath* there is a very important difference, the latter requiring abstinence from labor, the former merely requiring public worship in honor of the event commemorated, and allowing the remainder of the day to be spent in labor or amusement.

2. When it is once settled, that in a very early period of the church the first day was observed as a festival; when our opponents have fairly jaded themselves to a "weariness of the flesh," in their "much study" of the old fathers, to find proof of it;—though we never called it in question;—then the issue is, whether this festival was *ordained* by *Christ?*—whether the New Testament furnishes *inspired example* of such festival? Our opponents affirm; we deny. We maintain that in every passage of the New Testament, where the first day of the week is mentioned, the context furnishes a sufficient reason why it is mentioned, without the least necessity of supposing it to have been a festival season. No exception can be made to this, unless in regard to 1 Cor. 16 : 2. The reason why the Apostle in this place specifies the first, rather than any other day of the week, does not so clearly appear from the context; but the peculiar phraseology employed, "let each one of you lay by him," [himself,] is against the idea of any public meeting; and if no public meeting, of course no festival season. As every allusion to the first day of the week is sufficiently explained by

other circumstances noticed in the context, the *inferential* proof of its festival character is thereby destroyed. As for *clear, positive* proof of it, such as express precept or command, no person of modesty pretends it. Still less is there any proof of its *Sabbatic* character.

3. Another point wherein we are necessarily at issue with great numbers of Christians, is whether the *institution* of the Sabbath is separable from the particular *day* to be observed. They affirm; we deny. We maintain that God's blessing and sanctifying a particular day is the very thing in which the institution consists. To render this plain matter yet more plain, we invite close attention to the wording of the fourth commandment; premising, however, that the word Sabbath is not *translated* from a Hebrew word, but is the Hebrew word itself anglicized, just as baptism is an anglicized Greek word. The proper translation of the word is *Rest.* Now let the word Rest be substituted for Sabbath, and how clear it becomes—

"*Remember the Rest day to keep it holy.*" [Surely some particular day is denoted; for it is THE Rest day, not A Rest day.] *Six days shalt thou labor, and do all thy work; but the seventh day is the Rest of the Lord thy God.* [Is it any where historically recorded as a fact that God rested on THE seventh day? It is. Gen. 2 : 2. 'On the seventh day God rested from all his work which he had made.' Who does not see that that day on which God rested, was the *last* of the seven which constituted the first week of time?] *In it*—[in WHAT? why, in the seventh day, the last day of the week; for the pronoun *it* can have no other antecedent]—*thou shalt not do any work, thou, nor thy son, nor thy daughter, nor thy man-servant, nor thy maid-servant, nor thy cattle, nor the stranger that is within thy gates.* [WHY must no work be done on that particular day, the seventh or last day of the week? The reason follows.] *For in six days the Lord made heaven and earth, the sea and all that in them is, and* RESTED *on the seventh day,* [as the record in Gen. 2 : 2 proves. See also Heb. 4 : 4.] *Wherefore the Lord blessed the Rest day and sanctified it.*"

The conclusion is irresistible, that the Rest day spoken of is the particular day on which God rested from his work, which, as before shown, was the last day of tne week. That very day, and no other, God blessed and sanctified. The only reason assigned *why* he sanctified it, is " because that in it he had rested from all his work which God created and made." Gen. 2 : 3. The Rest day, then, which we are required to observe, is " the Rest of the Lord thy God :" which does not mean the rest which the Lord thy God has appointed, though it is true that he has appointed it ; nor does it mean a rest which becomes the Lord's by reason of our appropriating it to him ; but " the rest of the Lord thy God " means THE REST WHICH THE LORD THY GOD OBSERVED.

Now from all this we think it must be evident, that whoever observes any other Rest day than the seventh day of the week, does not observe the Rest—Sabbath—" of the Lord thy God." He may, it is true, appropriate it to the Lord his God, and in that sense call it theLord's ; he may ignorantly suppose that Christ in the Gospel has appointed it, and in that sense also call it the Lord's; but it can by no means be called " the Rest of the Lord thy God " in the sense of that expression in the fourth commandment. Hence, irresistible is our conviction, that he does not obey the commandment. O brother Christian, why will you persist in maintaining that your Sunday keeping is an act of obedience to the law of the Sabbath ?

Published by the American Sabbath Tract Society,
No. 9 Spruce-street, New-York.

No. 9

THE FOURTH COMMANDMENT.

FALSE EXPOSITION AND ITS CONSEQUENCES.

THE Fourth Commandment has been variously expounded by its professed friends. Among these expositions, none has been more injurious than that which represents it as requiring the observance, not of *the* Sabbath, and *the* seventh day, but of *a* Sabbath, and *a* seventh day—not of a certain and well-known time, but of an uncertain and varying time. Yet this is the exposition of it which is given both by commentators and writers on the subject of the Sabbath. It will be found, however, that this view is generally presented in order to prepare the way to introduce the first day of the week, under the specious name of Lord's Day, into the place of the Sabbath. Thus some are made to think, that the name Sabbath may as well be applied to the first day of the week as to the seventh. But to such an exposition there are several serious objections:—

1. It is a perversion of the original text itself. In every place where the weekly Sabbath and the seventh day are spoken of, the Hebrew article is uniformly used. This article is often used like our demonstrative *this*—but more commonly like our definite article *the*—never as our indefinite article *a* or *an*; and *Gesenius*, in answer to the question whether it may be used *indefinitely*, says, "The definite article cannot be rightly said to stand indefinitely." To this opinion agree all our translators, both ancient and modern, who have rendered the terms, both in the fourth commandment and all other places of the Scripture, by *the* Sabbath and *the* seventh day.

2. It makes the Fourth Commandment to be indefinite and absurd. If that commandment only requires

the observance of *a* Sabbath or *rest*, and that on *a* seventh day, then one man might keep the seventh day, another the third day, and another the fifth day, yet all obey the commandment. What confusion would thus result from carrying out this exposition to its legitimate results! But God's commandment is not yea and nay after this manner. It says, "*the* seventh day is *the* Sabbath of the Lord thy God." That man will not be held guiltless who misinterprets and misrepresents it, for however pious a purpose he may do so.

3. It is contrary to the teachings of the very men who give this exposition; for they affirm, that the fourth commandment required the keeping of *the* seventh day until Christ came. Now, if the Jews before Christ, were bound to keep a certain and definite day, and that *the* seventh day, then the commandment required a certain and definite day, and that *the* seventh day.

From these considerations it is evident, that those who represent the fourth commandment as requiring the observance of only *a* Sabbath, and that upon *some one* day of the seven indefinitely, are guilty of a false exposition of the commandment, and of handling the word of God deceitfully. They make a plain passage of Scripture to signify one thing for some thousands of years, and then ever afterwards to signify another thing. Thus do they make void the commandment of God, that they may keep their own traditions.

Now let us turn to a consideration of some of the *consequences* of this kind of exposition. Among these we will mention only three.

1 It overturns all certainty in explaining the Scriptures. If a man, in translating from a Latin or Greek author, should pervert his author's meaning in this manner, by using words in a different sense from that in which they were intended, he would be cast out and despised. But yet when a preacher represents the term *the Sabbath* as meaning simply *a rest*, that so he may call the first day of the week *a rest*, and therefore *the*

Sabbath, he deals worse with the Scriptures than the translator just mentioned does with his profane author Instead, however, of being cast out and despised, his speculations are allowed to go for truth. Thus unbelievers are encouraged in their infidelity; and occasion is given for them to say, that the Bible is interpreted by its friends to mean just what they please to have it. It is dangerous for men to use their wits thus to blind the eyes of their fellows.

2. It abolishes the Lord's Sabbath, and makes the Fourth Commandment to be a mere cipher. First, it abolishes the Lord's Sabbath, because it teaches that the observance of the seventh day, on which God rested and which he introduced into the commandment as one with the Sabbath, is not at all binding, but the day may be spent in any kind of labor. Is not this to abolish *the Lord's* Sabbath? Second, it makes the fourth commandment a cipher, because it takes away the *time,* which is the seventh day, and the *event commemorated,* which is God's resting from his creative work. Now read the commandment, as these expounders would have it, bereft of the *time* and the *event commemorated.* It then commands only *a rest,* without any precept or example as to its length or frequency. One person, therefore, may rest one hour in each day; another one day in a month; and a third one month in a year; and each may call this keeping the Sabbath. Does not this make the fourth commandment a mere cipher?

3. It abuses God's Word, and misleads his people. It abuses his word by representing that the Word teaches what it does not teach, and that it fails to teach what it attempts to teach. It misleads his people, on one side, by pressing the fourth commandment to sustain the first day of the week, which it says nothing about, thus laying a yoke upon the people, requiring them to observe a day, in regard to which they will finally be asked, Who hath required this at your hands? On the other side, it misleads the people, by encoura-

ging them to neglect a day which God hath sanctified, and commanded them to keep holy.

Such are some of the consequences of this false exposition of the fourth commandment. They affect both the sabbatic institution itself, and those whose duty it is to remember it. It is true that the persons who countenance such expositions are called very zealous and godly men ; but this, instead of bettering the case, makes it worse. If they were enemies to the commandment, such things might be expected, and would be comparatively unimportant; but that the wound should be inflicted by its friends, aggravates the evil. There is occasion to tremble for some religious teachers, who profess great interest in the Sabbath, but who yet refuse to hear the truth in regard to it. Some such there are, who, if the truth be presented to them, instead of inquiring if these things are so, imitate the Jews of old who, when they were cut to the heart, gnashed on their reprover with their teeth; and when they could endure it no longer, "stoppped their ears, and ran upon him with one accord." Such would do well to inquire if they are not in this thing teaching error for truth, and their own traditions for the commandments of God.

Published by the American Sabbath Tract Society.
No. 9 Spruce-street, New-York.

THE [No. 16.]

TRUE SABBATH

EMBRACED AND OBSERVED.

By Eld. SAMUEL DAVISON,

Many years a regular Baptist Minister; now Pastor of the Seventh day Baptist Church in Shiloh, New Jersey.

NEW-YORK:

PUBLISHED BY THE AMER. SABBATH TRACT SOCIETY

INTRODUCTORY OBSERVATIONS.

Having often been solicited to give an account of my conversion from the observance of what is commonly called the Lord's Day, or Sunday, to the observance of the ancient Sabbath of Jehovah, the seventh day of the week, I submit this brief narrative to public notice, not so much for the justification of my present practice, as in the hope that it may be the means of leading many other Christian people candidly to examine this subject, which, as it appears to me, is very essential to the restoration of primitive Christianity. The narrative derives its importance, not from the person of the narrator, but from the practical exhibition which it furnishes of the working of divine truth upon the mind.

THE TRUE SABBATH EMBRACED AND OBSERVED.

EARLY PREPOSSESSIONS.

My parents, and nearly all of my family connections, being members of Baptist churches, or attached to that denomination—and I having been a member of the same for above twenty-five years, and more than half that time an accredited minister among them—all my preferences and prepossessions were with their peculiarities as churches of the Lord Jesus Christ. If there was one characteristic doctrine of the Baptists which I esteemed above another, it was this: "We believe that the Scriptures of the Old and New Testaments were given by the inspiration of God, and are a perfect rule of faith and practice." I could say with the Psalmist, "My heart standeth in awe of thy word; for thou hast magnified thy word above all thy name."

MATURED ATTACHMENTS.

I believed firmly, that if there was a Christian people upon the earth who had kept the primitive faith from the days of the apostles, and had never symbolized with the errors of the church of Rome in her idolatrous and adulterous course, that people was the Baptist denomination. If there was any thing in my religious privileges in which I gloried, it was in thinking that I had never been deceived by the working of that mystery of iniquity. I was sensible that the Baptists had errors among them; but I regarded them as the errors of fallible human nature, and not as departures from the constitutional doctrine and law of the Holy Scriptures—

some of them superinduced by an unwatchful and familiar intercourse with our more erroneous Pedobaptist brethren, and hence mediately, though not directly, the effect of that great apostacy which was predicted as to come and deceive all nations. Holding these sentiments, I was ardently and conscientiously attached to that denomination, as the most scriptural people on earth. I did not doubt but that I should remain united with them in time, in death, and in eternal life.

—

REGARD FOR SCRIPTURAL CHRISTIANITY.

Notwithstanding my prepossessions and attachments, it has been my prevailing desire, from the time of my conversion, to be a Scriptural Christian; and since I became a teacher of others, I have felt a growing sense of obligation to know and teach the whole counsel of God aright. The words of the Lord Jesus Christ to his disciples, saying, "Call no man master," "Call no man father," have for years been so deeply impressed upon my heart, that I have scrupulously refused to call myself a Fullerite, a Calvinist, an Armenian, or after any human name. Although I have my preferences in reading and approving the sentiments of great and good men, the Bible alone is my creed book.

—

FORMER SABBATH SENTIMENTS.

My former Sabbath sentiments were formed according to the Puritan model. While a child, I learned Sutcliff's and Watts' Catechisms, in both of which it is taught, that the ten commandments are a rule of life to good men; and traditionally I was taught, that the Sabbath was changed from the seventh to the first day of the week in honor of the resurrection of Christ; and I fully believed this was confirmed by the various references to the first day contained in the New Testament.

—

DISTURBED ABOUT THE SABBATH.

I was first disturbed about the Sabbath seven years ago, when a brother sent me a tract upon the subject, called the *Investigator*. I read it with considerable interest, and was much perplexed in attempting to satisfy myself with my own views, as I went along in the perusal of it. I wished then, that there had been something more explicit upon the subject of the change of the day than what I could find in the New Testament. Not questioning, however, but that it was divinely changed, I quieted, rather than satisfied, my mind with what I supposed to be abundant apostolic example; and I remarked, that if our Pedobaptist brethren could produce from the Scriptures as clear examples of infant baptism, as we could of keeping the first day of the week for a Sabbath, I would admit its validity. Although I would not dare to say so now, then it sufficed to quiet my mind.

I had no farther solicitude upon the subject, until about midsummer of 1843. At that time, as several professors of religion of my acquaintance did not regard the day as I thought the Lord's Day ought to be regarded, I conculded to preach a sermon upon the subject, and commenced preparing one. I had then recently purchased Neander's History of the Christian Religion and Church during the First Three Centuries. I read this book with much satisfaction, as the work of an able and candid historian, who takes a philosophical view of the events and circumstances of society which operated to give character to those early ages of church history. In the section on Christian Worship and Festivals, I was surprised to find the following statement, viz: "OPPOSITION TO JUDAISM *introduced the particular festival of Sunday* very early indeed into the place of the Sabbath...... The festival of Sunday, like all other festivals, was always only a human ordinance; and it was far from the intentions of the apostles to establish a divine command in this respect—far from them, and from the early apostolic church, to transfer the laws of the Sabbath to Sunday. Perhaps at the end of the second century a false application of this kind had begun to take place; for men appear by that time to have considered laboring on Sunday as a sin." I was the more surprised at this statement, as I found Neander was not a Sabbath-keeper. He takes the high-church ground, acknowledging the right of the so-called apostolic or catholic church to alter or ordain the rites of Christian worship; which is, indeed, the foundation principle of all Papal, Puseyite, and Pedobaptist observances. I saw clearly enough, that if Neander was right, I had no better foundation for Sunday-keeping than hierarchists have for their Easter, Ascension, and Christmas Festivals, which I had always repudiated; or than Pedobaptists have for sprinkling infants. I therefore determined to give the subject

A THOROUGH EXAMINATION.

I commenced with human authors, and read Fuller, Buck, Doddridge, Paley, Wilson, Humphrey, Nevins, Kingsbury, Phelps, Whateley, and others; and I was astonished to find every one of them admitting, that there is no express command, precept, or passage of Scripture, to authorize the change of the Sabbath from the seventh to the first day of the week. They all attempt to support the practice by inferences and analogical reasonings from particular events. Not having veneration large enough to bow to their great names and acute reasonings, I was landed upon a lonely shore, without pilot or compass, with no guide but the truthful chart of Revelation. As I had often vowed in my heart to the Lord, that I would be a Bible Christian so far as I could discover the meaning of the divine Word, or know the revealed will of God; and had more than once told my Pedobaptist friends, when accused of sectarianism, that I would leave all for the truth's sake, if I could discover that I was wrong; I was greatly perplexed, for *I found a great fact*—The Sabbath was changed. The greater part of the world, the most estimable of Christians, do keep their weekly Sabbath on the first day! Can they all be wrong? I conversed with some, and found them more inconsistent in their reasons than the authors I read. For a time, to sanction the change of the Sabbath, I took what may properly be called prelatical ground. It may be stated as follows, viz: "The thing exists; and in the New Testament we find some things which appear to us so like it, that we conclude this and they are identical; though we cannot find the particulars of the change. And besides, we find some occurrences mentioned in the New Testament which seemingly happened in accordance with it and which afford reasons for it, and so we think they should be considered satisfactory evidences of the change existing at the time." But my confidence in this fact was overturned by discovering *another great fact*, viz: That the first day was not honored as a Sabbath during the first two centuries of the Christian era; and that when it did come to be so observed, it was not on the considerations that are now alledged, but on what appeared to me a wicked reason—mere spite to the Jews. I therefore commenced anew,

A THOROUGH EXAMINATION OF THE NEW TESTAMENT

But the more attentively I read it, with this object in view, viz. to find out the mind of Christ upon the subject of the Sabbath, the more plainly I saw that it was against me. I found that Christ and his apostles enjoined the observance of the law of the ten commandments as holy, just, and good —that law which says, "Remember the Sabbath day to keep it holy, ... the seventh day is the Sabbath of the Lord thy God." I found, also, that Christ had said, (Mark 2: 27, 28,) "The Sabbath was made for man; therefore the Son of Man is Lord also of the Sabbath day"—plainly incorporating it into the laws of his kingdom. Luke also says, many years after the resurrection, writing the account in his Gospel of that event, "The women rested the Sabbath day according to the commandment"—thus recognizing it, as it appeared to me, to be a commandment still in force.

THE RESURRECTION OF CHRIST.

The Resurrection of Christ being regarded as the great event which required the change in question, I carefully considered that matter. But I no where found it spoken of by the New Testament writers, as it is by divines of modern times. The only instance I could find of its celebration by the apostles, was in the ordinance of baptism, in these words, "If we have been planted together in the likeness of his death, we shall be also in the likeness of his resurrection." (Rom. 6: 5.) And again, "What shall they do which are baptized for the [resurrection of the] dead, if the dead rise not at all?" (1 Cor. 15: 29.) I concluded that there could not be two apostolic ways of celebrating it; and hence that I must look for some other reason to justify the change in question.

—

THE TIME OF THE RESURRECTION OF CHRIST.

I had always supposed that our Saviour rose on the morning of the first day of the week, and had no doubt about finding it plainly recorded that he did. But when I searched for it in the evangelists, I found the accounts very different from what I had supposed. Matthew 28: 1, reads, "In the end of the Sabbath." Mark 16: 1—"When the Sabbath was passed." Matthew—"As it began to dawn towards the first day of the week." Mark—"Very early in the morning, the first day of the week." Luke 24: 1—"Very early in the morning." John 20: 1—"Early, when it was yet dark,.... they came to the sepulchre, and found not the body of the Lord Jesus." As this did not tell the exact time of his resurrection, I set myself to see if I could find it by any other passages. On examination, it appeared plain to me, that as he was buried at sun-down, according to that law in Deut. 21: 23, to fulfill his own prediction, "So shall the Son of man be three days and three nights in the heart of the earth," his resurrection must have taken place at the same hour of the day, or rather evening—which would destroy its identity with the first day as now reckoned, and carry back his crucifixion to the fourth day of the week.

All we know of the time of the crucifixion, I found to be, that it was on the fourteenth day of the first month, the preparation day of the Passover

The fifteenth day was the Passover Sabbath, a high day with the Jews. (See John 19: 14, 31.)

If Jesus was thus crucified on the fourth day of the week, I found that it made a striking correspondence between the event and the prediction in Daniel 9: 7.

The reason why the Holy Spirit was poured out on the day of PENTECOST, I found to be, because it was the first annual national assembly after the crucifixion—the Saviour being put to death at the Passover, and Pentecost being fifty days after. This event, therefore, had nothing to do with the Sabbath.

—

CHRIST'S APPEARANCES.

The appearances of Christ to his disciples on the first day of the week, are considered as good reasons for sanctifying that day. It is supposed that he so designed them. But these did not appear to me as I expected, when I came to examine them carefully. I knew them as related by the evangelists, but I had them traditionally arranged and associated to suit the arguments for keeping the first day; and when I came to read them with an honest inquiry after the truth, they appeared very different from what I had supposed. I found that there were five appearances of Christ to his disciples on the first day following his resurrection; and neither of them occurred when the disciples were assembled for worship; neither were they accompanied by any such direction.

His first appearance was to the four women, as they returned from the sepulchre, where they had been with spices to embalm the body of Jesus. They were directed by an angel, and by Jesus himself, to go and tell his disciples that Christ was risen, and would meet them on a mountain in Galilee as he had promised them before his crucifixion. There was nothing in this like Sabbath-keeping!

The women having gone into the city, informed Peter and John, who went immediately to the sepulchre; and having looked in and satisfied themselves that the report of the women was true, Peter and John returned to the city. But Mary tarried still at the sepulchre, weeping, when Jesus appeared to her alone. (John 20: 16.)

Next he appeared to Peter. (Luke 24: 34, 1 Cor. 15: 5.)

Afterward he appeared to Cleopas and another disciple as they journied to Emmaus. (Luke 24: 13—35.)

At night, when they had retired for their evening repast, Jesus appeared in the midst of them, and partook with them of a piece of broiled fish and an honey comb. (Luke 24: 42.)

These were all on the first day of the week, and they appeared to me conclusive evidence, that the disciples had not yet received any intimations of a change of Sabbath time, there being no evidence of it in their conduct or discourse.

Eight days after this, Jesus appeared again to his disciples, Thomas being with them. (John 20: 26.) After these things, he shewed himself again to seven of his disciples as they were fishing at the sea of Tiberius. (John 21: 1—14.)

At another time, probably on the mountain in Galilee, he was seen of five hundred brethren at once. (1 Cor. 15: 6.)

After this, he was seen of James. (1 Cor. 15: 7.)

Then of the disciples when he was taken up into heaven. (Luke 24: 50, 51.)

Last of all, he was seen by Saul of Tarsus on his way to Damascus. (1 Cor. 15: 8.)

There are eleven instances mentioned of his meeting his disciples, and not one of them contains a single reference to the Sabbath in any way whatever, which fully convinced me that the pretence of the Sabbath being changed at the resurrection of Christ was wholly groundless. How any one, without very strong prepossessions and blindness, could think these things make a Sabbath, I could not see. Only five of these instances are said to be on the first day, and these were all private interviews! Saul of Tarsus might as well conclude that he ought to build a meeting-house where Jesus met him, as for the disciples to make a Sabbath of the first day because Jesus appeared to them on that day. After examining these things, it looked to me as though the Papists were quite as justifiable for changing the second commandment to make an image of Christ and his cross, as Protestants are for altering the fourth commandment to honor the resurrection. The Papists honor the crucifixion, and the Protestants the resurrection.

—

APOSTOLIC EXAMPLES.

I looked for apostolic examples. But alas, they all failed me. They did not afford me the evidences I had supposed they would. I found but one account of a Christian assembly on the first day of the week, which was at Troas; and that was an evening meeting, and a parting meeting which Paul held with his friends; and while he was holding that meeting, seven of his companions in travel went and removed the ship in which they were to sail from Troas to Assos, whither he followed them on foot to go aboard. I thought, Could they be keeping Sabbath in so doing? (See Acts 20: 1—14.)

"*The Lord's Day,*" I found mentioned but once in the New Testament, (Rev. 1: 10,) and there it does not tell what day of the week it was on, so that I judged it certainly must favor that day for which there is both Bible command and example, rather than that day for which there is nothing but custom and tradition. Thus it appeared to me, that all apostolic example was not only against the observance of the first day, but clearly in favor of the seventh; for I found that at Antioch in Pisidia, the Apostle observed the Sabbath with both Jews and Gentiles. (Acts 13: 14, 42, 44.) The same at Philippi. (Acts 16: 13.) And at Thessalonica. (Acts 17: 2, 3.) Also at Corinth, where the Apostle continued a year and six months, he observed EVERY Sabbath day. (Acts 18: 4, 11.)

The law of God, with all its awful sanctions, flaming from Mount Sinai, appeared to me to threaten my destruction if I dared to reject any part of its holy claims, for when I read what Jesus said, (Luke 16: 17,) "It is easier for heaven and earth to pass than for one tittle of the law to fail," I could not entertain a doubt but that it was obligatory upon his disciples.

THE DECISION.

These things greatly distressed me, and in the end separated me from Sunday-keeping forever. At this time I was not acquainted with a single seventh-day Christian. But a bookseller sent me some copies of the "Address of the Seventh-day Baptists to the Baptists of the United States," which was peculiarly opportune to my state of mind. It showed me the inconsistency of Sunday-keeping with all the foundation principles of the faith I had received, and the order I had observed; and served to bring me to a decision. Yet I did not dare to submit my mind at once to the force of truth, until I had repeatedly investigated every Scripture passage and event on which I had formerly relied for a justification of my faith. I endeavored to do this as independently of extrinsic considerations as I could; and each time brought me to the same conclusion. I could find no Scripture authority for a first-day Sabbath. Yet the conflict was not over. I suffered for some time that deep mental anguish which attends a conscientious mind, where enlightened judgment conflicts with all the inclinations, expectations, and kindliest associations of life. If ever an anxious mariner sailed tremblingly between Sylla and Charybdis, surely his condition was like mine at this time. To advocate the Sunday observance without Bible authority, I could not for conscience's sake. To embrace the no-Sabbath doctrine, I dared not; this was too dark and downward a leap from the highway of holiness for me to hazard; and the former was too disloyal and dishonest a course for me to pursue in the name of the King of saints. For a time I indulged a forlorn hope, that I might find some way of reconciling the matter so as to appear consistent without leaving the denomination. But accustomed to speak the honest sentiments of my heart, I found the subject naturally influencing my prayers and my preaching, and in other ways embarrassing me, so that it became a burden I knew not how to bear. I commenced keeping the Sabbath alone in my study. It seemed now as if God had shut me up to my own vows; *I was compelled to renounce all* for his truth, or prove apostate to the principles of godliness! Dark indeed appeared my prospects. I had a wife and eight children to support, and no human resource to look to but my salary. I felt, too, for the reputation, sentiments, and prepossessions of my wife and children, some of whom had already made a profession of religion, and for many other young converts recently gathered into the church of which I was pastor. But just at that time, I was called to baptize a young woman who had to leave father and mother, and brothers and sisters, and all she had on earth, for her faith in Christ. This greatly assisted me to determine to do so too.

The decision gave great relief to my mind. I could now with more confidence appeal to our Father in heaven for support and direction. I could with great comfort appropriate many precious promises of God's Word to my own case, and find them a precious cordial to my soul. Never have I found more enjoyment in divine things than since I thus renounced all for Christ. I found as the Psalmist expresses it, that "great peace have they that love thy law, and nothing shall offend them." "O taste and see that the Lord is good; blessed is the man that trusteth in him."

CONCLUSION.

The result has been happy in my own family. All in my house who have come to years of discretion have since united in walking according to the commandments. Although it was not easy at first to throw off early prepossessions, we have found no embarrassments from them since the decision was made. Many things which we feared have proved imaginary, and all necessary good has been added unto us; and the truth of God has more abounded toward us. Thus will it be with all them that obey God. "All his commandments are sure." "No good thing will he withhold from him that walketh uprightly." Its influence upon my religious feelings, and views of divine truth in general, has been to clear up some things that were previously obscure, and give a beautiful harmony to the requirements of the law and the doctrines of the Gospel. My hope is, when Babylon shall fall, to be found among them who keep the commandments of God and the faith of Jesus. (Rev. 14. 12.)

TAKING UP THE CROSS.

BY JOSEPH STENNETT.

Jesus, I my cross have taken,
All to leave and follow thee;
Naked, poor, despised, forsaken,
Thou from hence my all shalt be.

Let the world neglect and leave me;
They have left my Saviour too;
Human hopes have oft deceived me;
Thou art faithful, thou art true.

Perish, earthly fame and treasure;
Come disaster, scorn, and pain;
In thy service, pain is pleasure;
With thy favor, death is gain.

Oh! 'tis not in grief to harm me,
While thy bleeding love I see;
Oh! 'tis not in joy to charm me,
When that love is hid from me.

Published by the American Sabbath Tract Society,
No. 9 Spruce Street, N. Y.

No. 11.

Religious Liberty Endangered by Legislative Enactments.

AN APPEAL

TO THE

FRIENDS OF EQUAL RIGHTS AND RELIGIOUS FREEDOM,

IN THE

UNITED STATES,

FROM THE

SEVENTH-DAY BAPTIST GENERAL CONFERENCE.

MDCCCXLVI.

NEW-YORK:

PUBLISHED BY THE AMER. SABBATH TRACT SOCIETY.

No. 9 Spruce-Street

E. G. CHAMPLIN, STEREOTYPER AND PRINTER.

☞ The Seventh-day Baptist General Conference held its Forty-second Anniversary at Shiloh, N. J., on the 9th, 10th, 11th, and 13th days of September, 1846. During the session a resolution was passed expressing the settled conviction of the Conference, "that all legislation designed to enforce the religious observance of any day for a Sabbath, thereby determining by civil law that such day shall not be used for labor or judicial purposes, is unconstitutional, and hostile to religious freedom." A Committee was appointed to prepare an Address to the people of the United States in accordance with the opinion thus expressed. The following is the Address reported by the Committee, approved by the Conference, and referred to the American Sabbath Tract Society for publication.

THE APPEAL.

FELLOW-CITIZENS:—

We fully agree with you in the popular sentiment of our nation, that liberty is sweet—to men of noble minds, much more precious than estates, or treasures of silver and gold—dearer than our reputation and honor among the despots of the world. Was it not this sentiment, firmly-rooted in the minds of the Fathers of our National Independence, which led them to stake their "lives, their fortunes, and their sacred honor," rather than be the serfs of a British King and his aristocratic Lords? Applauding their spirit, we know that you will agree with us in the sentiment, that the preservation of that liberty which they achieved and perpetuated in our ever-glorious Constitution, is the highest civil duty which we owe to ourselves, to our posterity, and to our nation. All but coercionists will agree with us, that the preservation of our religious liberty is a sacred duty, which we owe alike to the cause of truth and our political happiness.

Give us your candid attention, then, while we present a brief statement of the wrongs we are suffering in these United States, despite the principles of the National Declaration of Independence, and the guarantees of our National Constitution.

Believing in the integrity of the provisional Government which made the Declaration of Independence, our fathers and predecessors in faith, fought side by side with yours for the liberty which that instrument declares to be the inalienable right of all men. They were equally zealous parties to he adoption of the Constitution of the United States—that Constitution which says there shall be "no law respecting an establishment of religion, or prohibiting the free exercise thereof;" "and the judges in every State shall be bound thereby, any thing in the constitution or laws of any State to the contrary notwithstanding." Although our brethren at Ephrata, in Pennsylvania, regarded warfare and the shedding of blood as inconsistent with the Christian profession, yet they were no less ardent admirers of those national instruments by which American liberties were asserted and established. Of this they gave ample proof, in the unwavering support which they ever voluntarily rendered to the National Government and its troops, by all the peaceable means at their command. History records an act of patriotism and piety, which reflects everlasting honor on their names. They voluntarily and compassionately received, at their establishment, between four and five hundred wounded Americans who had fallen in the battle of Brandywine, fed them from their own stores, and nursed them with their own hands, for which they never received nor asked a recompense of the American Government or people. It was enough for them, that they were their fellow men. But it stirred their hearts the deeper, that they knew they were bleeding in the cause of sacred liberty.

We are the descendants and successors in faith of these parties. We hold the same sentiments, and cherish the same principles, which they did at that time. Is it not surprising, then, that within seventy years after the signing of that Declaration, and in little more than half a century after the adoption of the Constitution, the lineal descendants of these parties, and their successors in faith and principles, should have their liberties so abridged by state authorities, as to give occasion for an appeal to the citizens of the whole nation, from whom the sovereign power emanates, for a redress of their wrongs? But so it is. Religious zealots, in our State Legislatures and on the Judicial Bench, have violated the Constitution of the nation, established an article of their religious creed, and made it penal for others of different sentiments to follow out their own honest convictions of duty to God. The consequence is, that eight of our brethren are at this moment under judicial sentence for their religious sentiments, and condemned to pay four dollars each, with costs of prosecution, or suffer imprisonment in the common jail. It is not pretended that they have injured the persons, or wronged the estates or interests of any of their fellow-citizens. Neither is it pretended that they are lewd or intemperate persons, or profaners of churches. The only pretence is, that they have injured the religious feelings of some others by peaceably working upon their own farms on the first day of the week, in obedience to the dictates of their own consciences and the law of God. And this is the second time, within the space of one year, that the persecution of these otherwise unoffending men, has been approved by the courts of Pennsylvania. In four other States of the Union, in defiance of the National Constitution, our fellow-citizens have suffered prosecutions, fines, and imprisonment, within the past year, upon similar charges. Beside this, in the States where toleration is provided for labor on our own farms and in our own work shops on the first day of the week, all contracts, legal and commercial transactions, if done even among ourselves, are declared null and void by the State Statutes. So that, even in these States, we are deprived of our constitutional and inalienable right to use one-sixth part of our time for commercial, legal, and judicial transactions; and then are tied up to our own premises, as though we were as dangerous to the religious interests of our fellow-citizens, as rabid animals are to their persons.

Applications were made to three State Legisla tures during the winter of 1845–6, for relief from these odious statutes. But those applications were all repulsed with supercilious denials. Forbearance is no longer a virtue. A succession of abuses and usurpations of our rights, has compelled us to take measures to resist, with all the legal means in our power, and with all that we can honorably acquire, whatever laws abridge the rights or coerce the consciences of ourselves or our fellow-citizens on religious or sectarian considerations. Appealing to Jehovah and his holy law for the rectitude of our principles and the righteousness of our cause, we have implored, and shall continue to implore, the interposition of his Providence to succeed our efforts.

Without wishing to disturb the peace of society, or wantonly to overturn the existing order of things, but actuated solely by a sense of duty to maintain the integrity of God's law, and preserve unimpaired our religious privileges, we appeal to you, fellow-citizens, in defence of the justice of our demands, by a fair representation of our Constitutional Rights.

The sixth article of the Constitution of the United States, section 2d, says, "This Constitution, and the laws of the United States which shall be made in pursuance thereof, ... shall be the supreme law of the land; and the judges in every State shall be bound thereby, any thing in the constitution or laws of any State to the contrary notwithstanding."

Section 3d says, "The members of the several State Legislatures, and all executive and judicial officers, both of the United States and of the several States, shall be bound by oath or affirmation to support this Constitution; but no religious test shall ever be required as a qualification to office or public trust under the United States."

In the amendments to the Constitution, article 1st, it is written, "Congress shall make no law respecting an establishment of religion, or prohibiting the free exercise thereof."

In view of these sections of the fundamental law of the nation, what can be more palpably unconstitutional than those State statutes which are so framed as to declare and establish the first day of the week as "the Christian Sabbath," or holy day. The State statutes which subject any citizen to fine or imprisonment for labor, or any legal transaction, on the first day of the week, as far as their influence extends, make void God's everlasting law, and subject the conscientious servant thereof to punishment for a strict conformity to it. The State statutes violate the Constitution of the United States in two respects. 1st. They violate that part of the Constitution which forbids the enactment of any "law respecting an establishment of religion;" because by them the religious observance of the first day is made a State establishment of religion as really and arbitrarily as the law of Constantine made it a part of the religion of the Roman Empire. 2d. They violate that part of the Constitution which forbids the making of any law "prohibiting the free exercise" of religion; because, by forbidding labor on the first day of the week, they prohibit a strict conformity to the law of God which says, "Six days shalt thou labor and do all thy work, but the seventh day is the Sabbath of the Lord thy God." With this view of the subject, we submit it to the common-sense of candid men to say, if every judicial officer who convicts or passes sentence upon his fellow-citizens for disobeying these arbitrary statutes on a charge of Sabbath-breaking, is not a perjured man. He swears or affirms to "support the Constitution of the United States, any thing in the Constitution or laws of any State to the contrary notwithstanding;" yet he administers a law which establishes a sectarian article of religion, and punishes conscientious men for a free exercise of their own religious opinions, and for doing what they esteem to be their duty to God.

Heretofore we have asked only for exemptions from these odious statutes for all such as observe the seventh day of the week as the Sabbath, and we have generally been permitted to pass peaceably along. But of late our growing numbers, and our increasing influence in the nation, together with the use of the public press in defence of our sentiments, have seemingly made us too odious in the eyes of some of our fellow-citizens to be suffered peaceably to enjoy our rights. Powerful efforts are being made to inflame the public mind against us, to influence the magistracy to enforce the Sunday laws now existing, and if possible to procure the enactment of others more stringent and restrictive. These things have thrown us unavoidably upon our constitutional rights. Experience teaches us that our peace and liberty are continually jepordized by the existence of statutes which can be so construed as to coerce us, contrary to our consciences, to do reverence to the first day of the week as a holy day. We therefore demand the entire repeal of all laws for coercing the observance of the first day, as being contrary to the spirit and the letter of the Constitution of the United States.

The view which we take of this subject is not from a partial construction of the Constitution. That instrument has been so construed by impartial and competent authority. The following extract from a letter written by GEORGE WASHINGTON, while President of the United States, and who was President of the Convention for framing the Constitution, to a committee of a Baptist Society in Virginia, in answer to an application to him for his views of the meaning and efficiency of that instrument to protect the rights of conscience, decides the intent of the framers of the Constitution, and consequently the intent of the Constitution itself. The letter is dated August 4, 1789, and reads as follows:—

"If I had the least idea of any difficulty resulting from the Constitution adopted by the Convention of which I had the honor to be President when it was formed, so as to endanger the rights of any religious denomination, then I never should have attached my name to that instrument. If I had any idea that the General Government was so administered that liberty of conscience was endangered, I pray you be assured that no man would be more willing than myself to revise and alter that part of it, so as to avoid all religious persecution. You can, without doubt, remember that I have often expressed my opinion, that every man who conducts himself as a good citizen is accountable alone to God for his religious faith, and should be protected in worshiping God according to the dictates of his conscience.

[Signed,] "GEORGE WASHINGTON." *

* This letter was translated into the German at Ephrata, Penn., and the present copy of the letter is probably a re-translation of it into English from the German.

The Congressional Committee on Post Offices and Post Roads, to whom were referred certain memorials for prohibiting the transportation of mails and the opening of post offices on Sunday, in the 43d session of Congress, A. D. 1830, reported unfavorably to the prayer of the memorialists. Their report was adopted and printed by order of the Senate of the United States, and the Committee was discharged from the farther consideration of the subject. That Committee take the same view of the intent of the Constitution as did General Washington. They say:—

"We look in vain to that instrument for authority to say whether first day, or seventh day, or whether any day, has been made holy by the Almighty." . . . . . "The Constitution regards the conscience of the Jew as sacred as that of the Christian; and gives no more authority to adopt a measure affecting the conscience of a solitary individual, than that of a whole community. That representative who would violate this principle, would lose his delegated character, and forfeit the confidence of his constituents If Congress should declare the first day of the week holy, it would not convince the Jew nor the Sabbatarian. It would dissatisfy both, and consequently convert neither." . . . . . "If a solemn act of legislation shall in one point define the law of God, or point out to the citizen one religious duty, it may with equal propriety define every part of revelation, and enforce every religious obligation, even to the forms and ceremonies of worship, the endowments of the church, and the support of the clergy." . . . . . "The framers of the Constitution recognized the eternal principle, that man's relation to his God is above human legislation, and his rights of conscience inalienable. Reasoning was not necessary to establish this truth; we are conscious of it in our own bosoms. It is this consciousness which, in defiance of human laws, has sustained so many martyrs in tortures and flames. They felt that their duty to God was superior to human enactments, and that man could exercise no authority over their consciences. It is an inborn principle, which nothing can eradicate." . . . . . "It is also a fact, that counter memorials, equally respectable, oppose the interference of Congress, on the ground that it would be legislating upon a religious subject, and therefore unconstitutional."

Impartial Judiciaries have taken the same view of these provisions of the Constitution, and have declared the laws enforcing the observance of the first day of the week unconstitutional, as may be seen in Judge Herttell's book, "The Rights of the People Reclaimed;" also in "An Essay on Constitutional Reform, by Hiram P. Hastings, Counselor at Law."

On the 2d of October, 1799, at New Mills, Burlington County, New Jersey, a Seventh-day Baptist being indicted before a Justice of the Peace for working on Sunday, and fined, he appealed. At the trial in Court, the foregoing letter from General Washington was produced by the Judge, and read in his charge to the Jury. The result was acquittal by the Jury.

In the year 1845, the Court of Hamilton County, Ohio, made a similar decision in a like case, and on similar considerations.

A Committee of the Common Hall of the City of Richmond, Virginia, to whom was referred the case of certain persecuted Jews, have made a like decision on the municipal laws of that City, which havé been construed to enforce keeping the first day.

The Post Office Laws are framed in accordance with these provisions of the Constitution. The Act of March 3d, 1825, section 1st, authorizes the Postmaster to "provide for the carriage of the mail on all post roads that are or may be established by law, and as often as he, having regard to the productiveness thereof, and other circumstances, shall think proper." Section 17th provides, "that every Postmaster shall keep an office, in which one or more persons shall attend on every day on which a mail shall arrive by land or water, as well as on other days, at such hours as the Postmaster General shall direct, for the purpose of performing the duties thereof; and it shall be the duty of the Postmaster, at all reasonable hours, on every day of the week, to deliver on demand any letter, paper, or packet, to the person entitled to, or authorzed to receive the same. The laws against labor on the first day, in each State where they exist, are obliged to except the mail-carriers and the postmasters. But we ask our fellow-citizens to consider by what show of justice, any local tribunal can punish a private citizen for doing that on his own account, which the servants and officers of the United States are doing at the same time, for the use of the people, and by a law of the same Government? Suppose a carriage conveying the United States Mail, should enter the City of Philadelphia on Sunday; and another carriage, containing goods or wares for the next day's market, should enter at the same time and by the same route; with what show of justice shall the driver of the market carriage be put under arrest and fined, and the driver of the mail carriage go free? Or suppose there should be a postmaster assorting his letters on the first day, and a fellow-citizen selling pens, ink, paper, and wafers, to write the same letters, in another part of the same building; with what show of justice shall the tradesman be fined and the postmaster go free? The officers of the United States Government have no national rights above the humblest citizen. The transgression of law by them is as really a crime as in the case of any other citizen. Our Government knows nothing of those kingly rights which set emperors, monarchs, and their servants, above law. If, therefore, there is no transgression of constitutional law in carrying the United States Mail on the first day, then there is none in a private citizen following his otherwise lawful and peaceable occupation on the same day.

In some quarters, during the last year, our motives and designs were grossly misrepresented by prejudiced persons, in our legislatures and elsewhere. We were represented as "wishing the legislature to change the Sabbath from the first to the seventh day of the week;" and were accused of "covertly wishing to compel our fellow-citizens to keep our Sabbath day." No insinuation could be more grossly deceptive—no accusation more flagitiously unjust to us as a people. We declare unequivocally, that we do not desire any such thing. We believe that keeping the Sabbath day is purely a religious duty. All we ask is, that our State Legislatures leave the matter where the Constitution of the United States and the laws of the General Government have placed it. They have no more right to determine this religious duty, than they have to determine the rites of Christian worship. We believe our fellow-citizens ought to be protected in the peaceable observation of their day of religious rest, as in the observance of every other religious institution, except where such observance is made a sanctuary for crime. We ask the same protection for ourselves on the seventh day of the week, and nothing more.

If the Constitution may be infringed upon to put down the observers of the seventh day, no one can say how long it will be before other minor denominations may be put down too. Already attempts are making to exact a confession of faith, unknown to the Constitution, as a qualification for a legal oath. If the religious sanctification of the first day of the week may be enforced by statutory requirements, so may the forms and hours of worship. He who says, that there is no danger of the latter being enforced, while statutory regulations violate two of the most sacred provisions of the National

Constitution, knows but little of the history of mankind, or pays but little attention to the tendencies of human nature. A single standing violation of the Constitution is an example and an authority for others to follow. One religious observance established by law, is the admission of the main principle of national hierarchy, and will come in time to be referred to as authority for similar infractions of the Constitution. The laws for the observance of the first day are in fact a union of Church and State. It is not pretended that they are designed to subserve directly a political or civil object. It is altogether a religious object which they subserve. It becomes every friend of equal rights, as he loves the Constitution of his country, to oppose these infractions of its just principles, until equal liberty is secured to all citizens by statutory provisions, as by the fundamental laws of the nation.

Our opponents often remind us of their pretence, that we are under no more restrictions than other citizens; we may do as we please about keeping the seventh day.. To this we reply, that the tyrants of the Roman people deprived the Republic of its liberties by professing themselves the guardians of their INTERESTS. "By declaring themselves the protectors of the people, Marius and Cæsar had subverted the Constitution of their country." Augustus established a despotism by artfully affecting to be governed himself by the same laws which he procured to be enacted to take away the rights of the people. These are the same principles upon which religious coercionists conjure us to be quiet under the loss of our constitutional rights. The progress of these things towards despotism is as dangerous in the American Republic as in that of Rome, and may be as rapid. Their success would be as deadly to human happiness, and all the best interests of mankind, in the nineteenth century, as they were in the decline and fall of the Roman Empire. Human nature now affords no better guaranty for the safety of *our* national rights, than it did to the Romans at the summit of their greatness. Liberty can be preserved only at the expense of perpetual vigilance, and by the popular support of individual rights. If ever the doctrine which has been urged before one of our legislative bodies, "The greatest good of the greatest number," should become a popular political axiom, to justify the course of the many in taking away the rights of the few, the halls of legislation will become scaffolds for the execution of liberty, and that odious principle will be the shroud in which it will be buried. Despots may establish a round of religious observances, and exact an unwilling and insincere conformity to their arbitrary prescriptions; but they can never convince the understanding nor win the heart of one who knows the voice of truth. They can only make him a slave, while the effects of their arbitrary prescriptions on the popular mind will be to wither up all interest in the religious tendencies of an observance sustained only by the enactments of heartless politicians. All that makes religion vital and effective for its own holy objects, expires when the sword is drawn to enforce it. Liberty, humanity, religion, and our National Constitution, then, require that the laws enforcing the observance of the first day of the week should be repealed.

As American Citizens, as independent Freemen, and as responsible Stewards of the glorious heritage bequeathed to us by the Fathers of the Revolution, we shall, with the aid of the Majesty of Heaven, maintain unimpaired the high privileges secured to us by the Charter of our Liberties.

We ask for no exclusive immunities. We disclaim all right of human government to exercise over, or fetter in the least, the religious rights of any being. Might is not right, neither does the accident of being a *majority* give any, claim to trample on the rights of the minority. It is a usurpation of authority to oppress the minority, or set at naught their indefeasible rights. In civil affairs we respect the authorities that be, but in religious service, resent being forced to keep the commandments of men. We recognize the laws of the land in all secular matters, and the laws of God, and of God alone, in religious faith and practice. These are the inalienable rights of all the members of a Republic. These are rights reserved by the people to themselves, in the formation of our Government, which no power can legitimately wrest from us, and with the help of God none shall.

No 12.

MISUSE OF THE TERM "SABBATH"

It is quite common, in these days, to hear the term *Sabbath* used to designate the first day of the week or Sunday. But such a use of the term is not only unscriptural, but calculated to mislead the people. Throughout the Bible, there is but one sacred day of weekly occurrence called the Sabbath, and that is the seventh or last day of the week. When, therefore, men talk about a *Christian* Sabbath and a *Jewish* Sabbath — a *first-day* Sabbath, and a *seventh-day* Sabbath — that so they may slily fix the term Sabbath upon the first day, and then persuade people that all those texts of Scripture which speak of the Sabbath day are meant of the first day, they pursue a course which is unauthorized, and deserve to be sharply rebuked There are circumstances, however, which many persons seem to regard as justifying the common practice of calling the first day by the name *Sabbath*. Let us examine some of them.

1. It is said that the term *Sabbath* signifies *rest;* therefore the first day, being commonly observed as a day of rest, may properly be called the Sabbath. In reply to this, it may be said, that when, by custom and common consent, any term is used to express a particular place or thing, it then becomes a proper name for that thing, and signifies only that thing to which it is applied. For instance,

a *tabernacle* means a place of worship. Yet, in New York, where this name is used to express a particular and well-known place of worship, it would be absurd and false to say you were at the *Tabernacle*, and mean the Church of the Messiah. So with the term Sabbath; although the word strictly means *rest*, yet after the Scriptures throughout the Old and New Testaments have used this term to express a particular rest, which occurred on the seventh day, it would be foolish and deceptive to speak of the Sabbath and mean the first day of the week. It may be farther said, that if this argument be good for calling the first day the Sabbath, and if the fact of its being a *rest*-day makes it the Sabbath, then may the Mohammedans properly call the *sixth* day the Sabbath, and the fact that they rest upon that day makes it the Sabbath. Yes, and those Mexican Indians, whom Cortes found keeping the *fourth* day, may properly call that day the Sabbath, and directly it is made such. Even those people in Guinea, whom Purchase describes as having a *rest*-day, but which, says he, "they observe not upon our Sunday, nor upon the Jews' Sabbath day, but hold it upon Tuesday, the *second* working day of the week," may properly call that day the Sabbath, and straightway it becomes such. Are the observers of the first day ready to rest upon such ground for calling that day the Sabbath, or to continue to call it Sabbath when there is no better ground? We hope not. And we feel bound, as those who respect the Bible, and dare not charge the Author of that Book with folly in calling the seventh day only the Sabbath, to protest against such abuse of the language of Scripture.

2. The second reason frequently urged, is, that he first day *comes in the room* of the seventh day,

and may therefore properly be called the Sabbath. Aside from the fact that the Scriptures say *not a word* about a substitution of the one day for the other, it may be said in reply, that if the argument be good, then the Lord's Supper may be called the *Passover*, and King Solomon may be called King *David.*

3. A third reason alledged for calling the first day the Sabbath, is, because it has long been the practice of Christians to call it so. In answering this assertion, it may be worth while to inquire what has been the practice of Christians in this matter. Few will deny, that wherever, in the New Testament, the word Sabbath refers to a weekly religious day, it is the seventh day. When the *first* day of the week is spoken of, it is under its appropriate title. For nearly the whole of the first century, then, we have the testimony of Scripture that the name *Sabbath* belonged exclusively to the seventh day. During the succeeding four hundred years, there were large numbers, both in the Eastern church, about Constantinople, and in the Western church, about Rome, who kept the Sabbath. And when ecclesiastical councils, in the fourth and fifth centuries, began to enact laws against them, they condemned Sabbath-keeping altogether. From this it is apparent, that the idea of calling the first day the Sabbath had not then entered their minds. What day was meant when the term Sabbath was used for five hundred years later still, the learned Dr. Peter Heylyn has told us in the following words:—" Wherever, for a thousand years and upwards, we meet with *Sabbatum*, in any writer, of what name soever, it must be understood of no day but *Saturday*." Indeed, if we search all the books which have been written on this and kindred sub-

jects up to the time of the Reformation, we shall not find that the first day was to any considerable extent regarded as the Sabbath or called by that name. Dr. Richard Whately, Archbishop of Dublin, in a late work on the subject of the Sabbath, says, "in fact, the notion against which I am contending, [viz. that the fourth commandment binds Christians to hallow the first day of the week, and that it may properly be called the Sabbath,] seems, as far as I can recollect, to have originated with the Puritans, not much more than 200 years ago, and to have been for a considerable time confined to them, though it was subsequently adopted by some members of our church."

So far is it from being true, then, that the first day has been universally called the Sabbath among Christians, that even now, by the best authorities upon such subjects, it is not called Sabbath at all. The Records of England up to the present time invariably call the *seventh* day the Sabbath. In the Journals of the House of Lords, whatever is entered as having been done on the seventh day, or Saturday, is under the date, *Die Sabbati*, upon the Sabbath day. The same is true of the House of Commons. The Rules and Records of the King's Bench, and the Latin Records in the Court of Exchequer and in Chancery, do likewise call the seventh day the Sabbath. These things may be known by any who will take the trouble to examine; and they show how groundless and erroneous is the supposition to which we are replying. Indeed, in many languages the seventh day is called by a name which indicates its sabbatic character. In Low Dutch it is called *rust-dagh*, the day of rest. In English, French, Italian, Spanish, Portuguese, Latin, Greek, and Hebrew, it has its right name, *the Sabbath*, the day of rest.

Now let us look at some of the *consequences* of calling the first day by the name of the Sabbath. It has given occasion for Papists to charge Protestants with neglecting the Scriptures to follow their traditions. The Papists claim, that the change of the Sabbath is the work of their own church, and that the Scriptures nowhere warrant the keeping of the first day, much less the calling it by the name of the Sabbath. Who will deny this latter position? Again, it has led some earnest and pious men to charge the teachers of religion with "befooling and misleading the people." Proof of this may be found to any extent in books writted on the subject in the seventeenth century. The charge is there distinctly and frequently made, of designedly using deceptive arguments.

We will not undertake to say, that those who are accustomed to speak in a manner so likely to deceive, design to do that. But we will say, that such would be the natural effect of their language. It would leave upon the minds of many an impression, that they were not only bound to pay peculiar respect to the first day of the week, but that the fourth commandment required of them such respect. For a religious teacher knowingly to make this impression, is to be guilty of directly fostering error. Nay, more; if he should call the first day the Sabbath, and refer to the fourth commandment as inculcating the duty of observing that day; or should, without direct reference to that law, express himself in such a way as to leave his hearers to suppose that it required the observance of the first day, he would be wanting in faithfulness to the truth, and exposed to the denunciation of those who add to or take from it.

No doubt many will think, that at a time when the prevailing tendency is to disregard all sacred seasons, it were better not to say these things, but to leave men under an impression that the law of God requires the observance of the first day of the week, and sanctions calling that day the Sabbath. But this prevailing disregard of the day of rest, is an important reason for urging an examination of the foundation upon which the Sabbath rests. Common prudence, to say nothing of Christian sincerity, would require us, in such circumstances, to place the duty upon its true ground. If it will not stand there, it will stand nowhere. It is a dangerous experiment to encourage or connive at misconceptions in a point like this. And even if we felt assured that it would be right, we are fully convinced that it would be inexpedient. It is exceedingly dangerous to acknowledge an unsound principle, although it may promise to conduct us to desirable results, or, at the worst, to produce no bad effects. It ought to be remembered, that it was in apparently trivial and harmless points, that those false principles were allowed, which have infused their poison into the Romish and other apostate churches — a poison which, commencing with the extremities, has worked its way rapidly towards the vitals, and diffused its effects through the whole system. It is not, then, a matter of small moment. The most important and disastrous consequences may result from baptizing a day of human invention with a name which the Scriptures apply exclusively to one appointed of God.

[No. 13.]

THE

BIBLE SABBATH.

By WILLIAM M. FAHNESTOCK, M. D.

"WE OUGHT TO OBEY GOD RATHER THAN MEN."

NEW-YORK:
PUBLISHED BY THE AMERICAN SABBATH TRACT SOCIETY,
No. 9 Spruce-Street.

THE BIBLE SABBATH.

Most professors of religion, who found their faith on the Word of God, attach much importance to a weekly day of sacred rest, however much they may differ in regard to the day to be sanctified as the Sabbath, or the manner in which its sacred hours are to be improved. It is not the design of the writer of this small tract, to enter upon the discussion of the multifarious points of disputation, which have been raised by most writers, in treating this question, but simply to exhibit the scriptural account of the day to be honored unto the Lord, with some cursory remarks on the prominent topics of the controversy, which can be, and which ought to be, determined by direct reference "*to the law and the testimony.*" Without, therefore, any pretensions to an extended confutation of men's hypotheses and men's subterfuges on this subject, he desires merely to present a concise epitome of *what saith the Scriptures* in reference to the day which legitimately challenges our profound veneration and implicit obedience; and will restrict his comments; on the bearings of the sacred text, to as few words as is practicable in a matter of such grave importance; that, in embracing and defending so sacred an institution, and in responding to the scriptural interrogation, "*Who hath required this at your hand?*" the reader may, confidently and without fear of contradiction, answer, "*The Lord thy God — the*

Almighty Jehovah!" and lay his finger on the clear, unequivocal, ungarbled, "*Thus saith the Lord,*" for his practice.

The *Scriptures* tell us, that God "rested on the *seventh day* from all his work which he had made; and God blessed the *seventh day* and *sanctified* it." Gen. 2: 2, 3. This is the first notice of the Sabbath in the Bible; and it is the first religious institution established by the Almighty for the benefit of all after generations. The rest of the testimonies of the Lord to the sacredness of his holy day, are like unto it, wherever they occur in the *Inspired Volume.*

During the sojourn of the children of Israel in the wilderness, the Lord, to supply their necessities, sent manna daily, save on the *seventh day;* thus recognizing strictly his holy Sabbath, by affording them a *double portion* on the *sixth* day, and requiring them to secure it at that time for the *seventh day.*

"And Moses said unto them, This is the bread which the Lord hath given you to eat. This is the thing which the Lord hath commanded. Gather of it every man according to his eating; an omer for every man according to the number of your persons, take ye every man for them which are in your tents. And the children of Israel did so, and gathered, some more, some less. And when they did mete it with an omer, he that had gathered much had nothing over, and he that had gathered little had no lack; they gathered every man according to his eating. And Moses said, Let no man leave of it till the morning. Notwithstanding, they hearkened not unto Moses, but some of them left it until the morning, and it bred worms and stank; and Moses was wroth with them. And they gathered it every morning, every man according to his eating; when the sun waxed hot it melted. And it came to pass, that on the *sixth day,* they gathered *twice* as much bread, *two* omers for *one* man; and all the rulers of the congregation came and told Moses. And he said unto them, This is that which the Lord hath said, To-morrow is the rest of the holy Sabbath unto the Lord; bake that which ye will bake to-day, and seethe that ye will seethe; and that which remaineth over lay up for you to be kept until the morning. And they laid it up till the morning, as Moses bade; and it did not stink, neither was there any worm therein. And Moses said, Eat that to-day; for to-day is the Sabbath unto the Lord; *to-day* ye shall not find it in the field. Six days ye shall gather it; but on the *seventh day*, which is the Sabbath, in it there shall be none. And it came to pass, that there went out some people on the *seventh day* for to gather, and they found none. And the Lord said unto Moses, How long refuse ye to keep my commandments and my laws? See, for the Lord hath given you the *Sabbath*, therefore he giveth you on the *sixth* day the bread of *two days;* abide ye every man in his place on the *seventh day*." Exod. 16: 15—30.

This was *before* the giving of the law, and is irrefragible evidence of respect unto the Sabbath *before the law was promulgated.*

When the Decalogue, written on stone by the finger of God, was committed to the Israelites, the obligation to honor the Sabbath—the *seventh day*—was emphatically *renewed*, and most explicitly defined and enjoined.

"Remember the Sabbath day to keep it holy. Six days shalt thou labor and do all thy work; but the *seventh day* is the *Sabbath* of the Lord thy God; in it thou shalt not do any work, thou, nor thy son, nor thy daughter, thy man-servant, nor thy maid-servant, nor thy cattle, nor thy stranger that is within thy gates; for in six days the Lord made heaven and earth, the sea, and all that in them is, and rested the *seventh day;* wherefore the Lord blessed the *Sabbath day* and *hallowed* it." Exod. 20: 8—11.

The same is reïterated by the same writer in another place.

"Six days shall work be done; but the *seventh day* is the Sabbath of rest, an holy convocation; ye shall do no work therein; it is the *Sabbath of the Lord* in all your dwellings." Lev. 23: 3.

The reader will observe, that this commandment does not ordain a *new* and *peculiar* institution, but *reminds* the Israelites of one which had been established long prior to their existence as a nation, to be had in remembrance and to be rigidly observed. "Remember the Sabbath day to keep it holy." The reader will also observe, that it does not simply appoint *a* Sabbath, or a seventh part of time to be consecrated as holy time, but that the precise time, the particular day, is specifically certified by Jehovah himself—that it is *the day*, and not the *institution*, which the Lord blessed and hallowed; that it was not the *sabbatic law*, but the *day of rest*, which was enjoined. The law was predicated on the *sanctified day*, not the day accommodated to the institution; and that there might be no mistake on the subject, the law defines the day *as it found it*, and assigns clearly and most unequivocally the reason for its observance. It aims simply at hallowing the *day*, the precise, particular day; which is still more emphatically expressed in the original, יום השבת, "the *day* of *the rest*," because *in it*, the day, God rested from all his work, and subsequently enjoined like rest, on the same day, and for the same purpose, upon all his people. This Bible truth ought to be sufficient to overset all the sophistry of equivocators, in their attempts to blind the inquirer, by astutely insinuating the idea, that the *sabbatic law* only demands the consecration of *a seventh portion of time*, which position, they, in turn, as stoutly repudiate, when any one sees proper to choose any other seventh part of time than the day which they propound for them. To proceed; Nehemiah says:—

"In those days saw I in Judah some treading wine presses on the Sabbath, and bringing in sheaves and lading asses; as also wine, grapes, and figs, and all manner of burdens, which they brought into Jerusalem on the Sabbath day; and I testified against them on the day wherein they sold victuals. There dwelt men of Tyre also therein, which brought fish and all manner of ware, and sold on the Sabbath unto the children of Judah, and in Jerusalem. Then I contended with the nobles of Judah, and said unto them, What evil thing is this that ye do and profane the Sabbath day? Did not your fathers thus, and did not our God bring all this evil upon us, and upon this city? Yet ye bring more wrath upon Israel by profaning the Sabbath. And it came to pass, that when the gates of Jerusalem began to be dark before the Sabbath, I commanded that the gates should be shut, and charged that they should not be opened till after the Sabbath; and some of my servants set I at the gates, that there should no burden be brought in on the Sabbath day. So the merchants and sellers of all kinds of ware lodged without Jerusalem once or twice. Then I testified against them, Why lodge ye about the wall? if ye do so again, I will lay hands on you. From this time forth came they no more on the Sabbath. And I commanded the Levites that they should cleanse themselves, and that they should come and keep the gates to sanctify the Sabbath day." Neh. 13: 15—22.

To turn to the New Testament, our blessed Redeemer proclaimed himself Lord of the Sabbath, (Mark 2: 28,) thereby incorporating it in the new dispensation. He also declared most distinctly, that he did not come to destroy the law, but to fulfill it; that not one jot or tittle should pass from the law, till all be fulfilled. Matt. 5: 17, 18. Luke also affirms, in reference to the course of the disciples after the crucifixion, that they "rested the Sabbath day *according to the commandment*." Luke 23: 56. This was *after* Christ had declared that all his work was *finished*—the new covenant perfected, and he had been nailed to the tree. This doubtless refers to the commandment to observe the *seventh day*. No one disputes it, as no command was given to observe any other day. And from the Acts of the Apostles, we find that they made *it* the day of their special ministrations of the Word, as their Lord and Master had done before them.

"But when they departed from Perga, they came to Antioch in Pisidia, and went into the synagogue on the *Sabbath day*, and sat down. And after the reading of the law and the prophets, the rulers of the synagogue sent unto them saying, Ye men and brethren, if ye have any word of exhortation for the people, say on. Then Paul stood up, and beckening with his hand, said, Men of Israel, and ye that fear God, give audience." Acts 13: 14, 15. "And when the Jews were gone out of the synagogue, the *Gentiles* besought that these words might be preached to them the next *Sabbath.* * * * And the next *Sabbath day* came almost the whole city to hear the word of God." Id. verses 42, 44. Paul "reasoned in the synagogue *every* Sabbath, and persuaded the Jews and the Greeks." Id. 18: 4, 5.

All the *promises,* and all the *penalities* connected with the observance or the desecration of the Sabbath, refer to the *seventh day Sabbath,* and to no other *in future.*

"Blessed is the man that doeth this, and the son of man that layeth hold on it; that keepeth the Sabbath from polluting it, and keepeth his hand from doing any evil." Isa. 56: 2.

"If thou turn away thy foot from the Sabbath, from doing thy pleasure on my holy day; and call the Sabbath a delight, the holy of the Lord, honorable; and shalt honor him, not doing thine own ways, nor finding thine own pleasure, nor speaking thine own words; then thou shalt delight thyself in the Lord; and I will cause thee to ride upon the high places of the earth, and feed thee with the heritage of Jacob thy father; for the mouth of the Lord hath spoken it." Id. 58: 13, 14.

"Thus saith the Lord: Take heed to yourselves, and bear no burden on the Sabbath day, nor bring it in by the gates of Jerusalem; neither carry forth a burden out of your houses on the Sabbath day, neither do ye any work, but hallow ye the Sabbath day, as I commanded your fathers. * * * And it shall come to pass, if ye diligently hearken unto me, saith the Lord, to bring in no burden through the gates of the city on the Sabbath day, but hallow the Sabbath day to do no work therein, then shall there enter into the gates of the city, kings and princes, sitting upon the throne of David, riding in chariots and on horses, they and their princes, the men of Judah and the inhabitants of Jerusalem; and this shall remain forever. * * * But if ye will not hearken unto me, to hallow the Sabbath day, and not to bear a burden, even entering at the gates of Jerusalem on the Sabbath day; then I will kindle a fire in the gates thereof, and it shall devour the palaces of Jerusalem, and it shall not be quenched." Jer. 17: 21, 22, 24 25, 27.

No where in the Inspired Word have we any other

weekly Sabbath appointed. No where has that Sabbath ever been *abrogated* or *superseded*. No where in the Scriptures is any other day called the Sabbath-day. No where is any other day *required* to be observed *as the Sabbath*. If, then, HE, the Almighty, gave the *seventh day*, and sanctified and hallowed it *as his Sabbath*, and has not abrogated it—has not absolved us from its duties, nor delegated authority to others to do so—it remains in as full force as when first instituted by Jehovah himself, and will stand in the Judgment against all the crafty inventions and futile subterfuges of perverse, rebellious man.

The foregoing summary is a plain, unvarnished, unmutilated *scriptural account* of God's rest-day, which HE enjoined on all mankind, for all ages, for all nations, tongues, and kindred. Some persons, nay, the great mass of the Christian world, have been taught, that the Sabbath alluded to is a "*Jewish Sabbath*," and "*has been done away;*" in proof of which position, they adduce the passages in Paul's Epistle to the Colossians—"Let no man, therefore, judge you in meat, or in drink, or in respect of an holy-day, or of the new moon, or of the Sabbath-*days*, which are a shadow of things to come; but the body is of Christ."* Col. 2: 16, 17. "Who blotted out the hand-writing of ordinances, that was against us, which was contrary to us, and took it out of the way, nailing it to his cross." Col. 2: 14. This, I must remark, proves

* The Sabbath was no type of Christ—a *shadow*, of which Christ was to be the *body*. It was instituted before the *transgression;* consequently, the term *Sabbath-days*, here, has no relevancy if applied to the *weekly* Sabbath; but it evidently alludes to the *festival days* among the Jews, usually called *Sabbaths*, as all the Israelites had at those periods to *refrain from labor*—"such as the festivals of the Passover, Pentecost, the Feast of Tabernacles, &c., &c , which are alluded to in Leviticus, 19: 3—30. *Keep my Sabbaths*."—CALMET.

too much; for if it has abrogated the seventh-day Sabbath, it has blotted out the sabbatic law also; unless it be shown, that *it* is reserved, or that another has been re-enacted, clearly and expressly ordained. If so, let its advocates point to a single requirement, an unequivocal injunction, to observe any other day as the Sabbath, and it will terminate all controversy on the subject. The "hand-writing of ordinances," which was "nailed to the cross," was merely "the ceremonial law," the onerous burdens of the Levitical ritual, not the "moral law of commandments"—the Decalogue! If the opposite view be correct, then the Sabbath, or any "rest-day," is "against us," contrary to our nature and wants, and is not for our good, and ought to be annulled and obliterated forever. Then, also, we are driven to the doctrine of the "Friends," that all days are alike holy under the gospel dispensation. The advôcates for the first day of the week can not consistently escape this dilemma. They must accept the Sabbath hallowed by the Lord, or hallow all days alike.

Much as man has attempted to obscure and pervert this holy institution, the Word of Truth is clear, express and emphatic, in regard to the perpetuity of the particular day to be hallowed, as well as it is explicit in the precise time to be sanctified. The Scriptures no where speak of a "*Jewish Sabbath*" or a "*Christian Sabbath.*" The Sabbath of the Bible is but one, and has but one name—"*the Sabbath of the Lord thy God;*" which the Scriptures declare is the *seventh day,* instituted more than two thousand years before there was a Jew in the world, and, consequently, could not have been a "Jewish Sabbath." The Sabbath, Christ, who is "Lord of the Sabbath," asserts, "was made for man"—the whole race of man—not for a particular nation or people, but for *mankind at large.*

It is proper here to remark, that this sneering at.

the "*Jewish Sabbath*," which in times past was, and still is, by weak minds, constantly resorted to, in the absence of legitimate argument, to prejudice the populace against giving this subject a fair and impartial examination, and thereby to lead them to prejudge the case, has, within a few years past, been abandoned by all sensible and consistent advocates for the *sabbatic institution*. They find that it stultifies their own pretensions, and has done much damage to themselves in sustaining the claims of sacredness for any other day; for, while they maintain that the ancient Sabbath was a Jewish institution, they unwittingly prove that there is no longer any Sabbath to be observed, since they fail to show that another has been ordained or established for the Christian Church. If a "Jewish Sabbath," it was done away with by the Jewish dispensation; and if no other Sabbath has been expressly appointed by Divine authority, the Christian Church is certainly left without the Sabbath, or any substitute possessing any of its sacredness—a sacredness which can only be derived from an *express* and *explicit* mandate from the Lord of the Sabbath. That puerile quibble, the *nick-name* "Jewish Sabbath," has, therefore, been abandoned by the most prominent writers of the present day; who generally fall back and found the *institution* (the origin and grounds for its perpetuity) long anterior to the "Jewish," the Mosaic dispensation—even back to the Sabbath of Paradise. Thus Dr. Barnes, of Philadelphia, in a series of sermons on this subject, delivered and published in the fall of 1845, advocates this position, and contends strenuously for the *Ante-Mosaic Sabbath*. The same view was inculcated by the "National Lord's Day Convention," held at Baltimore, November, 1844; and it has been reiterated more distinctly and emphatically by "The Rhode Island Sabbath Union," in an address to the people of that State, in 1846, to which, among others, we find attached the name of Dr. Wayland, the honored President of Brown University. The Committee of the Rhode Island "*Sabbath* Union," in calling attention to the *claims of the Sabbath*, remark:

"The Lord of the Sabbath has here said, '*The Sabbath was made for man*.' Man is here used, most certainly, as a *generic* term, and, therefore, presents a universal proposition. The Sabbath was not made for *man*, for man as a genus, as a race, unless it was made for every individual of the race; for the first, and for the last man; for the first generation, and for every other. The Sabbath, then, must have existed from the beginning, and is as old as the human race. Our Lord says, moreover, '*The* Sabbath was made for man.' He says not, the Jewish Sabbath, or the Christian Sabbath, but *the* Sabbath, the common, the universal one, which belongs to mankind. Is this not the very language to denote a universal and perpetual institution?

"Let us look at the connection of the Sabbath with the work of creation. 'God blessed the *seventh* day and sanctified it.' If the Creator had merely *rested* on the seventh day, it would have been an impressive consecration. But when he proceeds to bless and sanctify it, there is authority, a positive Sabbath, forming a part of the primeval arrangement, when God fixed the order in which the world should go—six days labor and one day rest, over and over forever. The first week of the world, then, was not completed till there had been a Sabbath, as well as a first day or a sixth. Is not this indicative of the universality and perpetuity of the institution?"

Here we might rest the question, with perfect safety, if the mass of mankind would be content with the plain teachings of the Bible; but, having "itching ears," they, unfortunately, are too apt to leave "the law and the testimony," and cleave to "the commandments of men;" which teach them, that "*Christ* OR *his Apostles*" have transferred the sacredness of the seventh day to the first day of the week. The writer, therefore, feels constrained to bring before his readers the passages on which that notion is predicated, to exhibit the weakness of their untenable position, and thereby establish the Sabbath of the Bible.

What saith the Scriptures to support the claims of the first day of the week to be *holy time?* The first notice we have of the disciples being together on "the first day of the week," on which the assumed "change" is predicated, is found in the Gospel by John:—

"Then the same day at evening, being the first day of the week, when the doors were shut *for fear of the Jews* (mark that!) came Jesus and stood in the midst, and saith unto them, Peace be unto you. And when he had so said, he showed unto them his hands and his side. Then were the disciples *glad* when they saw the Lord." John 20: 19, 20.

This passage contains no command, no intimation whatever, to sanctify that day. It does not even claim that they were there for any sacred purpose, much less to celebrate the Sabbath, or institute a new day of worship, but simply for common protection, "for fear of the Jews;" and a design to comfort them in their trepidation is all the legitimate inference we can draw from the circumstance of Christ's appearing unto them. All the Apostles were not together; *Thomas was absent!* If they had met together to *sabbatize*, he, certainly, would have been with them. Not having been present, and not having seen the risen Saviour, while doubting and disputing on the subject of his resurrection, "*eight days afterward*," Christ appeared again, to confound the incredulity of Thomas, and for no other ostensible purpose.

'Thomas, one of the twelve, called Didymus, was not with them when Jesus came. The other disciples therefore said unto him, We have seen the Lord. But he said unto them, Except I shall see in his hands the print of the nails, and thrust my hand into his side, I will not believe. And after *eight* days the disciples *were within*,* and Thomas with them: then came

---

* *Within* does not imply that they were assembled at any public place *for worship*, or to celebrate a *holy day*. *Within* may simply mean, that they were together in the place of their common lodgment—where they abode together.

Jesus, *the door being shut*, and stood in the midst, and said, Peace be unto you. Then said he to Thomas, Reach hither thy finger, and behold my hands; and reach hither thy hand, and thrust it into my side, and be not faithless, but believing. And Thomas answered and said unto him, My Lord and my God." John 20: 26,

So much, *and that is all*, is the authority adduced by the advocates for the sacredness of the first day for Christ having changed the day of rest, the Sabbath, or having given his sanction to the change. Ought such a vague *inference* overturn the fiat of the Almighty—change times and laws ordained by Jehovah to endure forever? Is the "being together," save one, of the twelve, "for fear of the Jews," and "being within eight days afterward," any evidence of their being there to celebrate the "Sabbath" or Lord's day? Is there, in these transactions, any re-enactment of the sabbatic law, which some persons maintain was abrogated by the "blotting out of the handwriting of ordinances?" Is there any injunction issued by them—the apostles—requiring the disciples to honor, hallow, and sanctify the first day of the week, in any of the above proceedings?

The next Scripture assumed for the substitution of the first day of the week in the place of the Sabbath of the Lord, is found in the Acts of the Apostles:—

"And upon the first *day* of the week, when the disciples came together to break bread, Paul preached unto them, ready to depart on the morrow, and continued his speech until midnight. And there were many lights in the upper chamber where they were assembled together. And there sat in the window a certain young man named Eutychus, being fallen into a deep sleep; and as Paul was long preaching, he sunk down with sleep, and fell from the third loft, and was taken up dead And Paul went down, and fell on him, and embracing him, said, Trouble not yourselves, for his life is in him. When he, therefore, was come up again, and had broken bread, and eaten, and talked a long while, even till break of day, he departed." Acts 20: 7—11.

It is necessary to a proper understanding here, to

bear in mind—1st. That it was the custom of the disciples, in the days of the apostles, to meet together, and break bread, *every* day. "They continued steadfast in the apostles' doctrine and fellowship, and in breaking of bread, and in prayers." "And they, continuing *daily* with one accord in the temple, and breaking bread from house to house, did eat their meat with gladness and singleness of heart." 2d. That in those times a day was counted "the evening and the morning were the first day." "From even unto even shall ye celebrate your Sabbaths." Lev. 23 : 32. Thus it appears, by this passage, that they had simply met, as was their uniform, daily custom, to celebrate the breaking of bread on the evening (the commencement of the day), it being the last evening Paul was to be with them; and in all probability the circumstance would not have been noticed so particularly, but to introduce the case of Eutychus, in confirmation of Paul's miraculous powers. The passage does not prove any thing for the sacredness of the first day of the week, but proves much against it; for, if the first day of the week is holy time, Paul, in preaching till midnight, and departing on the morrow, would be a Sabbath-breaker for traveling on that day. He would have kept the evening only. "From *even* unto *even* shall ye celebrate your Sabbaths." The same disregard for the sacredness of the first day of the week was manifested by the Redeemer himself, in traveling on the "resurrection day" to Emmaus, a distance of seven and a half miles, while a "Sabbath-day's journey" was restricted to *one mile:* slender evidence, indeed, of the Saviour's having transferred the holiness of the *Sabbath* to "the first day of the week," or having "sanctioned" it, as is often claimed by its advocates.

The next passage adduced is found in Paul's First Epistle to the Corinthians—"Upon the first *day* of the week, let every one of you lay by him in store, as God hath prospered him, that there be no gatherings when I come." 1 Cor. 16 : 2. First *day?* Day is not in the original, but is supplied, and is so designated by being italicized. So the true reading is, "In the first of the week." However, if it mean the first day, Sunday, it makes it a commercial day, a day of business, a day of reckoning, not of *rest*, as it requires a man to cast up his accounts, to find what amount he can "lay by."

The last text, and the one most relied upon, is from John's Revelation—"I was in the spirit on the Lord's day." Rev. 1 : 10. There is nothing in this passage, or in the context, to indicate that it was the first day of the week. It is a mere *assumption*, without any Scripture to fortify the position. The best biblical critics admit that there is no scriptural evidence to identify the expression with the first day of the week If we follow the Protestant rule, to prove Scripture by Scripture, and not evade the plain teachings of the Bible, it will be an easy matter to see a much more apt application of the expression. Many of the best commentators suppose that it alludes to the Gospel-day. "Your father Abraham rejoiced to see *my day;* he saw it, and was glad." John 8 : 56. Was not this a day which approximates (if it will not be admitted to be identical) not only in *idea*, but in a *kin-name*—the *day of Christ*—the Gospel-day? Paul speaks of it as something yet to come. "That ye may approve things that are excellent; that ye may be sincere and without offense, till the *day of Christ.*" "Holding forth the word of life, that I may rejoice in the *day of Christ*, that I have not run in vain, neither labored in vain." "Who shall also confirm you unto the end, that ye may be blameless in the day of our Lord Jesus Christ." "Now, we beseech you, brethren, by the *coming* of our Lord Jesus Christ, and by our gathering together unto him, that ye be not soon shaken in mind, or troubled, neither by spirit, nor by word, nor by letter, as from us, as that the day of Christ is at hand." "That the spirit may be saved in the day of the Lord Jesus." Phil. 1 : 10; 2 : 16; 1 Cor. 1 : 8; 2 Thess. 2 : 1, 2, 3; 1 Cor. 5 : 5. Again, it is maintained by some expounders, that allusion is had to the Judgment Day. "The day of the Lord will come as a thief in the night, in which the heavens shall pass away with a great noise, and the elements shall melt with fervent heat; the earth also, and all the works therein, shall be burned up." 2 Peter 3 : 10. Therefore John, in saying, "I was in the spirit on the Lord's day," simply asserts, that in prophetic vision his spirit reached forward to the great day for which all other days were made, and beheld the momentous transactions of that awful crisis, which he was directed to reveal to the churches on earth.

From this brief examination, it appears, that the term "Lord's day," as here used, does not refer to any particular day of the week. But if it refer to any special day of the week, as some suppose, it must refer to the seventh; for that is the sanctified, hallowed *rest-day* of the Bible, and is the only day which the Lord calls his holy day (Is. 58: 13), and therefore must be the Lord's day. If, however, the term "Lord's day," used by John, does not refer to the gospel day, or the day of judgment, nor to the Lord's "holy day," the seventh-day Sabbath, but alludes to a festival day to commemorate the resurrection, as is assumed, where is the command requiring it to be kept holy? And where is the evidence in the Scriptures, that it was kept *as the Sabbath*, or in *place of the Sabbath?*

Even were there any intimations given by the prophets or the apostles, (which we deny,) that the resurrection day should be regarded as the "ceremony-worship-day" under the gospel dispensation, where is the evidence in the Scriptures that the first day of the week is or was the resurrection day? It is assumed, not proved. The Bible and human theories are at conflict on this subject. It is generally assumed, that the Redeemer was crucified on Friday, and rose early on Sunday morning. This makes Christ a liar; for he said, "As Jonas was *three days* and *three nights* in the whale's belly, so shall the Son of Man be *three days* and *three nights* in the heart of the earth." Matth. 12: 40. Crucified on Friday, and rising on Sunday morning, would make but part of three days, and only two nights. Christ said three days *and* three nights, and he certainly must be right. Therefore, crucified on Friday, he could not have risen on Sunday. The New Testament does not assert that he rose on the first day of the week; it only says, that he was *seen* on the first of the week, not first *day*. In all the places in which allusion is had to this matter, (Matth. 28: 1; Mark 16: 1, 9; Luke 24: 1; John 20: 1, 19), the original says, in the first of the week—*day* is not once named, but is supplied in our version, as is indicated by being italicised. But even if the term first of the week implies first day, the Scriptures no where assert that he *rose* on that day. Being *seen*, and *rising*, are two entirely different matters. So is a *part* of three days and two nights different from three days and three nights. If Jesus had said, "*three days and nights*," it might not involve the present difficulty; but no one questions that Jonas was three whole days and three whole nights in the whale's belly. Then, as the Redeemer makes that the simile of his own confinement in the heart of the earth, the antitype, to be verified and accredited, must be like unto the type. He must have been there the *three days* and the *three nights*, according to his word. It is vain presumption, arrant blasphemy, to make it any less to gratify a human theory. Let God be true, though it make all men liars.

In the absence of all direct *scriptural evidence* to sustain the assumption, that the first day of the week is the "*resurrection day;*" and in the absence of all such evidence, that the Lord designed to elevate the first day of the week to the special regard of the Christian Church, and confer upon it the sacredness of the ancient Sabbath; would we not, at least, have some intimation of it in the writings of the prophets, in which all the important circumstances of the Redeemer's life and mission are foreshadowed? Where, reader, will you find any thing in them that predicts any *change* of the *holy Sabbath* to the *resurrection day?* If found, let it be adduced. The Sabbath is a standing monument against *Atheism*, for all ages, declaring the workmanship of God; yet some *assume*, that as *redemption* is a greater work, and a more important work, than the *creation* of the universe and the living *souls* which inhabit all the spheres, therefore the *resurrection day* ought to be honored as the *rest-day*. Has not the *Lord* the right to determine this matter? If HE deemed it important that the *resurrection day* be thus distinguished, would HE not have *declared it*, expressly, unto us? Would HE have left us to *infer* it? Can we, will we, be justified in casting aside the *explicit* command of the Most High, in this matter, to substitute our *fancied* day of greater *importance* than the one the *Almighty* has *ordained?* "Wherefore kick ye at *my* sacrifice and at *mine* offering, which I have commanded?" 1 Sam. 2 : 29. "It is hard for thee to kick against the pricks." Acts 9 : 5.

If, then, there is no evidence in the Scriptures, that the *first day of the week* is the "*resurrection day*," (which, even if satisfactorily established, would not invalidate our position, nor entitle it to supersede the holy Sabbath); and, more particularly, if there is no evidence in the Inspired Volume, that the term "Lord's day" is intended to designate the *first day of the week;* we are reduced, by every principle of reasoning, to regard the *seventh day*—the Heaven-heralded Sabbath—as the only "Lord's day," the only "rest-day," sanctified and hallowed by the Almighty as holy time.

All days, in one sense, are Lord's days; but there has never been but one *Heaven-appointed* weekly *Sabbath,* and that, most unequivocally, is the *seventh day.* "Remember the Sabbath day to keep it holy"—"the *seventh day* is the Sabbath of the Lord thy God." Ex. 20: 8. If that sacred injunction has been abrogated, we should expect—(for it would be unreasonable to recognize its repeal or transfer, without as explicit and as authoritative a mandate from the Court of Heaven)—at least a *re-enactment* somewhat thus: "*From the resurrection of the Lord Jesus, ye shall no longer* SABBATIZE, *but shall give heed to the assembling of yourselves* ON THE FIRST DAY OF THE WEEK; *in it ye shall do no work; and, to avoid the appearance of symbolizing with my ancient people, the Jews,* call it no longer the *Sabbath,* but designate it by the term *Lord's day!*" Is there any intimation of such an *abrogation,* or such a *transfer* of the *sacredness of the Sabbath* to *Sunday,* in the *inspired volume?* Not the semblance of it. Even if the early disciples, without any intimation from the *Lord of the Sabbath,* but of *their own accord,* chose to set apart a special day as a *festival day,* as they were wont to do for *martyrs* and *saints,* it can not, certainly, *supersede* the *institution of Jehovah;* neither can they confer upon it the sacredness belonging, by the *decree of the Most High,* to *his rest-day.* Indeed, this is so evident, that the erudite and frank NEANDER expressly says, "*Opposition to Judaism introduced the particular festival of Sunday,* very early, indeed, into the place of the *Sabbath*.... Sunday was distinguished as a *day of joy*, by the circumstance that men did not fast upon it, and that they prayed standing up, and not kneeling, as Christ had raised up fallen man to heaven again through his resurrection. The *festival of Sunday*, like all other festivals, *was always only a* HUMAN ORDINANCE; and it was far from the intention of the apostles to establish a *divine* command in this respect—far from them, and from the early apostolic church, to *transfer the laws of the Sabbath to Sunday*. Perhaps at the end of the second century, *a false application of this kind* had *begun* to take place; for men appear by that time to have considered laboring on Sunday as a sin."*

Such, then, is the scriptural account of the Sabbath, and such the frank admission of one of the most distinguished ecclesiastical historians, who could have no motive in perverting or misrepresenting the facts in the case, but who has always shown himself above all mean subterfuges for any purpose whatever. His testimony might be fortified by many names of high authority among writers of eminence, who do not contend for sabbatizing on the seventh day, yet whose candor and honesty constrain them to make the like admission.

Thus it will be seen, that the observers of the seventh-day Sabbath can look up with full confidence of having a "thus saith the Lord" for their practice; while the observers of the first day of the week must confess, with confusion of face, that they are but following "the commandments of men," and can only plead "the nakedness of the Fathers," as Whitby terms their inconsistencies. Will the Lord admit

---

* The History of the Christian Religion and Church during the First Three Centuries. By Dr. Augustus Neander. Translated by Henry John Rose, B.D. New York, 1848, p. 186.

such a "vain oblation?" Will he suffer such a perversion of his holy institution to go unreproved? Where, reader, can you find in the Bible any authority for appropriating the title of the holy rest-day, the Sabbath, to the first day of the week? If you can not, is it not "robbing God" thus to falsify his Word? Is it not base felony every time any worm of the dust thus perversely uses the term which HE, the Sovereign of the Universe, has attached to his holy day—thereby wantonly "changing times and laws"—overturning the decrees of the Lord God? Is it not wresting the Word to your own destruction? If the Lord charge man with robbery in withholding perishable tithes and offerings, and curse him for that delinquency, how much greater, think ye, must be the condemnation of those who set at naught his prerogative to institute and ordain the service of the sanctuary? He alone has the right to impose religious ordinances; and it is but the reasonable service of his creatures to obey, implicitly, his righteous mandates—the sacred injunction, to hallow and sanctify his holy Sabbath. "Will a man rob God?" asks the Almighty, through his prophet; "yet ye have robbed me, saith the Holy One. Ye are cursed with a curse; for ye have robbed me, even this whole nation." Mal. 2: 8, 9. Where, then, will you find your excuse for this perversion of the Word of God, when that Word shall come to judge you? for it is the Word, the written Word, (given to be a lamp unto your feet and a light to your path,) which shall judge you at the last day. Of old it was said, "From the days of your fathers ye are gone astray from mine ordinances, and have not kept them." Mal. 3: 7. The apostle of the Gentiles speaks of those in his day who corrupted the Word. 2 Cor. 2: 17. In another place it is asked, When wilt thou cease to pervert the right ways of the Lord? Acts 13: 10. To which interrogation all are obnoxious who seek out inventions of their own, or follow "the commandments of men," which subvert the testimony of the Lord.

Canst thou, reader, contend with the Almighty? It is a fearful thing to fall into the hands of the living God, when he shall lay judgment to the line, and righteousness to the plummet, and shall *sweep away the refuge of lies.* Isaiah 28: 17. The *true principle*, reader, and the only *safe principle*, is, to "*let God be true*, though it *make every man a liar.*" Rom. 3: 4. "Ye are my friends," says Christ, "if ye do whatsoever I command you." John 14: 15. "He that saith, I know him, and keepeth not his commandments, is a liar, and the truth is not in him." 1 John 2: 4. "In vain do they worship me, teaching for doctrine the commandments of men." Matt. 15: 9. "What thing soever I command you, observe to do it; thou shalt not add thereto, nor diminish from it." Deut. 12: 32. "Turn not from it to the right hand or to the left." Josh. 1: 7. "Add not unto his words, lest he reprove thee, and thou be found a liar." Prov. 30: 6. "If any man shall add unto these things, God shall add unto him the plagues that are written in this book; and if any man shall take away from the words of this prophecy, God shall take away his part out of the book of life, and out of the holy city, and from the things that are written in this book." Rev. 22: 18, 19. Ponder well this subject, reader, and render unto God the things that are God's, that it may be well with thee, and thou be admitted into the rest reserved for those who "delayed not to keep the commandments"—for those who keep his covenant and walk in the way of the Lord.

No. 14.

DELAYING OBEDIENCE.

To have the understanding enlightened in regard to duty, and the conscience so thoroughly awake as to make one feel uneasy in the neglect of it, and yet to be surrounded with advisers, wearing the name and title of Christians, who are continually urging farther delay, is about as uncomfortable a position as a person of fervent piety needs to be placed in. To rebuke such advisers in the faithfulness of the gospel, and yet, at the same time, to behave towards them with becoming meekness, is not the easiest thing in the world. Nevertheless, the idea that we may postpone our obedience to God for a little season, notwithstanding our convictions, is not to be tolerated.

Suppose, for example, that a person becomes convinced, that it is his duty to observe the Sabbath of the Bible—the seventh day of the week. Forthwith he is assailed by his associates with the suggestion, that he ought not to be in a hurry—that he ought to take plenty of time for consideration, at least a year. Plausible as such advice is, we offset it with a simple passage of Scripture. "I thought on my ways, and turned my feet unto thy testimonies; I made haste, and delayed not to keep thy commandments." Ps. 119: 59, 60. Here the Psalmist testifies, that he turned his feet to obedience, so soon as, by thinking on his ways, he found that he was walking astray. He made no delay about it; he did not go about to consult the wise men of the nation; he did not examine the writings of the rabbis and doctors, to see if there was not some way of getting round the duty, he *made haste* to render obedience. But, now-a-days, as soon as a person's conscience begins to lash him for neglected duty, he is advised to be very careful about running too hastily. Well, we would not wish one to be *too* hasty; but, on the other hand, it may be well to consider whether there is not such a thing as being *too tardy*. Conviction of duty is not to be trifled with. When any one does violence to his conviction, he feels that he disobeys God; and such disobedience is sure to be followed by disastrous results. The voice of conscience grows more feeble, and (if the disobedience be persisted in) becomes, at length, hushed in silence. It may continue to reprove with regard to other duties, but with regard to that particular one which has been made the object of willful neglect, it reproves no more. As a necessary consequence, the soul suffers the loss of all those blessings which obedience in that one thing would bring.

Nor is this all. Conscience, having yielded to corruption in one instance, becomes ready to yield in another. Its sternness has been overcome, and it no longer guards the soul with that security which it had been wont to do. It is to the soul what the sense of modesty is to the female; and, as the female cannot allow her sense of delicacy to be trifled with without incurring the risk of a total loss of virtue, so the conscience cannot, in a single instance, be abused, without incurring the danger of becoming "seared with a hot iron." We will not undertake to say, that this is, in every case, the result; but we *do* say, that there is great danger of it. We insist, therefore, that when one understands what is duty, he ought to lose no time in putting it in practice. Let him remember, too, that the wrath of God is revealed against those "who hold the truth in unrighteousness." Rom. 1 : 18.

But the possibility that one may be mistaken as to his duty, is often urged as a reason for delay. There may be something in this; at least, it seems plausible. Generally, however, this objection is more specious than solid. At all events, it is so with regard to those things which are the subject of direct and unequivocal command. With regard to the Sabbath, we have no hesitation in saying, that it savors of "the wisdom that is earthly." The object of those who urge it is to induce a deference to the views of those who have acquired great skill in explaining away the divine law. But we hold, that however doubtful may be the teachings of Scripture with regard to such questions as are purely doctrinal, or however obscure the language in which its prophecies foretell coming events, with regard to the common, practical duties of life, the Word of God is so plain that there is no need for a child to be mistaken. Were it otherwise, it would be unsuited to the wants of mankind. For, inasmuch as every one must give account for himself, and not another for him, it is necessary that each one should be able to decide his duty for himself. People of small intellectual capacity must be able to make this decision, as well as those of more expanded powers; and children, as well as those of mature age. Hence duty must be revealed in very simple language. And how simple the language in which our duty to keep holy the Sabbath day is revealed! "*Remember the Sabbath-day to keep it holy—the seventh day is the Sabbath.*" Who can fail to understand it? What untutored peasant cannot comprehend it? What child does not perceive its meaning? The command to refrain from the adoration of images is not more plain. Yet, when a person of ordinary mental powers is convinced by it, and begins to think about rendering obedience, straightway he is admonished that he does not understand it, and that he would do well to consult some learned men, some spiritual rabbis or doctors of divinity, before taking any decided steps!

And what do the learned doctors say, upon being consulted? Why, that it is the duty of men keep holy the first day of the week. But how do they make it appear? Do they produce any precept from the Scripture, plain and unequivocal, like the fourth commandment? Not by any means. They can present nothing which is level to the comprehension of a child. Whatever they say on the subject, is entirely above the understanding of children, and entirely above the understanding of ignorant people. They talk about the magnitude of redemption, as compared with the work of creation; they have something to say about redemption being finished on the first day of the week, by the resurrection of Christ from the dead; they lay a few such theological propositions together, and finally draw out the inference, that the first day of the week is a holy day. But the plain, ordinary mind, does not understand this. The child fails to comprehend it. It is true, he hardly dares to indulge the thought that learned men may be mistaken; nevertheless, he is puzzled, extremely puzzled, to understand it. Is not this conclusive proof, that no such duty is enjoined in the Book of God?

We cannot, therefore, subscribe to the idea, that a person must, in reference to the Sabbath, or in reference to any other plain command of Heaven, wait to consult friends, and learned teachers, and the writings of fallible men, before rendering obedience. If God has spoken, "see that ye refuse not him that speaketh." We do not believe that any one can begin to obey God too soon.

Published by the AMERICAN SABBATH TRACT SOCIETY,
No. 9 Spruce-street, N. Y.

[No. 15.]

AN APPEAL

FOR THE

RESTORATION OF THE BIBLE SABBATH:

IN AN

ADDRESS TO THE BAPTISTS,

FROM

THE SEVENTH-DAY BAPTIST GENERAL CONFERENCE.

NEW YORK:
PUBLISHED BY THE AMERICAN SABBATH TRACT SOCIETY,
No. 9 Spruce-Street.
1852.

THE ADDRESS.

The Seventh-day Baptist General Conference, to the Members of the Baptist Denomination throughout the United States, holding to the Observance of the First Day of the Week as a Divine Institution:

Beloved Brethren:—

When our Divine Redeemer dwelt on earth, he prayed that all his disciples might be "made perfect in one." As this prayer was in harmony with the sure word of prophecy, which instructs us to look for a time when "the watchmen shall see eye to eye, and sing with united voice," we are sure that it will ultimately be answered. We see nothing, however, to warrant us in looking for such a happy consummation, while we contemplate the multiplied divisions of the Christian world, perpetuated as they are by the selfishness of human nature. Here the prospect is dark indeed. But we have an unshaken confidence in the power of God to bring about his own purposes, notwithstanding all the devices of men. "The hearts of all are in his hands, and he turneth them whithersoever he will." He that made "the multitude of one heart and of one soul," in the first age of the church, can again concentrate his scattered bands, break down every wall of separation, and enlighten every mind by the effusion of his Spirit. Then shall Zion move forth, "clear as the sun, and terrible as an army with banners."

We rejoice, brethren, that you, as well as ourselves, are looking for this day of glory. Moreover, we have knowledge of your firm persuasion, that this glorious union of the now scattered forces of Israel, can be effected only upon the basis of divine truth. With a single glance you see the fallacy of that reasoning, which calls upon you, for the sake of union, to sacrifice the least particle of God's Word. Taught by the Spirit of God, you have learned that the smallest atom of truth is more precious than fine gold. That meager piety which finds "non-essentials" in the appointments of Jehovah, you cannot abide. Your language is, "We esteem ALL thy precepts concerning ALL things to be right, and we hate EVERY false way."

We know, moreover, that it is the desire of your hearts, that all dissensions between Christians should be for ever ended. For this object you are laboring and praying; and while you are doing so, you have the enlightened conviction, that your labors and prayers will be successful, in proportion to the amount of truth with which your own minds are imbued, and which you can bring to bear upon the minds of others. Laboring as you do to expound to others the way of the Lord more perfectly, we cannot suppose that you are yourselves unwilling to learn. We therefore approach you with confidence, affectionately and earnestly requesting you to take into consideration the subject which is the only ground of difference between you and us. In our estimation, it is a subject of great importance; and though some of you have made it a matter of thought, we are persuaded that the great body of your denomination have dismissed it without any particular investigation. Indeed, we speak not unadvisedly when we say, that on this question the whole church of God have been hushed to sleep. In urging it upon your attention, we think you will not charge us with wishing to raise disturbance in Zion. We indulge the hope that you will impute to us the same disinterestedness of motive by which you yourselves are actuated when you boldly proclaim your denominational sentiments upon every high place, and scatter your publications in every direction. Your course springs not from any wish to foment disturbance, but from the pain which your hearts feel to see the institutions of Christ made void by the traditions of men. Our action in this matter springs from the same principle. We feel in regard to the Sabbath just as you do in regard to baptism. We declare before God and the Lord Jesus Christ, that we are moved by a desire for your good and God's glory.

When we look over your large and influential denomination, we find that, in reference to the subject upon which we now address you, you are divided into about three classes. I. Those who, acknowledging the perpetuity of the Sabbath law, enforce the observance of the Sabbath by the fourth commandment, but change the day of its celebration from the seventh to the first day of the week. II. Those who see the impossibility of proving a change of the day, and therefore regard the commandment as abolished by the death of Christ. But, at the same time, they consider the first day of the week as an institution entirely new, to be regulated as to its observance wholly by the New Testament. III. Those who consider neither the Old nor the New Testament to impose any obligation upon them to observe a day of rest, and advocate one merely on the ground of expediency.

I. To those of you who acknowledge the obligation of a Sabbath, but change the day of its celebration from the *seventh* to the *first* day of the week, we would say, that while from the Law only you infer any obligation to sabbatize at all, yet make the particular time of sabbatizing to stand upon New Testament authority, we do not see how you can relieve yourselves from the charge of departing from the great principle contended for by Baptists, viz. That whatever is commanded by an institution, is to be learned from the law of the institution, and not from ther sources. On this principle, you reject the logic of Pedobaptists, who, while they find the ordinance of *baptism* in the New Testament, go back to the law of *circumcision* to determine the subjects. You tell them, and very justly too, that the *law* of the institution is the *only rule* of obedience. But do you not fall into the same error when the argument has respect to the Sabbath? We can see no more fitness in applying the law of the Sabbath to the first day of the week, than in applying the law of circumcision to the subjects of baptism. For the law of circumcision was not more expressly confined to the fleshly seed of Abraham, than was the law of the Sabbath to the seventh day of the week. The true principle is, that every institution is to be explained and regulated by its own law. Therefore, if the first day of the week is an institution binding upon us, the law to regulate its observance should he looked for where we find the institution. Be pleased, brethren, to review this argument, and see if you are not treading on Pedobaptist ground.

In justification of this change of the day, we often hear you plead the example of Christ and his apostles. But where do we find any thing to this effect in their example? Did the apostles *sabbatize* on the first day of the week? Did the churches which were organized by them do so? Observe, the question between you and us is NOT, Did they *meet together* and *hold worship* on that day? BUT, Did they *sabbatize?* that is, Did they REST FROM THEIR LABOR on the first day of the week? Did they observe it AS a Sabbath? This is the true issue. We have often asked this question, but the only answer that we have received has been, *that they assembled for worship.* But this is not a candid way of meeting the point. It is in reality an answer to a very different question from the one we ask. Brethren, act out your own principles. Come up fairly to the question. When you ask a Pedobaptist, Did Christ baptize or authorize the baptism of little children? you expect him to make some other reply than, "*He put his hands on them and prayed.*" When you ask, Did the apostles baptize unconscious babes? you are not well pleased with the reply, *They baptized households.* Your question was with regard to *infants*—the *baptism* of them. If, therefore, when we ask you, Did the apostles and primitive Christians *sabbatize* on the first day of the week? you merely reply as above, we do not see but you are guilty of the very same sophistry you are so ready to charge upon your Pedobaptist brethren. Your adroit evasion of the real question seems to place you much in the same predicament as were the Pharisees, when Christ asked them whence was the baptism of John. It appears as if you reasoned with yourselves, and said, "If we shall say they *did* sabbatize on the first day of the week, the evidence will be called for, and we cannot find it; but if we shall say they did *not,* we fear the day will lose its sacredness in the eyes of the people." We do not by any means wish to charge you with a Pharisaic lack of principle, but we put it to your sober judgment, whether your position is not an awkward one. Brethren, reconsider this point, and see if you are not on Pedobaptist ground.

If the apostles did not sabbatize on the first day of

the week, then it follows, as a matter of course, that whatever notoriety or dignity belonged to that day, they did not regard it as a substitute for the Sabbath. Consequently, unless the Sabbath law was entirely abrogated by the death of Christ, the old Sabbath, as instituted in Paradise, and rehearsed from Sinai, continues yet binding, as "the Sabbath of the Lord thy God."

But more than this. Even if it could be proved, that the apostles and primitive Christians *did* actually regard the first day of the week *as a Sabbath*, it would not follow that the old Sabbath is no longer in force, unless it could be proved that they considered the new as a SUBSTITUTE for the old; or, that so far as the particular day was concerned, it was of a CEREMONIAL character. But where do we find proof for either of these points? In the whole record of the transactions and teachings of the apostles, where do we find this idea of *substitution?* No where. Where do we find evidence that, so far as the *particular day* was concerned, it was *ceremonial*, and therefore to cease at the death of Christ? No where. The argument that proves the *Sabbath law* not to be ceremonial, proves the same of the *day*. Did the *Sabbath law* originate in Paradise, when man was innocent, and had no need of a Redeemer? So did the *day*. It was then sanctified and blessed. Does the *Sabbath law* take cognizance of the relation on which all the precepts of the moral law are founded, viz. the relation we sustain to God as *creatures* to *Creator?* So does the *day*. It is a memorial of this relation, and of the rest entered into by God after he, by his work, had established the relation. It appears, then, that neither the *Sabbath law*, nor the *day* it enjoins, was of a ceremonial character. True, it is not *moral*, in the strictest sense, but rather *positive*. Nevertheless, by divine appointment it is in the same category with the moral law, and must be considered a part of it. If this reasoning is correct—and if it is not, we hope you will point it out—it would not follow that the old Sabbath is done away, because Christ and his apostles sabbatized on the first day of the week; but only that there are *two* Sabbaths instead of *one*.

But could Christ or his apostles consistently alter the law of the Sabbath? In all his ministry, Christ acted under the *appointment* of the Father, and according to such *restrictions* as were contained in the law and the prophets. By those restrictions, no laws were to be set aside at his coming, except such as were peculiar to the Jewish economy; such as "meats, and drinks, and divers washings, and carnal ordinances, imposed until the time of reformation." Heb. 9: 10. To set aside these, the law gave the Messiah an express grant. Heb. 10: 9. But the very moment he should attempt to go beyond the limits of that grant, he would destroy all evidence of his being the Messiah promised and appointed. For it was by his exact conformity to the law, that his claims were established. Hence, early in his ministry, he declared that he "came not to *destroy* the law or the prophets." Matt. 5: 17. Most cheerfully do we recognize him as God over all, and blessed forever; yet we are well satisfied that, even in virtue of his divinity, he could not consistently set aside any laws except those which were "a shadow of things to come." Otherwise we should have God *denying* himself—God *contradicting* himself! The New Testament records not a single instance of his claiming a right to do so. When he avowed himself Lord of the Sabbath, he only claimed to determine what was the proper method of keeping it—what were breaches of it, and what were not. The Sabbath was made *for* man, and consequently it was his prerogative to decide what acts and duties answered to the nature and design of the institution. *Therefore*, the Son of Man is Lord of the Sabbath. Mark 2 : 28.

In regard to the obligation resulting from apostolic example, it appears to us that you have fallen into some errors. We are not convinced that the example of the apostles can be justly pleaded for any thing else than the order and arrangement of the *church.* However proper it may be to imitate them in other respects—in the duties of the moral law, for instance—yet, if it were not known to be proper, independent of their example, we cannot suppose their example would make it so. We must first ascertain, by some settled and infallible rule, whether their practice is worthy of imitation. In regard to the ordering of *church affairs*, there can be no doubt, for they were sent upon this very errand, with the promise of the Holy Spirit to qualify them for the work. But the Sabbath is not a *church ordinance.* It is not an institution for the church *as such*, but for *all mankind.* All reasoning with reference to it, from apostolic example, must therefore be very inconclusive. Even if we should admit that the *church* is bound by such example to regard the first day of the week, yet this is the utmost extent to which our admissions can go. We cannot see how the institution becomes binding upon the world at large. Consequently, we are compelled to maintain, that an institution which was originally given for all mankind, remains unaltered. We are willing that the example and practice of the apostles should regulate the *church* as to its ordinances and government, and herein we claim to follow them as strictly as you do ; but when they are pleaded for any thing more, we want first to know whether they conform to the express law of God. Otherwise we must consider them as no more binding than an apostle's quarrel with Barnabas. Acts 15: 39.

If this argument is well founded, we are led to a very satisfactory disposal of a question often proposed, viz., Why do we never read in the New Testament of Christian assemblies being convened *as such* on the Sabbath? For if the Sabbath be not a *church ordinance,* but an institution for mankind at large, it can be of no importance for us to know what Christian assemblies *as such* did with regard to it. All that is of real importance for us to know, is the precise bearing of the institution upon man *as* man—upon man *as* a rational and accountable creature. On this point the information is clear and decisive.

The controversy between us and you appears to be brought down to a very narrow compass. *Did the Apostles and primitive Christians sabbatize on the first day of the week?* And, *Is it the duty of all men to imitate their example, or only the* CHURCH? If, upon a solemn and prayerful consideration of this subject, you are persuaded that there is no proof that the early Christians regarded the first day as a Sabbath, (substituted in place of the seventh,) and will honestly avow your conviction, we have no fear that the controversy will be prolonged. For, should you still be of opinion that some sort of notoriety was attached to the day, and that Christians met for worship, we shall not be very solicitous to dispute the point. The apostolic rule, "Let every man be fully persuaded in his own mind," will then govern us. See Rom. 14: 5, 6. Our concern is not that you keep the first day of the week, but that you keep it *in place of the Sabbath,* thus making void the commandment of God. If once you discover, that Sunday is not the Sabbath by divine appointment, and therefore cannot be enforced upon the conscience, we are persuaded that your deep sense of the necessity of such an institution, will soon bring you to the observance of the one originally appointed.

II. But we proceed to address those of you who regard the sabbatic law as having been nailed to the cross, and consider the first day of the week as an institution entirely new, regulated as to its observance wholly by the New Testament.

You, whom we now address, are exempt from some of the inconsistencies which we have exposed; but your theory labors under very serious difficulties, and is to be regarded, on the whole, as more obnoxious to the interests of religion, than the one we have been considering.

According to your position, the New Testament recognizes no Sabbath at all. Do not start at this charge. That it is repugnant to your feelings, we allow. You have never thought of any thing else than *entire abstinence from labor* on the first day of the week. It is your day of *rest*, as well as *worship*. But on what ground do you make it a day of rest? What *example* have you for doing so? What *law* of the New Testament requires you to lay aside all your secular business? As sin is the transgression of the law, and where no law is there is no transgression—1 John 3: 4, Rom. 4: 15—how do you make it appear to be sin to work on the day in question? It is by the commandment that sin becomes exceeding sinful. Rom. 7: 13. By what commandment do you make it appear sinful to work on Sunday? These are questions of the highest importance.

Now suppose one of your brethren attends public worship on the first day of the week, and—to make his conformity to what is supposed to be apostolic example as perfect as possible—participates in the breaking of bread. He then goes home, and labors diligently till the day is closed. By what law will you convince him of sin? Not the law of the Sabbath as contained in the Decalogue, for that you hold to be abolished. Not any law of the New Testament which says, "Keep the first day of the week holy; in it thou shalt not do any work," for there is no such law. Not the law of apostolic example, for there is no proof that the apostles ever gave such example. The very utmost that you can with any show of reason pretend of their example is, that they met together for worship and breaking of bread. To this example your brother has conformed to the very letter—who can say he has not in spirit also? What now will you do with him? "The Bible, and the Bible only, is the religion of Protestants." The Bible, therefore, is the Rule by which he is to be tried. Convict him of sin by this Rule, if you can.

But the case becomes still more difficult, when you come to apply it to those who are without the pale of the church. We have already seen, that apostolic example concerns merely the ordering and arrangement of the *church*. Attempt now to convince the unbeliever of sin in working on the first day of the week. In order to do this, charge apostolic example upon him. What is his reply? "I know not," says he, "that I am bound to imitate them in this matter. How does it appear that I am? I will admit, for argument's sake, that they celebrated the resurrection on Sunday by religious worship; but they also broke bread and partook of it by way of celebrating his death. If their example binds me in one particular, why not in the other? Prove to me," says he, "that any but the church assembled on the first day for worship, and I will do so too. But in the absence of all such proof, I must conclude that their example has nothing to do with me; unless, indeed, you can make it appear, that their example and practice were in conformity to some law, which commanded them as rational creatures, independent of their relation to Christ and his church. When you can produce that law, then I shall feel bound to obey it, and imitate the apostles in their obedience to it; but not till then." Such is the reasoning by which an unbeliever may set aside all your attempts to charge sin upon him. Where, brethren, is your law which, like a barbed arrow, pierces the very soul, and fastens guilt upon the conscience? Where is that law which speaks out its thunders, saying, "Thus saith the Almighty God, the Lord, the Maker of heaven and earth, It is the Sabbath day; in it thou shalt not do any work?" To throw aside the law, which cuts and flames every way, reaching soul and spirit, joints and marrow, in order to deal with the ungodly by mere apostolic example, is like muffling the sword, lest it should give a deadly wound. Apostolic example is indeed powerful with those whose hearts have been made tender by the Spirit of God, but with others powerless.

We are persuaded, brethren, that your conscientious scruples about laboring on the first day of the week, never resulted from the mere contemplation of apostolic example. Such example, it is true, is all the law you acknowledge; but this is the theory you have adopted since you came to maturity, and began to think for yourselves. Your scruples have an earlier and different origin. They commenced with your childhood, when you were taught to consider the day as holy time. It was then carefully instilled into your mind, that God had, by express law, forbidden you to desecrate the day, and that you would incur his displeasure in case you should do so. The idea was then imbibed, that if you did not keep the day, you would violate the fourth commandment. This idea has grown with your growth, and strengthened with your strength. It has obtained such commanding influence over your feelings, that you cannot comfortably forbear keeping a day of rest, though your theory does not require it. Even to this day a strong impression rests upon your minds, that the fourth commandment contains much of moral excellence—too much to be thrown altogether away, notwithstanding your system of theology teaches its abrogation. Such is the true secret of your tenderness of conscience. Apostolic example has in reality nothing to do with it. Following the secret monitions of conscience, your prosperity is promoted in spite of your theological system. But sound reason discovers, that your experience and your theory are in opposition to each other. Some of the more thinking ones among you are aware of this, and are continually aiming at such a modification of their theory, that their experience will harmonize with it. But be assured, that there will be an everlasting conflict, till you are brought to acknowledge fully and heartily the claims of the sabbatic law.

We are aware of that system of theology which regards the New Testament as furnishing the only code of laws by which men are bound since the death of Christ. We have looked at this doctrine with attention; and so far as the order, government, and ordinances of the *church* are concerned, we admit its truth. As the laws and ordinances of the *Jewish* church were determined by the *Old* Testament, so the laws and ordinances of the *Christian* church are determined solely by the *New* Testament. Therefore, we should say at once, the argument is yours, if the Sabbath were a church ordinance. In such case, however, none but the church has a Sabbath. But the question is not concerning church ordinances. In these we follow the New Testament as closely as yourselves. The question is concerning an institution which has respect to mankind at large—to man *as* man; for the Saviour teaches us that the Sabbath was made *for* man. Now, it will be a very hard matter to prove, that when men as rational creatures are concerned, the only code of laws by which they are bound is the New Testament. Let us put the matter to the test. How will you prove that it is unlawful for a man to marry his sister, his daughter, or any other of near kin? The New Testament utters not a word on the subject. It is not enough to say, It is implied in the law which forbids adultery; for it must first be proved to be a species of adultery to do so. Nor will it do to say, The common sense of mankind is a sufficient law on the subject; for the moment we suppose that its unlawfulness is to be determined in this way, we abandon the argument that the New Testament is the only code of laws, and resort to the common sense of mankind as furnishing a part of the code. But if the common sense of mankind shall furnish a part of the code by which we are bound, who shall undertake to say how large a part? Besides, on this principle, the book of divine revelation is not complete and perfect. It is a lamp to our feet only in part, and the common sense of mankind makes out the deficiency! You are, therefore, driven to take your stand again upon the New Testament. Finding you there again, we repeat the question, *How do you prove by your code that a man may not marry his sister?* It is impossible. You must, of necessity, look to that division of the Scriptures usually called the Old Testament; for the New says not one word about it.

Let us turn now to the 18th chapter of the book of Leviticus, and we shall find a collection of laws exactly to the point. "None of you shall approach to any that is near of kin to him," &c. v. 6. The degrees of kindred are then expressly marked. Will it be objected, that these laws were given particularly to the Jews, and to no other people? We admit they were given to the Jews, as indeed was the whole system of revelation in that age; but we cannot admit that they concerned no other class of people. For it is expressly shown in that chapter, that the matters of which they took cognizance, were regarded as abominations in the Gentiles. Because of such things, the fierce wrath of Jehovah came down upon the Canaanites, and they were cast out from the land as loathsomeness. v. 24, 30. If these things were viewed as abominable in the Canaanites, they surely were not *ceremonial* pollutions. They were not mere *Jewish* laws. The fallacy of the doctrine is therefore sufficiently exposed.

We think you have fallen into error concerning the nature and design of that division of the Scriptures commonly called the New Testament. We regard it not as the *Law Book* of mankind, in the strict and proper sense; but rather as a *Treatise on Justification*, or an *Expose of the Way of Salvation*, in which are contained such references to the law, and such quotations from it, as are necessary to the complete elucidation of the subject. The preparation of this treatise was of necessity delayed until the great Sacrifice for sin had been offered, and our High Priest had entered into the holy place. For, as the sacrifice and intercession of our High Priest constitute the sole foundation of our justification, so "the way into the holiest of all was not yet made manifest, while the first tabernacle was yet standing." Heb. 9 : 8. So much of the plan of salvation was illustrated to the people, as could be by means of the ritual service; and that, together with the prophecies, laid a foundation for them *to believe* that, *in some way or other*, they would be just before God. So that by *faith* the patriarchs were justified. Heb. 11. They knew it was to be *somehow* through the work of Him who was typified and promised as the great Redeemer. But they could not understand the plan until the Redeemer came and died for them.

Because this expose of the way of salvation could not be made until after the death of the High Priest, *therefore* it was not proper to organize gospel churches. The only church that was suitable for that age was found in the Jewish nation, and from its very nature was unfit for the world at large. It was, therefore, confined to that people. Moreover, because it was not proper to organize gospel churches until the way of salvation was fully laid open, it was also not proper to lay down the laws and ordinances of the church until that time. This accounts for the laws of the church being found only in the New Testament.

Now, if the New Testament is to be regarded as an exhibition of the way of salvation, with such references to the Old as are necessary for the elucidation of the subject, rather than as the Law Book for mankind at large, the idea that the Sabbath ought not to be looked for in the Old Testament falls to the ground. Nevertheless, to some minds it appears strange, that while the New Testament writers mention all the other duties of the Decalogue, this of Sabbath keeping is apparently omitted. In speaking of the sins of which Christians were guilty before their conversion, not one word is said about Sabbath breaking, though upon other sins they dwell with emphasis. But this admits of a very easy solution. Those writers addressed two classes of converts—those from among the Jews, and those from among the Gentiles. As to the former, they were already rigid to an extreme in keeping the Sabbath. All that was necessary to do in their case, was to vindicate the institution from Pharisaic austerities, and determine what was lawful to be done, and what was not lawful. This was done by Christ. But as for the Gentile converts, to charge them with having been guilty of the sin of Sabbath breaking in their state of heathenism, would have been manifest impropriety. For the Sabbath being for the most part a *positive* rather than a *moral* precept, it could not be known without a revelation. But as the Gentiles had no revelation, this is a good reason why the apostle dwelt not upon this sin to charge it upon them, but only upon those which were more obviously breaches of the Moral Law. Thus it appears, there was no necessity for any more particular mention of the Sabbath to be made in the New Testament than what is made.

But it is not our object in this Address to cover the whole field of argument. We design simply, by presenting some of the strong points, and exposing your inconsistencies, to stir up your attention to the subject. We are sure that the great majority of you have never given it a thorough investigation. For a complete discussion of the whole ground, we refer you to our publications. Will you read them? Will you anxiously inquire, What is truth? Will you pray over the matter, saying, "Lord, what wilt thou have us to do?" Or, will you sleep over it, as if it were of no great practical importance?

III. But we must address that class of Baptists who consider neither the Old nor the New Testament to impose any obligation to observe a day of rest, and advocate one merely on the ground of expediency. In some sections of our country, Baptists would consider it almost a slander upon their denomination to intimate that there were persons among them of such anti-sabbath principles. But any one who is conversant with the order at large, knows very well that it is true. There are those who boldly avow such doctrine, and many others who do not deny that it is their real sentiment, though they are not forward to proclaim it upon the house-tops. Whether this class embraces a very large proportion of the denomination, it is not necessary to inquire. It is our impression, that the proportion is sufficiently large to justify an effort for their conversion to right views of Divine Truth.

If there is no day of rest enjoined by divine authority, and the observance of one rests wholly upon expediency, we see no reason, except that the voice of the multitude is against it, why you cannot as well observe the *seventh* as the *first* day of the week. There would be no sacrifice of conscience in so doing, while it would be a tribute of respect to those who feel that the keeping of the seventh day is an indispensable part of duty. But it is not on this principle, particularly, that we desire you to change your ground. Feeling that it is not *our party* that must be honored, but rather *divine truth*, and our party only *for the sake of* the truth, we would much rather correct your doctrinal views.

Of course, you do not deny that a day of rest was once enjoined upon God's chosen people. It is only under the gospel that you suppose all distinction of days to be annihilated. If, then, it is *expedient* that a day of rest should be observed, it follows irresistibly, that the annihilation of all distinction in days, by the gospel, was very INEXPEDIENT! And thus, whatever blessings the gospel dispensation brings to the human race, a strict following out of its principles would be INEXPEDIENT! And, farther, that the *law*, which enjoined a day of rest, had more of an eye to expediency than the *gospel* has! Consequently, that the gospel, though declared to be *faultless*, and capable of *perfecting* those who believe, must nevertheless, FOR EXPEDIENCY'S SAKE, borrow a little help from the abrogated rites of the law! In other words, God, in setting aside a day of rest, committed an oversight, and left his work for man to mend! Brethren, we see not how it is possible for you to escape such monstrous conclusions. They are the legitimate result of your principles—principles which you must have adopted without considering where they would land you. For we are not disposed to believe you so completely destitute of piety, as willingly to abide by the result of them. We entreat you to reconsider them, and adopt such as are more in accordance with the spirit of our holy religion.

When you advocate the observance of a day of rest on the ground of *expediency*, we are persuaded that you do so in view of the bearing you perceive it to have upon the well being of mankind. But still the question will arise, Has the gospel less regard to the well being of mankind than the law had? Look at the humanity of the sabbatic institution. How necessary that both man and beast should rest one day in seven. How evident that they cannot endure uninterrupted toil. How perfectly well established, that, if doomed to constant labor, they sink under the premature exhaustion of their powers. So well is this established, that we cannot put such a low estimate upon your judgment as to suppose it necessary to enter upon any proof of it. But the question returns, Does the gospel breathe less humanity than the law? Or, consider the bearing of the institution upon the interests of religion. It affords opportunity for men to be instructed in the great things which pertain to their salvation; and if there were no Sabbath to call them away from their labors, it would be impossible to bring religious instruction into contact with their minds. Does the gospel afford less advantage in this respect than the law did? Did the law provide a season for instructing the people in religion as it *then* stood? and does the gospel provide no season for instructing them in religion as it *now* stands? Must they be instructed in *types*, but not in the *substance?* —in *prophecy*, but not in the *fulfillment* of prophecy? No one will be responsible for the affirmative of these questions.

If the New Dispensation actually has abrogated the Sabbath, we do not believe that it is *expedient* to ob serve it. We cannot believe, however, that an institution so important to the civilization, refinement, and religious prosperity of mankind, has been abrogated. We refer you to our publications, and to the publications of those who have, in common with us, defended the perpetuity of the sabbatic law; and we entreat you to reconsider your ground. The doctrine of expediency! What a fruitful source of corruption has it been to the church of God! There is not an antichristian, popish abomination, but what pleads something of this kind. Do, dear brethren, let it be expunged from your creed

Brethren of the Baptist Denomination: You are a great and growing people. Your influence is felt throughout the length and breadth of our land. We rejoice in your prosperity. "May the Lord make you to increase and abound in love one towards another, and toward all men." In your prosperity we behold, in a measure, our own. Your baptism is our baptism. Your church government is our govern ment. Your doctrinal principles are ours; and there is nothing which constitutes any real ground of separation, except the great and important subject we now urge upon your attention.

The popularity you have gained as a denomination, however, is not owing to your Sabbath principles. It is founded entirely on your views concerning the initiating ordinance of the gospel. These views are characterized by that perfect simplicity which marks every divine institution.. Hence you have won the affections of the common people, while, if you had attempted to operate on them by a more complicated theory, failure would have been the result.

This induces us to urge upon your notice the *exceeding simplicity* of the Sabbatarian argument, compared with all those theories which stand in opposition to it. It is adapted to persons of weak capacities, of whom there are thousands in the kingdom of Christ. Any illiterate person can open the Bible, and point to chapter and verse, saying, "The seventh day is the Sabbath of the Lord thy God." This is plain; he can understand it. But tell him that redemption was a much greater work than creation; that redemption was finished by the resurrection of Christ; that an event so important ought to be commemorated; and that, in order to do this, the day of the Sabbath was changed from the seventh to the first day of the week; for all which there is not a single "thus saith the Lord;" nothing but the uncertain deductions of human reason. Can he understand it? No. It requires an elevation of intellect which God has not given him. The inferences and deductions are beyond his capacities. How then is he to render an *intelligent* obedience? If he conform his practice to the theory thus set before him, it will not be because he understands it, but because he is willing to trust the guidance of his mind to those who, he thinks, know more than he does himself. This, therefore, is strong internal evidence that the keeping of the first day is not of God. For God's Book is adapted not only to those of elevated intellect, but to the ignorant and rude. Every thing concerning our practice is plain even to wayfaring men. Were it otherwise, we should conclude that the Bible is not an inspired production. If it did not come down to the capacities of all, we should infer that it was not made by Him who made all minds. Indeed, it would not, in such case, be a *revelation* to all, but only to the more talented. But it is a revelation to *all;* and he that obeys God, must do it for himself; he that repents and believes, must do so for himself; and at the great day, every one of us shall give account for himself unto God. It is of the highest importance, therefore, that every one know *for himself* the foundation of his faith and practice.

In thus urging the simplicity of the argument for the Sabbath, we are but doing what you do in regard to Baptism. Compare the cases. A man of considerable intellect can reason from the Abrahamic covenant, lay propositions together, and draw inferences and deductions, until, finally, he makes it pretty clear to his own mind, that the children of the flesh, these are the children of God; Paul to the contrary notwithstanding. But how is it with some good old Baptist sister, who can hardly join two ideas together, and draw a logical inference from them? Why, she cannot tell about this reasoning from the Abrahamic covenant. It is something she does not understand. But she can open her Bible, and point to chapter and verse for believer's baptism. She puts her finger upon something that is just adapted to her capacities. As she has a soul to save, an obedience to render, and an account to give, all for herself, her practice is accordingly. Brethren, think this matter over, and see whether your reasoning on the Sabbath is not very much akin to that of those who reason from the Abrahamic covenant to Baptism. Think seriously, whether it does not render *intelligent* obedience impossible to vast numbers of Christians. Think whether a course of reasoning which darkens a very simple subject, is not more specious than solid.

Again, your children are to be early instructed in this matter. How do you succeed in making them understand it? Is your little child capable of comprehending all this argument, which you found upon the finishing of redemption by the resurrection of Christ? Can you point him to any plain passage, where Christ authorizes a change of the Sabbath? How do you feel when the little creature says, in the simplicity of his heart, "Father, mother, does not the fourth commandment require the observance of the seventh day of the week? But do we not keep the first day? I should think this is not keeping the commandment." One would think you would be forcibly reminded of that scripture, "Out of the mouths of babes and sucklings thou hast ordained strength." Ps. 8: 2.

The extensive operations in which you are engaged for the conversion of the world, render it in the highest degree important that you should not err on a question like this. If you are right, you ought to be very certain of it. Among the heathen, you are extending the observance of Sunday as a sacred day. If you are thus sowing the seeds of error instead of truth, the evils who can calculate? Hence you cannot too early begin to review your ground. Consider the difficulties your missionaries already have to encounter, because of unscriptural sentiments propagated among the heathen by those who nevertheless loved their souls. The poor, perishing idolaters are witnesses of the clashing of doctrine between Jesus Christ's men, and they ask, "*Why is this? You have come to give us a gospel which professes to make its followers 'perfect in one,' and yet you yourselves are divided.*" You cannot in conscience abandon your principles, however, nor dare you, in your translations, give to a sentence or a particle one single turn, which will not fully express the mind of the Holy Spirit. Dare you, then, without feeling the most entire certainty, teach them that God says, "Remember the first day of the week to keep it holy?" The responsibility of the missionary, in this respect, is not less than where his translation is concerned. Does he feel the same awful sense of responsibility?

From the heathen turn to the contemplation of the Jewish nation. The time cannot be far distant, when those who, "as touching the election, are beloved for the fathers' sakes," shall be called to behold the glory of God, in the face of Him they have so long rejected. But in order to this, a voice from the divine word cries, "Cast ye up, cast ye up, prepare the way, take up the stumbling block out of the way of my people." Have Christians seriously considered what this stumbling-block is? For our own part, we are persuaded that nothing can be more justly called by this name, than the general abandonment, on the part of Christians, of the Sabbath of the Lord. The Jews, taking it for granted, without examination, that this abandonment is really taught by the Christian religion, suppose that its author cannot be the true Messiah. They have seen, through every period of their nation's history, that God has put signal honor upon this institution. They have seen its sacredness elevated high above that of the ceremonial institutions. They have heard their prophets dwell upon the profanation of it as the crying sin of the land, on account of which the sore judgments of Heaven came down upon it. It is true, some teach that the whole Mosaic system was clothed with as much sacredness as the Sabbath; and that it was not for the sin of Sabbath breaking, any more than for a disregard of the ritual service in general, that they suffered the wrath of Jehovah. But such persons must have paid only a superficial attention to the subject. The attentive reader cannot fail to be struck with the fact, that while in the prophets the Sabbath is exalted as of vast importance to the nation, and all its prosperity, and the favor of God, seemingly, suspended on the proper keeping of it, ceremonial usages are comparatively depreciated.

Since the Sabbath holds such a sacredness throughout the ancient oracles of God—since the Israelites have taken their lessons of obedience to it under "the rod of his wrath"—since no grant was given to the Messiah to set it aside, nor the least intimation ever made to the Jews that it would be set aside—can we wonder that they think that teacher to be an impostor who should break this commandment, and teach men so?

But there is a crisis approaching—the day is near, and it hasteth greatly—when it will be indispensable that all those who truly love the Lord Jesus Christ, have their "loins girt about with truth." Popery is preparing for another desperate struggle. The great principle of the Reformation, that "the Scriptures are the only rule of faith," is to be discussed anew. In the Church of England, this discussion has already commenced. Rome has opened her sluices, and antichristian corruption again threatens to flood the church of God. As the water naturally seeks such channels as may be already prepared, so will it be with this doctrine. What branch of Zion will be next troubled? Probably that which makes the next widest departure from the great Protestant principle. Then that which is next in order; and so on. For it can not reasonably be expected to stop, until it reach that order of people which is governed by the Bible alone.

Upon all others the desolation must be more or less extensive. For those who acknowledge the principle of departing from the Bible in ever so small a degree, may be expected to exemplify it to an indefinite extent, when the circumstances of the times are so modified as to give occasion for it. As for yourselves, you do not avow the *principle* of departing from the Scriptures, but profess to hold it in abhorrence. The language of your *creeds* is explicit on this point; and we know of no denomination so forward to plead a strict conformity to this principle as yourselves. Yet it is impossible for you to pretend, with any show of modesty, that the Scriptures expressly enjoin the keeping of Sunday as a Sabbath to the Lord. You cannot say, from Scripture authority, that the apostles observed it as such. Nevertheless, your creed declares that it ought to be so observed; and your practice accords with your creed. Wherefore, it is as evident as mathematical demonstration, that you do depart from the great Protestant principle. Consequently, if our views be correct in regard to the crisis which is at hand, the time cannot be far distant, when your own denomination will in some modified form be affected with the deprecated evil, and you will be compelled to abandon every principle and practice which can give it the smallest advantage.

Do you think, brethren, that in your present position you are prepared for the great struggle? When the Puseyite, replying to those who contend for the Protestant maxim, refers to the observance of Sunday, and says, "Here we are absolutely compelled to resort to the aid of ancient usage, as recorded, not by the inspired, but by the uninspired writers," are you ready for the issue? Can you confute what he says? When another one says, "The *seventh* day is the Sabbath of the Lord thy God; we celebrate the *first.* Was this done by divine command? No. I do not recollect that the Saviour, or the apostles, say we shall rest on the first day of the week instead of the seventh;" and then concludes, "The same reasons which urge you to dissent from the observance of the three grand festivals of the Church of England, ought to operate with you respecting the Sabbath;"—are you prepared to join issue with him? Can you justify yourselves on your own principles? If you can, we will confess our short-sightedness. But indeed we fear, we tremble, in view of the crisis which is approaching, when we look at the traditional usages prevailing among Christians, and consider with what a tenacious grasp they are held. O Lord God Almighty! thou who hast sworn that 'thy kindness shall not depart from thy church, nor the covenant of thy peace be removed,' let not thy truth fall in the contest.

We mean not to goad your feelings, by charging upon you any of the abominations of Popery. We are sure you would not cherish one of them, if you were conscious of it. But we take it for granted, that those who are forward to take the mote out of their brother's eye, are willing to have the beam taken out of their own. You have charged pedobaptist denominations, over and over, with upholding popery's chief pillar. You have told them, that their zeal against the man of sin would avail them but little, until they first rid themselves of his traditions. You have talked feelingly of the sin of encumbering the ordinances of God with human inventions. You have read the church of Christ many a good lesson on the importance of holding the truth in its purity. In all this you have, doubtless, been sincere. We have no fault to find with you; for you have only followed the Bible direction, "Cry aloud, spare not, show my people their transgression." In conformity with this direction, we would endeavor to act our part as faithful reprovers. Yet our desire is, to do it with meekness, considering ourselves, lest we also be tempted. It may be—we know not—that some of the abominations of the man of sin are cleaving to us. If so, "let the righteous smite us, it shall be a kindness; let them reprove us, it shall be an excellent oil, which shall not break our head."

Turn, brethren, to the seventh chapter of the prophecy of Daniel, and twenty-fifth verse. You there find one spoken of who "shall speak great words against the Most High, and shall wear out the saints of the Most High, *and think to change* TIMES *and* LAWS." You have had no difficulty in finding in this prophecy a reference to the law of baptism, as one of the *laws* which this great power has changed; but you have not shown satisfactorily what are the *times*. You have usually referred them to the numerous festivals and holy-days, which have been multiplied by the church of Rome. But these were *times* ESTABLISHED; not *times* CHANGED. Will you please to expound this passage a little more clearly? Will you tell us whether, under the gospel, there is any sacred time except the Sabbath? We will not be unreasonably confident, but we are much mistaken, if you can give any clear and satisfactory construction to this prophecy, without finding that something of Rome still cleaves to you.

Suffer us here to declare our conviction, that you could take no more effectual step toward converting the Christian world to right views about baptism, than to embrace the Sabbath of the Bible. In your discussions with Pedobaptists, you are constantly referred to the change of the Sabbath, as proof that some things may be binding which the Scriptures do not expressly enjoin. You have never met this argument fairly and fully. To be sure, you always make an attempt to meet it. But how do you do it? By proving that Christ expressly enjoined his followers to *sabbatize* on the first day of the week? By showing from express Scripture testimony, that the apostles *did actually rest from their labors* on that day? No. Neither of these things have you ever shown; nor can you show them. The whole head and front of your proof—if proof it may be called—amount only to this; that the apostles and primitive Christians *met together for worship* on that day. It is true, by such a course you have generally talked your opponents into silence, because by exposing fully the defect of your reply, it would only render their own transgression the more glaring. But while you *silenced* them, you did not *convince* them. While they saw that for one of *your own* customs you could not plead a "thus saith the Lord," they felt comparatively easy under all your rebukes, and naturally enough thought it not *very* important, that *they* should have a "thus saith the Lord" for the sprinkling of babes.

But a most important consideration, in view of this subject, is the influence of your large and powerful denomination upon an unconverted world. Whatever your theory about the perpetuity of the sabbatic law—whatever your doubts and scruples about the use of the term *Sabbath* under the gospel—you cannot rid yourselves of a deep sense of the importance of a day of rest to the world at large. Hence the resolutions of your churches and conventional bodies, with regard to the profanation of what you call the Lord's day. Hence your plain, out-spoken censures of running cars, stages, steamboats, and other public conveyances, on this day. Hence your griefs and lamentations over those who make it a day of recreation or mirth. Hence your readiness to coöperate with those bodies which are organized to suppress, if possible, the violation of what is called the Sabbath. We admire the *principle* which governs you in all this; but we lament that it is not regulated by a better understanding of the subject. If you would promote right principles, you must be careful that your proofs, and examples for illustration, are pertinent and free from all uncertainty. We are fully persuaded, that your *Recommendations* and *Pledges*, your *Resolutions* and *Associational Acts*, will always meet with defeat, until you can fortify them by a law of God, so clearly expressed, that it will urge and goad the violator's conscience wherever he may go. The consciences of guilty men cannot be reached by the method you are pursuing. You behold them desecrating the Sunday, and, in order to make them lay it to heart as a sin, you bring down upon them—what? Apostolic example? New Testament intimations, and far-fetched inferences? No. None of these do you think of employing. But the *Law*, the all-searching, sin-rebuking *Law* of God, is the only means you think of in such a case. Nothing else suits your purpose, be your *theory* what it may. But hear their reply. "Is the law of the commandment upon us TO-DAY? That it was YESTERDAY, we allow; for it says, '*the seventh day*.' That the law of the commandment lies against us *every* day, you will not pretend; but only *one* day in seven. If that one day was *yesterday*, you are yourselves as guilty as we; and we, therefore, feel comparatively comfortable. To be sure, some sense of the necessity of keeping the Sabbath holy, does at times rest upon our minds; and our consciences, for the moment, reproach us; but when we see you, and all the Christian world, living in the neglect of it, we feel quite easy again, and think our sin to be but a light one." Such may not be their precise language, but it is the exact expression of their hearts' feelings. Thus even the Law fails in your hands, because you attempt to make it speak *what it will not speak.*

If you ask *us*, "Do *you* meet with success in attempting to reach the consciences of guilty, unbelieving men?" we reply, that we have no difficulty, except so far as you, and the whole body of observers of the first day, stand in the way. We bring them to admit, openly and honestly, the claims of God's law, and a sense of guilt momentarily rests upon them. But immediately they turn to contemplate *your* practice, and their hearts become hardened. We do, therefore, affectionately, but earnestly, invite you to consider, how tremendous is your influence toward perpetuating Sabbath profanation in the land. Your numbers, your learning, your talents, your wealth, your general respectability, all combine to operate with overwhelming effect in this matter.

Our observations, if correct, go to show what a source of danger the Sunday heresy is to the Moral Law. The Sabbath is a most important precept of this law; "the golden *clasp*," as an old writer quaintly observes, "which joins the two tables together; the *sinew* in the body of laws, which were written with God's own finger; the intermediate precept, which participates of the sanctity of both tables, and the due observance of which is the fulfilling of the whole law." This important precept is either set aside entirely, or its edge and keenness so muffled by a transfer to another day, that the united efforts of the church can do little or nothing toward impressing it on the conscience. Here, then, is a relaxation of the standard of morality; and while the standard is relaxed with regard to this one precept, in vain do we look for the Law, as a whole, to appear glorious in the eyes of men.

This remark will be strengthened, if we consider to what inconsistencies the advocates of Sunday are driven. Some, in their zeal to defend it, even go so far as to deny the Moral Law to be a rule of conduct to Christians. Others, though they admit the Law to be a rule of conduct, cannot relieve themselves of at least *seeming* to undervalue it. When the Sabbath discussion is out of sight, they speak out clearly, and without equivocation, giving the fullest proof that they regard the Law as the unchangeable standard of obedience. But at other times they reason from the New Dispensation in a manner so vague and indefinite, that one is puzzled to tell whether they regard the Gospel as enforcing strict obedience to the Law or not. Now he that is established in the clear truth, is hampered with no such difficulties. There is, with him, not only the naked and abstract admission, that the Moral Law is unchangeably binding, but there appears such a beautiful and perfect conformity between this admission and the principles he inculcates, that the most common minds are struck with it, and every doubt is scattered.

While you are fettered by such difficulties, is there no danger that the Law will lose its sacredness in the eyes of the peeple? Surely there is. There is danger, also, that your system of theolegy will be corrupted in other particulars. Error goes not alone. Could an opinion exist in the mind, circumscribed and isolated, without affecting any of our other principles, it would be comparatively harmless. But it is not more a truth, that a man who utters one falsehood is obliged to tell twenty more to hide it, than that he who supports one error is obliged to forge numberless others to give consistency to his creed. It is also a truth, which reflection and daily observation will confirm, that nearly if not quite all the heresies which ever infested the church of God, are traceable to some loose notions concerning the Moral Law. Nothing, therefore, can be more necessary, than that our creed give the greatest possible prominence to the Law as a standard of holiness; and that our customs be in perfect conformity with our creed.

Brethren, can we hope that the subject on which we have addressed you will receive your prayerful attention? Almost your entire denomination has slumbered over it; but may we not hope, that you will now awake? May we not hope, that it will be discussed in your private circles, and in your public assemblies; in your Bible classes, and in your Sunday schools; that it will be studied by your ministers, and by the people in general; and that every one will, in the deep desire of his soul, pray, "Lord, open thou mine eyes, that I may discern wondrous things out of thy Law."

But if, on the other hand, we see a disposition to pass it by with cold neglect—an unwillingness to look the question in the face—an attempt, on the part of your teachers and leaders, to hush it up as a matter of no importance—a studied effort to lead the people away from it, when they are disposed to examine—or teaching them that it is the spirit, rather than the letter of the law that God requires—we shall be constrained to apply the language of Him who spake as never man spake—"EVERY ONE THAT DOETH EVIL HATETH THE LIGHT, NEITHER COMETH TO THE LIGHT, LEST HIS DEEDS SHOULD BE REPROVED." John 3: 20.

THE

ROYAL LAW CONTENDED FOR:

OR,

Some brief Grounds serving to prove that the Ten Commandments are yet in full force, and shall so remain till Heaven and Earth pass away:

ALSO,

The Seventh Day Sabbath, proved from the beginning, from the Law, from the Prophets, from Christ, and his Apostles, to be a duty yet incumbent upon Saints and Sinners.

By a Lover of Peace with Truth, Edward Stennet.

They that forsake the Law praise the wicked, but such as keep the Law contend with them. Prov. 28: 4.

Let us hear the conclusion of the whole matter, Fear God and keep his commandments, for this is the whole duty of man. Ecc. 12: 13.

The Sabbath was made for man, and not man for the Sabbath; therefore the Son of man is Lord even of the Sabbath. Mark 2: 27, 28.

Then shall I not be ashamed, when I have respect to all thy commandments. Ps. 119: 6.

London, Printed in the Year 1658.

NEW-YORK:

REPUBLISHED BY THE AMERICAN SABBATH TRACT SOCIETY.

PREFACE BY THE TRACT SOCIETY.

THE friends of the Sabbath will doubtless receive this little volume as a valuable relic of the past—as a word from one of the tried and faithful friends of the truth, one who not only loved the day of God's weekly rest, but greatly delighted in the promise of a future and glorious sabbatism with the people of God. Edward Stennet, the author, was the first of the series of Sabbatarian ministers of that name, who for four generations continued to be among the foremost of the Dissenters in England, and whose praise is still in all the churches. He was an able and devoted minister, but dissenting from the Established Church, he was deprived of the means of support; and, his family being large, he applied himself to the study of medicine, by the practice of which he was enabled to give his sons a liberal education. He suffered much of the persecution which the Dissenters were exposed to at that time, and more especially for his faithful adherence to the cause of the Sabbath. For this truth, he experienced tribulation, not only from those in power, by whom he was a long time kept in prison, but also much distress from unfriendly dissenting brethren, who strove to destroy his influence, and ruin his cause. He wrote several treatises upon the subject of the Sabbath besides this, but they are very rare, and perhaps cannot all be found in a perfect state of preservation. It would be well, no doubt, to revive all of them, and, if practicable, republish them in the same form as this, that they might be bound together, and placed, as they deserve to be, in every Sabbath-keeper's library. They all breathe the genuine spirit of Christianity, and in their day were greatly conducive to the prosperity of the Sabbath-keeping churches

NEW-YORK, July, 1848

THE ROYAL LAW CONTENDED FOR

SOME BRIEF GROUNDS, SERVING TO PROVE THAT THE TEN COMMANDMENTS ARE YET IN FULL FORCE, AND SHALL SO REMAIN TILL HEAVEN AND EARTH PASS AWAY.

1. The matter of the ten commandments was written in the heart of Adam before his fall, as doth appear in Gen. 1: 27, *God created man in his own image, in the image of God created he him;* also in Eccl. 7. 29, *God hath made man upright, but they have sought out many inventions.* And the Apostle plainly asserts, that the gentiles, which had not the law, (in the letter of it,) did by nature the things contained in the law, which showeth the work of the law written in their hearts. Rom. 2: 14, 15. Now if the gentiles had the word of the law written in their hearts in their sinful state, doubtless they had it in more perfection in their state of innocence, as considered in Adam; for the letter of the law was added because of transgression. Gal. 2: 19. Now if there was transgression before the letter of the law was added, that implies that there was a law before then; in that the letter of the law is said to be added, it implies that the matter of it was in being before, but much worn by sin; and that is one reason why the Lord was pleased to add the letter.

Let it be considered, how it can stand with Scripture or right reason, that Jesus Christ should abrogate this law. Did Christ blot out this law from the hearts of all men by his death? Then all men have not the law of nature to guide them; for we cannot be so gross as to imagine that the law is put into their hearts upon a new account, for that were to bring all men under the new covenant.

2. God spake all these commandments unto the people, and they heard his voice, (Deut. 5: 22—24,) with great majesty and glory, and he added no more; and he wrote them upon two tables of stone, and delivered them unto Moses—all of which holds forth their perpetuity; they are spoken by God, they are written by him in tables of stone; so was never any ceremony. Job desired that his words might be graven with a pen of iron and lead in a rock of stone forever. Job 19: 24.

3. Afterward the first tables were broken, which I suppose did signify the Israelites' breaking of the first covenant; for Moses broke them on account of their having made a golden calf, and so had broken the covenant. Whereupon Moses was then commanded to hew two tables like the first, and God wrote the same words again upon them, (Deut. 10: 1—4,) and they only of all the laws were put into the ark, and when the ark is set in its proper place between the cherubim there is nothing in it but the two tables. 1 Kings 8: 9. Now the ark was a type of Christ, and the putting of the law into it did signify the putting of it into the heart of Christ, (Psalm 40: 6—8, *Thy law is in my heart,*) and from thence they are transcribed into the hearts of the seed of Christ. See Jer. 31: 33, where God promises to put his law in their inward parts, and write it in their hearts. Now what law is this that must be put into the heart, when the law of sacrifice is abolished? Compare Heb. 10: 6—9, with the fore-mentioned Psalm. That this is the law that is here spoken of is manifest if we consider how proper and suitable it is for the heart of a believer. Paul calls it the law of his mind in Rom. 7: 23, and in verse 22 he professeth he delights in the law of God after the inward man; and God saith he will put the law in his heart and write it

there; both which phrases hold it forth to be the same law that was written by God and put into the ark. Man's heart is the tables, and God himself is the writer; the matter written is the law. Hear what Wisdom saith to this: *My son, keep my words, and lay up my commandments within thee; keep my commandments and live, and my law as the apple of thine eye; bind them upon thy fingers, write them upon the table of thy heart.* Prov. 7: 1—3. Now what laws are these but the table laws? And Wisdom's son is to have them written upon the fleshy tables of his heart.

4. When God promiseth to exalt his first-born higher than the kings of the earth, and that his covenant should stand fast with him, and that his seed should endure forever, and his throne as the days of heaven, (Psalms 89: 28, 29,) yet he saith, *If his children forsake my law, and walk not in my judgments; if they break my statutets, and keep not my commandments; then will I visit their transgression with a rod, and their iniquity with stripes. Nevertheless, my loving kindness will I not utterly take away, nor suffer my faithfulness to fail.* Verses 30—32. Mark it, this covenant was with Christ, (though with David in the type,) in behalf of all the seed; and the chastisements must be the portion of the seed if they break the law of God, though his covenant stand fast. Now as this covenant reaches all the seed, so doth the law and the punishments for the breach of it; and if so, then what law is it that reaches all the seed, if not the law of the ten commandments, with those laws which are comprehended in them.

5. These commandments are eminently distinguished and marked out from all the ceremonial laws, both to show their eminency and perpetuity: they are said to be the work of God, in Exod. 32;

16; and the Psalmist saith, *The works of his hands are verity and judgment.* And these works are called, *all his commandments,* in Psalm 111: 7, and they are ten. Deut. 4: 13. And therefore I conceive Wisdom's son is to bind them upon his fingers, to show the number of them, there being for each finger one, and that both hands might be active in them. And Zacharias and Elisabeth were said to walk in all the commandments and ordinances of the Lord. Luke 1: 6. They are distinguished from the ceremonial ordinances, and called all the commandments, to set forth their number, as before said, and their eminencey; and therefore they are so frequently called in the Scripture, *the commandments of God,* distinct from the other laws, which were shadowy in the time of the law of shadows, (as these places of Scripture, besides many others, do show, viz., Deut. 5. 31, 6: 11, 7: 11, 8: 11, 11: 1, 30: 16, 1 Kings 2: 3, 8: 58, 2 Chron. 19: 10, Neh. 1: 7, and 10: 29, &c.,) and distinct from the testimony of Jesus in clear gospel times. In Rev. 12: 17, note that the dragon's war is with the remnant of the woman's seed which kept the commandments of God and the testimony of Jesus. And again, here are they that keep the commandments of God and the faith of Jesus. Rev. 14: 12. And when the man would know what he should do to be saved, Christ told him that he knew the commandments. A cloud of witnesses would come in, if need were, for the confirmation of them. But farther observe what the Scripture saith to their duration. The Paslmist saith, *All his commandments are sure, they stand fast for ever and ever, and are done in truth and uprightness.* Psalm 111: 7, 8. Note it; all his cammandments, which are the works of his hands, as aforesaid, stand fast for ever and ever; that is, not only in the time of the ministration of the letter, which was in a sense for ever, but for ever and ever, that is, under both ministrations, that of the letter and that of the spirit, in Old Testament times and in the New. Search and see if you can find any word that doth speak of any thing that is said to abide or stand fast for ever and ever, which comes short of the time aforesaid. And when God hides his face from the house of Jacob, then is the time that the testimony is bound up and the law is sealed among the disciples, (Isa. 8: 16, 17,) clearly relating to the time that the Jews rejected the gospel, and the disciples are commanded to make use of the law as well as the testimony to try the doctrines of others by. Isa. 8: 20. All which shows the perpetuity of this law of God, which will farther appear if we consider Deut. 7 : 9. Our Lord saith in Matt. 5: 17, 18, *Think not that I am come to destroy the law or the prophets; I came not to destroy, but to fulfill.* But the question will be, what law this is? To me it appears to be the law of the ten commandments; for these reasons:

1st. Because this comes in as the motive to provoke his disciples to let their light shine in the world, that men might see their good works and glorify their Father which is in heaven. Matt 5: 16. Therefore it must be such a law as the doing of it holds forth good works to public view.

2d. It is such a law as Christ professes he came not to destroy; but the ceremonial law he destroyed in this very sense, so that none are to be in the practice of it; he blotted out the hand-writing of ordinances that was against us, and contrary to us, and took it out of the way, nailing it to his cross.

3d. Destroying of the law is here put in direct opposition to fulfilling of it; to destroy is to take out of the way or to blot out as before; but to fulfill the law is to do that which is contained in the law; therefore saith Christ to John, when he went to be baptized, *It becometh us to fulfill all righteousness,* (that is, to perform it.) Matt. 3 : 15. And the Apostle saith, that love is the fulfilling of the law. What law? Why this, *Thou shalt not commit adultery, Thou shalt not kill, Thou shalt not steal,* &c. *Love worketh no ill to his neighbor; therefore love is the fulfilling of the law.* Rom. 13 : 8—10. So that, to fulfill the law of the ten commandments, is not to blot them out or make them void; that were to destroy them, which Christ came not to do, but, on the contrary, to do the things contained in them, which he did exactly in his life, and so was offered up a Lamb without spot.

4th. This is such a law as must stand in force, every jot and tittle of it, till heaven and earth pass away. Matt. 5 : 19. But heaven and earth are not yet passed away; therefore this law stands firm. But because it is said in the text, Till all be fulfilled, hence some affirm that all was fulfilled at the death of Christ, and this fulfilling of it holds forth the abrogating of it. But did heaven and earth pass away then? or did Christ, by his taking upon him all that guilt which was due to us, and by his perfect fulfilling of it in his walk, take us from our obedience? God forbid. Because Christ fulfilled the righteousness of the law, must we not fulfill it? The Apostle saith that for this end Christ died. *For what the law could not do, in that it was weak through the flesh, God sending his own Son in the likeness of sinful flesh, and for sin condemned sin in the flesh; that the righteousness of the law might be fulfilled in us, who walk not after the flesh but after the spirit.* Rom. 8 : 3, 4. But what is the fulfilling of the righteousness of the law, but to do the righteous things contained in the law? And in this sense every true believer doth fulfill the law, though his completeness be in Christ; for love is the fulfilling of the law, (Rom. 13: 10,) so that the commanding power of the law is such a just measure, that every one that loves acts his part towards the fulfilling of it.

5th. It farther appears to be the ten commandments, by the use Christ makes of what he had before asserted: *Whosoever therefore shall break one of these least commandments, and shall teach men so, shall be called least in the kingdom of heaven.* Matt. 5: 19. That is, forasmuch as that law must stand till heaven and earth pass away, and I came not to destroy it, therefore beware of breaking it, for whosoever you are that break any part of it, and shall teach men so, you shall be called the least in the kingdom of heaven; *but whosoever shall do and teach them, the same shall be called great in the kingdom of heaven.* To prevent farther mistake, he repeateth the law in many particulars, and gives the sense, showing how far their righteousness should exceed the righteousness of the scribes and pharisees. By all of which it plainly appears, that this law, which Christ came not to destroy, is the law of the ten commandments, or the laws that were comprehended in them.

6. The Apostle confirmeth and establisheth this law after the death of Christ, as plainly appears in the third chapter of Romans, the drift of which is to set Jews and Gentiles in a like condition by nature—all breakers of the law of God, and so become guilty before him, (verse 19,) and that therefore no flesh could be justified by the deeds of the law, the law being for another purpose—to convince of sin, (verse 20,) or to bring sin to their knowledge. He proves that Jews and Gentiles, circumcised and uncircumcised, are justified by and through faith, and not by the law of works. Verses 27—30. But lest the Gentiles should think, because they could not be justified by the works of the law, that there-

fore they might look upon the law as a thing done away or made void, he puts this question to the uncircumcised Gentiles, *Do we then make void the law through faith? God forbid; yea, we establish the law.* He settles this question, whether the law be in force to believing Gentiles or no, with a God forbid; which shows the greatness of his zeal against such a persuasion, it being the same answer which he gives to another gross question, whether we should continue in sin that grace might abound; and, as if that were not enough, he adds to it, Yea, we establish the law.

7. This same Apostle doth prove that the law was in force at the time of his conversion. He saith he had not known sin but by the law; he had not known lust except the law had said, *Thou shalt not covet.* Rom. 7 : 7. He was alive without the law once, but when the commandment came, sin revived, and he died, (verse 9,) that is, not without the letter of it, for that he had, and did in a great measure conform to, but without powerful convictions for sin by the law; and in this sense then the commandment came, sin revived, and he died that before was alive in his own apprehension. *For without the law sin was dead,* (verse 8,) and by the law is the knowledge of sin; and sin, taking occasion by the commandment, deceived him, and slew him. *Wherefore the law is holy, and the commandment is holy, just and good,* (verses 11, 12;) not that the holy and just law was made death unto him—God forbid—but sin, that it might appear sin, by this good law wrought death in him, that by the commandment sin might appear exceeding sinful. Verse 13. And if so, then this law did not die with the body of Christ; though we are dead to the law by the body of Christ, that we should serve in newness of spirit, and not in the oldness of the letter,

and that we should be married to another, even him who is raised from the dead; we being dead to that spirit of bondage in which we were held, that we set our obedience to the law no longer in the room of Christ as our head and husband; Christ by his blood having purchased us from that power that the law had over us by reason of sin. So that our service is not to satisfy the law, as a woman serves to please her husband that she is bound to; but we are not dead to serving in newness of spirit in obedience to Christ as our husband. Rom. 7: 4—6. In this sense the Apostle delights in the law of God after the inward man, (verse 22,) though the other law in his members stood in great opposition to it. Verse 23. Mind this chapter well, and it will appear so plain that he that runs may read, that the Apostle intends no such thing as to take us from our obedience to the law, nor yet the abrogating of the law, but the contrary.

8. The same Apostle urges the law, in the very letter of it, to the Ephesians. He saith, in chapter 6 : 1—3, *Children, obey your parents, for this is right; honor thy father and thy mother, which is the first commandment with promise.* He proves his exhortation to be right from the commandment, and he takes notice of the order of the commandments; it is the first commandment of that second table, and it hath a promise annexed to it. He speaks in the present tense; he does not say it *was* the first commandment, but it *is* the first with a promise, *that thy days may be long on the earth.* He urges the promise to them for their encouragement; and to prevent mistakes, he shows the extent of it, that it was not only to the Jews, that they should live long in the land of Canaan, but to the Gentiles also; therefore the interpretation says, *that thy days may be long on the earth.*

9. James gives a full confirmation to what I am treating of. He convinces them of sin by this law, in having the faith of Jesus Christ with respect of persons, as appears by chapter 2: 10, 11, *For whosoever shall keep the whole law, and yet offend in one point, he is guilty of all.* He shows what law he means, and how it is that he who offends in one point is guilty of all; because, *He that saith, Do not commit adultery, saith also, Do not kill; now if thou commit no adultery, yet if thou kill, thou art become a transgressor of the law.* And John saith, *Whosoever committeth sin transgresseth the law, for sin is the transgression of the law,* (1 John 3: 3, 4;) and in the next verse he explains what law he means, and saith, it was such transgression that Christ was manifested to take away. Now if this law of God was done away by the death of Christ, sin could not be a transgression of it so long after; neither could any be convinced of sin by it, because it was not. But the Apostle saith, *Whosoever commiteth sin transgresseth the law;* which shows it was in force then, and not only so, but that likewise it should so remain.

10. Let it be considered whether this opinion that the law is done away doth not clash with redemption itself. The Apostle states that all men were under the law, and by breaking of it they came under the curse. Gal. 3: 10. And Christ was made under the curse, to redeem his people from under the curse of the law, that the blessing of Abraham might come upon the Gentiles through faith. Verses 13, 14. Now if we were not under the commanding power, we could not be under the curse, (for that follows disobedience,) and if so, then Christ was not made a curse for us; neither can the blessing of Abraham come upon the Gentiles upon that account, if the Jews only were under the law, and

under the curse of it. Christ's dying to redeem them from the curse, could not bring the blessing of Abraham upon the Gentiles. And again, the Apostle saith, *that Christ was made under the law, to redeem them that were under the law, that we might receive the adoption of sons.* Gal. 4: 4, 5. Now if we were not under the law, we could not be redeemed by Christ's being under the law, nor receive the adoption of sons thereby; but it is manifest that every one is under the commanding power of the law, and by nature under the curse; and Christ hath only redeemed his people from the curse, but they are not redeemed from their obedience to the law of God. I find no Scripture that saith so; but the contrary.

11. God complaineth of the blindness of his servants, and of the deafness of his messengers that he sent, (Isa. 42 : 19, 20,) and their blindness and deafness appears in this, that they did not hear nor understand God's design in the gift of his Son, that it was not to destroy the law or to slight it, but to magnify it and make it honorable. Verse 2. Previously it was in tables of stone, but now in the fleshy tables of the heart; service was then done from a spirit of bondage, but now from a spirit of adoption. And in this sense I conceive the law to be magnified and made honorable, and upon this account God is well pleased for his righteousness' sake, that is, I conceive, for his Son's sake.

12. This opinion, that the whole law is abolished, doth pull up true magistracy by the roots, the office of rulers being for the punishment of evil doers, and for the praise of them that do well. But if the statutes and judgments be not in force, there is no corporeal punishment to be inflicted upon any, though thieves, murderers, or the like; and so there is no room for the magisterial power at all, but men

are left in this respect as the beasts of the field, to shift one among another as well as they can. But the Apostle saith, *The law is made for the lawless and disobedient, for ungodly and for sinners, for unholy and profane, for murderers of fathers and murderers of mothers, for man-slayers,* &c. 1 Tim. 1: 9, 10. Now that this is the law of penalties, is manifest, in that it is said it was not made for a righteous man; but the ten commandments were for the righteous, for the Psalmist saith, *Make me to go in the path of thy commandments, for therein do I delight. O how love I thy law! It is my meditation all the day.* Psalm 119: 35, 97.

And how shall we have governors as at the first, and counsellors as at the beginning, (Isa. 1: 26,) if they have no law to govern by? If any say we shall have laws from Christ, and shall not need those laws that were for the commonwealth of Israel, I answer, I know no word of God that doth give us ground to hope for any other laws of Scripture then what we have. And suppose that God should revive his work and bring his enemies under, and put opportunity into the hands of men fearing God and hating covetousness to rule the nation, and to make laws according to Scripture, what could they do if the Scripture were not their statute-book, if they should turn law-makers? Would not that be their sin, there being no warrant in the Scripture for it? And would it not bring all into confusion again, and make another Babel? For the great question which is to be resolved in the latter days, will be, Who is our statute-maker?—which the saints put out of question in Isa. 33: 22, *The Lord is our Judge, the Lord is our Statute-maker, the Lord is our King, he will save us,* (and not king Omri with his statutes.) Mich. 6: 16. And when the saints come to own this truth in good earnest, their opponents' tacklings will be loosed; they shall neither strengthen their masts, nor spread their sails. And Malachi tells us what laws our King hath made, which the saints are to own when the day of the Lord shall burn as an oven all the proud, and the Sun of Righteousness arise upon all that fear him; when they shall tread down the wicked with so much ease that they shall be as ashes under the soles of their feet, so that it shall be counted the Lord's doings. And in the day that the Lord shall do this, *Remember ye the law of Moses, my servant, which I commanded unto him in Horeb for all Israel, with the statutes and judgments.* Mal. 4 : 3, 4.

I shall now endeavor to answer some objections which are usually brought against this truth, though several of them are partly answered in the grounds before mentioned. I shall therefore say the less, and begin to speak something to that Scripture in 2 Corinthians, third chapter, on which the objectors chiefly build their persuasion; and indeed at the first glance thereon, without comparing it with other Scriptures, it hath more color for such a purpose than all the Scriptures that ever I heard brought; from which Scripture this is objected, that the ten commandments were the ministration of death and the letter, and are done away.

Answer. That they were the ministration of death and of the letter is granted, for the Scripture saith so; but the Scripture doth not say that they are done away, as will appear, if we consider the drift of the Apostle. He endeavoreth to show the difference between the ministration of the spirit and of the letter, the one being a bare reading of the law, from which no life was communicated to those that heard it. The Apostle calls it the ministration of condemnation, that is, it lays open sin, and the curse for sin, but it is the gospel ministration which holds forth justification and strength against sin; not that the ten commandments in themselves were death to any—God forbid! as the Apostle saith in Rom. 7: 13; but sin, when it is finished, bringeth forth death; and the commandments preach death to the transgressors of them, so that they are called the ministration of death and condemnation, because man hath broken them, and so is under the curse of them, which Christ hath delivered believers from, (Rom. 3: 13;) and the ministration of it is really done away, that is, as I said before, the reading of the law by a typical priesthood, which the Jews would have set up in the room and place of the ministration of the spirit. And whereas they lived under the hearing of the bare letter of the law, which gave no strength to perform, we live under the hearing of the gospel, which is spirit and life. John 6: 36. But that the matter of the law, or commanding power of it, should be done away, this Scripture doth not in the least prove, but it is used in the hand of the Spirit to convince of sin. This the same Apostle proves in Rom. 7: 7, where he saith, *I had not known sin but by the law; I had not known lust except the law had said, Thou shalt not covet.* This will appear evident if we consider the same chapter from verse 8 to verse 14.

Obj. 2. Another Scripture is frequently urged from Acts 7: 37—*A prophet shall the Lord your God raise up unto you of your brethren, like unto me; him shall ye hear.* From which it is concluded, that we are to hearken only to Christ and not to Moses.

Ans. If by hearing of Christ you mean hearing only what he spake with his own lips when he was on earth, then we are not to hear hear his apos-

Jes. But if you mean, by hearing of him, to hear what he spake upon earth and what he spake by his Spirit in his apostles, then why are we not to hear what he spake by his Spirit to his prophets, seeing we are built upon the foundation of the apostles and prophets, Christ being the chief corner-stone. Eph. 21: 20. And if those who are of this persuasion would be true to their principle to hear Christ, hear him what he saith in Luke 16: 31—*They have Moses and the prophets, let them hear them; for if they will not believe Moses and the prophets, neither will they be persuaded though one rose from the dead.* And he counsels to keep the commandments, (Matt. 19: 17, 18,) and reproves for the breach of them, as also for the making them void by traditions, (Matt. 15: 6,) as might be made to appear by many other Scriptures. Therefore there is nothing of weight in this objection to shake the thing asserted. But for a more full answer to this objection and the former, I must needs entreat the reader to see my other book on the Sabbath.

Obj. 3. Moses was faithful over his house as a servant, so Christ is faithful over his house as a son. Now, if Christ hath not given us all the laws that we are to observe, this is to make Christ less faithful than Moses.

Ans. Doubtless Christ as a son is faithful over his house, as Moses was faithful over his house as a servant. But we are to consider, what was Moses' house, and what is Christ's house. Moses' house, I conceive, was the Tabernacle; his faithfulness did appear in that he did all things according to the pattern showed him in the Mount. Christ's house is the saints, the true tabernacle which the Lord hath pitched and not man, (Heb. 8: 2, 5,) of which the other was a shadow. And as Moses as a servant gave forth ordinances for his house, so Christ as a son has given out ordinances for his house. But the ten commandments are a law which belongs to men as they are men, though they be no part of Christ's house, it being, as before proved, the law written in their very hearts.

Obj. 4. But when certain of the sect of the pharisees arose and said it was needful to be circumcised and keep the law of Moses, the Apostle proves them to be tempters of God, in putting a yoke upon the neck of the disciples, which neither they nor their fathers were able to bear. Acts 15: 5, 10.

Ans. Are the ten commandments such a yoke as is not to be borne? Is it a yoke to have no other God but Jehovah, and to abstain from murder, theft, adultery, and the like? For so it must be, if you judge that the whole law is here slighted. But the thing under discussion here is, whether such and such laws are to be kept or not, and the stress that is laid upon the keeping of them, namely, the pressing of them as things without which they could not be saved, as in Acts 15: 1; and therefore the Apostle, in answer to this, shows that the Gentiles had received the gospel and did believe, God having given to them the Holy Ghost, and put no difference between them and the Jews, purifying their hearts by faith, (verses 7—9,) and that through the grace of Jesus Christ both Jews and Gentiles should be saved, (verse 11;) and as the Apostle opposeth the keeping of these laws for such a purpose as to be saved thereby, so the bare keeping of them is forbidden. And therefore James saith, (verses 19, 20,) *My sentence is, that we trouble not them which from among the Gentiles are turned unto God, but that we write unto them that they abstain from pollutions of idols, from fornication, from things strangled, and from blood.* So that the Apostle's judgment is, that the Gentiles should keep some part of the law. And therefore the question was not, whether any part of the law should be kept; and the reason why they would write no more seems to be in verse 20, *For Moses of old time hath in every city them that preach him, being read in the synagogues every Sabbath day.* So the apostles and elders write, in verse 24, *Forasmuch as we have heard that certain men that went out from us have troubled you with words, subverting your souls, saying, Ye must be circumcised and keep the law, to whom we gave no such commandment.* Now can we be so gross as to think, that it is subverting men's souls, and contrary to the commandments of the apostles and elders, to bid them love the Lord their God with all their hearts and with all their strength, and to worship him alone, and not to take his name in vain, and the like? This is to keep the law. But the difference was about other laws as well as circumcision, and they are as really forbidden to keep them, as they are forbidden circumcision; and therefore it cannot be the law of the ten commandments, but the law of shadows, as is manifest by chapter 21. When Paul came to Jerusalem, the brethren told him that it was reported that he taught all the Jews which were among the Gentiles to forsake Moses, saying, *that they ought not to circumcise their children, neither to walk after the customs,* (verse 21;) therefore they counseled Paul to purify himself, with some others, that it might be seen that he walked orderly and kept the law. Verse 24. *But as touching the Gentiles which believe, we have written and concluded that they observe no such things.* Verse 25. So that it is very clear, that it is circumcision and the customs that is here called the law of Moses, which the Gentiles were commanded not to keep. But to think that the Gentiles should be forbidden to keep the law of God that was written in their natures is abominable, and contrary both to Scripture and reason.

Obj. 5. But the Scripture saith, *Cast out the bond-woman and her son, for the son of the bond-woman shall not be heir with the son of the free-woman;* which bond-woman was an allegory of the covenant from Mount Sinai, and therefore to be cast out.

Ans. The Apostle is here showing how impossible it is for works and grace to stand together in point of justification; for this people were seeking to be justified by the works of the law. He shows the difference betwixt the two covenants, one of works gendering to bondage, *the righteousness of the law being this, that the man that doeth these things should live in them,* (Rom. 10: 5;) the other of grace or free promise, without any respect to man's righteousness. He shows that the sons of the covenants are like unto their mothers; the sons of the one covenant are born after the flesh, the sons of the other by promise; and those that are born after the flesh persecute those that are born after the Spirit. Nevertheless, what saith the Scripture? *Cast out the bond-woman and her son, for the son of the bond-woman shall not be heir with the son of the free-woman;* that is, the covenant of works with those that seek to be justified thereby, *Christ being the end of the law for righteousness to every one that believeth.* Rom. 10: 4. But if we should understand the ten commandments in themselves to be the bond-woman, then it is impossible for them that keep them to be heirs or children of the promise, but they must be cast out as children of the bond-woman, which is very erroneous, and contrary to the current of the Scriptures. For the doers of the law are justified before God, (Rom. 2: 13,) though not for doing. And mark how the Apostle forbids this notion in Romans 3: 31—*Do we then make void the law through faith? God forbid! Shall we continue in sin,* or transgress the law, *that grace may abound? God forbid!* Rom. 6: 1, 2. *Is the law sin? God forbid!* Rom. 7: 7. *Was the law, which was good, made death unto me? God forbid!* Verse 13. *Shall we transgress the law because we are not under the condemning power of it,* (Christ having redeemed us from it?) *God forbid!* Rom. 6: 15. Certainly the Scripture did foresee how apt men would be to slight and make void the law of God under specious pretences, as their being believers, and Gentiles which had not the law given to them, but that they are under grace, and the like. *If the uncircumcision keep the righteousness of the law, shall not his uncircumcision be counted for circumcision?* Rom. 2: 26.

Consider these quries—1. If the whole law was done away by the death of Christ, why did the Apostle spend so much time to prove that by the works of the law none could be justified, (Gal. 3,) seeing there was no law to work upon? Would it not have been a nearer way to have told them that the law was abolished?

2. If the whole law was done away at the death of Christ, how can any part of it be now in force? If it be said it is upon a new account, show me any one law that Christ hath once destroyed and again revived, seeing the Apostle saith, if he should build again the things that he destroyed, he should make himself a transgressor. Gal. 2: 14.

3. What Scripture proves that we have any one of the ten commandments given out on a new account?

4. If the whole law be done away, what law is there for the punishment of evil-doers, thieves, murderers, and the like?

5. If the ten commandments are to be abolished, how is it that the Lord hath annexed so many great and precious promises to the keeping of them and delighting in them, as in Psalms 1: 1—4, and many other places, which do of right belong to such as keep the commandments? Rev. 22: 14.

6. How is it that the Apostle saith, the law is good if a man use it lawfully, (1 Tim. 1: 8,) if at the same time there be no law?

7. If the law was done away at the death of Christ, when was it given again upon a new account? If it was given before his death, (in the 5th chapter of Matthew,) then how is it that the law that was given on Sinai stood in force till that time? Could they both stand in force at once? If not till after the death of Christ, then when was it given out, seeing that we find not any of the commandments so much as mentioned for a long time after the death of Christ? Can we think the saints and the world were left without a law?

8. How is it that we contend for governors as at the first, and counsellors as at the beginning, seeing there is no law for them to rule and govern by, if this doctrine be true, that the whole law is done away?

Thus I have endeavored in a measure to prove, that the ten commandments are not only in force to unbelievers, but also to believers. But believers are not under the law so as to be justified or condemned by it; not under it as a covenant of works and ministration of death, but under it as a righteous rule of life—a holy, just, and good law; so they are under it, and do delight in it. Rom. 7: 22; Psalms 119: 70, 72, 97; 1 Cor. 9: 21. *It is time for thee, Lord, to work; for they have made void thy law,* (Psalms 119: 122.) *Therefore I esteem all thy precepts concerning all things to be right, and I hate every false way,* (Verse 128.)

THE SEVENTH DAY IS THE SABBATH.

If the ten commandments be in force, every jot and tittle of them, it must necessarily follow that the seventh day is the Sabbath, and is to be observed according to the commandment. But because there is much opposition against this truth, I shall offer something in particular to it, which may tend to the clearing of it.

1. It was instituted by God before the fall of man, as appears in Gen. 1: 31—*And God saw every thing that he had made, and behold it was very good.* But when man sinned, God changed his voice, and then the ground was cursed for his sake. Gen. 3: 17. Farther, God was six days upon his work of creation, and rested not until the seventh day. Now, betwixt the end of the sixth day and the beginning of the seventh day, there is no interval or space of time, (chap. 1: 31, 2: 2;) then why should it be thought that the Sabbath was a shadow to hold forth rest by faith, and why should we run into such imaginations concerning the cause of God's instituting the Sabbath, seeing God so plainly declared it himself, namely, *that he blessed the seventh day and sanctified it, because that in it he rested from all his works which God created and made.* Gen. 2: 3.

2. The reason that the Lord gave when he commanded the observance of the seventh day, was as before, *because that in six days the Lord made heaven and earth, the sea, and all that in them is, and rested the seventh day, wherefore the Lord blessed the Sabbath day and hallowed it,* (Exod. 20: 11;) and it is as a motive to provoke man to follow the Lord's example from the beginning, both in work and rest

Six days, saith the Lord, *thou shalt labor and do all thy work, but the seventh day is the Sabbath of the Lord thy God; in it thou shalt do no manner of work.* And if thou wouldest know a reason why thou shouldest do so, it is because I the Lord thy God did so. And truly, to me it is clear, that one main reason why the Lord took so much time as six days to create all things in, and rested the seventh day, was to show man an example, and what he ought to do. Doubtless God could have made all things in a moment; but six days he works, and rests the seventh day, that man might do the same, and thereby not only hold forth the creating power of God, and the method that he was pleased to take in the creation, but also his great mercy in instructing and commanding man to work six days and rest the seventh, that he might be refreshed.

3. It plainly appears, that this institution was in force and to be observed from the beginning, though no mention is made of the patriarchs observing it, no more than of their sacrificing and doing many other things, which it is judged that they did, notwithstanding we hear nothing of them. But consider, God rested the seventh day and sanctified it. Now to profane that which God sanctifies doubtless is a sin; and had they done servile work upon the Sabbath, they had profaned it. Neh. 13: 16, 17. And what the Lord said to Peter, in another case, may be rightly said in this, namely, *What God hath sanctified, that call not thou common or unclean.* Acts 10: 15. And the Lord, when he gave forth this command, saith, *Remember the Sabbath*, to note the importance of it, and the antiquity of it, it being no new thing, but from the beginning; and that the Lord urges, in verse 11, as the cause why it was to be observed. Israel observed the Sabbath before the giving of the law on Mount Sinai, as appears in

Exod. 16: 23, 25, 26. But mark what Nehemiah saith to this in, chapter 9: 13, 14, *Thou camest down also upon Mount Sinai, and spakest with them from heaven, and gavest them right judgments and true laws, good statutes and commandments, and madest known also unto them thy holy Sabbath.* Mark, this commandment is singled out from all the rest, and is said to be made known to them, which shows that it was in being before, though probably they might lose the observation of it, by reason of their hard bondage in Egypt. However, it is plain that they had need of the knowledge of the Sabbath, and God makes it known unto them. And Christ leads us plainly to the first institution of it when he saith, *The Sabbath was made for man, and not man for the Sabbath.* He points to the making of it, and for whom it was made, not for the Jews only as Jews, but for man, before there was any such distinction as Jew and Gentile; and in that it was made for man, which was the public person or representative of the whole of mankind, it was made for all men, Adam standing as a public person before his fall.

4. Our Lord Jesus doth show the true end of God's giving the Sabbath, and also how it ought to be kept, and shows the pharisees their mistake in the observation of it, they being so rigid that they would not suffer good works and works of mercy to be done, though there were necessity for the doing of them, as will appear if we consider the following Scriptures: The pharisees asked Christ if it was lawful to heal on the Sabbath day, that they might accuse him, (Matt. 12: 10,) and his answer was this, *What man is there among you that shall have one sheep, and if it fall into a pit on the Sabbath day, will he not lay hold on it and lift it out? How much then is a man better than a sheep? Wherefore it is lawful to do good on the Sabbath day.* Matt. 12:

10—12. Again, the pharisees told Christ that his disciples did that which was not lawful, because they pulled the ears of corn upon the Sabbath day. But mind the answer of Christ, *Have ye not read what David did when he was a hungered and had need, how he entered into the house of God, and did eat the shew-bread, which it is not lawful for any to eat but the priests?* Mark 2: 24—26. *Have ye not read in the law, that the priests in the temple profane the Sabbath day and are blameless?* Matt. 12: 5. It was not unlawful to pluck the ears of corn when they went through their neighbor's field, for that they might do by the law of God, (Deut. 23: 25,) and that the pharisees knew very well; but they thought it was unlawful because they did it upon the Sabbath day. But mark the answer of Christ, how he cleared the disciples; it was unlawful for David to eat the shew-bread, but he was a hungered and had need, and therefore to be excused. If the disciples had pulled the ears of corn when they had no need, upon the Sabbath day, it had been doing of needless work, and so had been unlawful. But the text saith they were a hungered, therefore they might do it, it being a work of mercy as David's was. And the same may be said of the priests' profaning the Sabbath, who, notwithstanding, are said to be blameless. Their preparation of the sacrifices was allowed, which work in itself would have been counted servile work, but that it was for such a merciful end, namely, the sins of the people; therefore saith Christ, *Had ye known what this meaneth, I will have mercy and not sacrifice, ye would not have condemned the guiltless.* Matt. 12: 7. Clearly proving that the Sabbath was to be observed, (but not so as to break another command, to neglect mercy, which the pharisees would do,) and that his disciples, in having mercy on their bodies, were no Sabbath-breakers.

Farther, observe what Christ saith in Mark 2 : 27, *The Sabbath was made for man, and not man for the Sabbath.* The pharisees made themselves slaves and bond-men by making the Sabbath a yoke, (whereas it should have been a delight, Isa. 58 : 13,) by superstitious outside performances, as though man had been made for the Sabbath. But Christ tells them, it was made for man, that is, for the good and benefit of man, that he might rest from his labors and be refreshed, as they were in Exod. 31 : 17. And thus you see how clearly our Lord hath given the sense of this law. It is lawful to do well upon the Sabbath day, to visit the sick and to heal them, and to do works of mercy to our own and others' bodies, the Sabbath being made for man.

5. Jesus Christ declares himself to be Lord even of the Sabbath day, (Matt. 12 : 8,) and he takes his title thus: *The Sabbath*, saith he, *was made for man, and not man for the Sabbath ; therefore the Son of Man is Lord even of the Sabbath day.* Here seems to be two things from whence Christ takes this title. First, the Sabbath was made for man, that is, as before was said, for Adam, and so for all men, being made for him before his fall. Now, Christ being the Son of Man, the chief man, or second Adam, the man of God's right hand, the heir of all things, is of right Lord even of the Sabbath day. Second, the Sabbath was made for man, that is, for the good of man, and in mercy to man, as is said before. Therefore, Christ being the author of all good, the giver of all mercy, he is Lord of it; and, therefore, Christ doth not slight the Sabbath (as some do imagine) by saying he is Lord of it, as though he were not to keep it, or that his intent was to change it. That were to strip himself of his title, or else to entitle himself Lord of that which was not. But in that it is said Christ is Lord of the Sabbath, it

proves the Sabbath to be in force. As Christ proves the resurrection, in Mark 12 : 26, 27—*I am the God of Abraham, the God of Isaac, the God of Jacob ; I am not the God of the dead, but of the living*—so Christ is Lord of the Sabbath day. He is not Lord of the dead types and shadows, or of that which is not in being, but he is Lord of the lively oracles, of which I consider the Sabbath to be one. Acts 7 : 38.

Objection. But did not Christ break the Sabbath, and teach men so to do, in bidding the impotent man take up his bed and walk, it being unlawful to carry a burden upon the Sabbath day ?

Answer. The scribes and pharisees said so, indeed, and that his bed was a burden; but they were very unfit judges, they being ignorant of the right manner of observing the Sabbath, and seeking likewise to take advantage against Christ in his words and actions. Their saying the man's bed was a burden, and that it was unlawful for him to carry it, doth prove no more that was it so, than their saying that the disciples did break the Sabbath in plucying the ears of corn, and Christ in healing the diseased. But was not this a work of mercy, the man having been lame so long in the porch now being cured ? Was it not meet that he should be released from the place, and take his bed with him to lay on at night ? (for it is likely he had no other.) And who can say that it was a burden ? In some countries that which they call a bed is no heavier than a good cloak or coat. But consider what gross wickedness naturally flows from this opinion. The objectors themselves, and all, must acknowledge that the whole law was in force till the death of Christ—the very shadows, till he nailed them to his cross ; then the fourth commandment doubtless was in force.

Now, to say that Christ broke it, and taught men so, is to say that Christ sinned, and taught men to sin, (for sin is the transgression of the law,) and this roots up redemption by Christ; for if Christ was a sinner, he could not be a Saviour. He had not been a meet offering for the sins of others; he had been a sinner himself. But he was offered up a Lamb without spot, (Heb. 7: 26, 1 Peter 1: 19,) and was made sin for us, that knew no sin, (2 Cor. 5 : 2;) and therefore this objection is made so gross, that every sincere heart that sees the tendency of it will not touch it; and indeed I had not mentioned it here, but that many through weakness have taken it up as a sufficient ground to prove the making void of the Sabbath, for want of looking into the bottom of it.

6. Another ground to prove the Sabbath yet to be in force, may be taken from the words of Christ to his disciples in Matt. 24: 20—*But pray ye that your flight be not in the winter, nor on the Sabbath day;* which is part of the answer Christ gave them when they came privately to him to ask him when the destruction of the temple should be, the signs of his coming, and the end of the world. It is generally conceived that this part of Christ's answer relates to the destruction of Jerusalem; and, indeed, that is the shortest time that can be thought it relates to, as appears by the question which was asked him. But suppose it to be so; doth it not plainly appear from hence, that the Sabbath was to remain in full force after the death of Christ? The destruction of Jerusalem was about forty years after the death of Christ, and yet he commands his disciples to pray that their flight be not in the winter, neither on the Sabbath day. Now, can we think that Christ would lay such a foundation for superstition, as though the Sabbath was to be at the ruin of Jerusalem, when it was to cease at his death? Or can

we think that Christ would teach his disciples to pray false, or to pray that their flight should not be on the Sabbath, when indeed there was to be no Sabbath? This is gross to imagine; for as sure as winter was to remain winter, so the Sabbath was to remain the Sabbath. And if their flight had been upon it, it would have been the more tedious, it being a day of rest and refreshment to them, wherein they used to rejoice and praise the Lord, as appears by that song for the Sabbath day, in Paslm 92. But although this Scripture looks to the destruction of Jerusalem, yet I conceive that it looks farther, even to that distress that Jerusalem shall be in at the second coming of Christ, and that for these reasons:—

1st. Those things that Christ spake of were accomplished in a measure in the apostles' days; and yet they are not completely fulfilled. For instance, Christ told his disciples that they should be delivered up to be killed, and they should be hated of all nations for his name's sake. This was in the apostles' days, and hath been since; and false prophets did arise then, and so they have since. So that those things which Christ spake looked to several times, and therefore, I conceive, he saith, *Verily I say unto you, this generation shall not pass till all these things be fulfilled.* So I judge that what he spake concerning Jerusalem had not only respect to that destruction that came upon it during that generation, but also to that great calamity that should be upon it in the last days.

2d. This will more plainly appear, if we consider the words of Christ, *But pray ye that your flight be not in the winter, nor on the Sabbath day; for then shall be great tribulation, such as was not since the beginning of the world to this time, no, nor ever shall be.* Matt. 24: 20, 21. Now, with this compare

Zech. 14: 2, *For I will gather all nations against Jerusalem to battle, and they shall be taken, and the houses rifled, and the women ravished.* And in the third and fourth verses it is said, *Then shall the Lord go forth and fight against those nations, as when he fought in the day of battle, and his feet shall stand in that day upon the Mount of Olives.* With which compare Dan. 12: 1, 2, *And at that time shall Michael stand up, the great Prince which standeth for the children of thy people; and there shall be a time of trouble, such as never was since there was a nation, even to that same time; and at that time thy people shall be delivered, every one that shall be found written in the book. And many of them that sleep in the dust of the earth shall awake, some to everlasting life, and some to shame and everlasting contempt.* Now, if that great destruction of Jerusalem produced such great trouble as never was, nor ever should be again, how is it that there shall be such great trouble as never was since there was a nation, when Michael stands up to deliver the people, every one that is written in the book, and Jerusalem is taken, and the houses rifled, and the women ravished, when the Lord comes forth to fight against those nations, and his feet shall stand upon the Mount of Olives, according to that text in Acts 1: 11, *So shall he come in like manner as ye have seen him go into heaven;* and when the seventh angel pours out his vial, (Rev. 16: 17, 18,) which time I conceive is one and the same with that in Zechariah and Daniel—and the angel is Michael, the great prince which Daniel speaks of, whose feet shall stand upon the Mount of Olives—then is the time of great trouble, and such an earthquake as was not since men were upon the face of the earth, so mighty an earthquake and so great. So that to me it appears, that these three Scriptures do correspond with the words of Christ, pointing out the same time; and if so, then the Sabbath shall remain till the coming of Christ, and so shall stand till heaven and earth pass away, according to the passage in Matt. 5: 18; and for ever and ever, according to that in Psalm 111: 8; and the destruction of Jerusalem seems to be a type of that great destruction that shall be at Christ's appearance. And, as Jerusalem was taken when some from all nations were gathered together, as history reports, and on the Sabbath day it was destroyed, so it appears that the strength of the saints will be gathered together at Jerusalem, because all nations will gather against it, and Jerusalem's strait will be upon the Sabbath day, as seems to appear by the words of Christ, for then, saith he, shall be great tribulation, such as never was; (then! when? why, when their flight shall be upon the Sabbath day;) and this great tribulation is when Jerusalem shall be taken, the houses rifled, and the women ravished, as was said before; *at which time Michael shall stand up and fight against these nations, as when he fought in the day of battle; and the slain of the Lord shall be many, even from one end of the earth to the other,* (Jer. 25: 31—33,) *and the Mount of Olives shall cleave in the midst thereof, and there shall be a very great valley, into which the saints shall flee,* (Zech. 14: 5.) Then shall the Sabbath be swallowed up in the great Sabbath of a thousand years, that glorious and holy rest which the saints shall enter into, and live and reign with Christ. Rev. 20: 4.

7. Another ground is taken from the practice of Christ's disciples after his death, as recorded in Luke 23: 5, 6, *And they returned and prepared spices and ointments, and rested the Sabbath day according to the commandment.* Some say, that if we do observe the Sabbath, we must do all those sacrifices which

the Jews did upon it. But at this time the veil of the temple was rent in twain from top to bottom, and the shadows were done away by the body of Christ, and yet they kept the Sabbath, not through fear or ignorance, but according to the commandment, which is to rest from their labors; and so they did, for the text saith, *they returned and rested.* There is no sacrifice expressed in the commandment. *The stranger and the cattle were to rest on the Sabbath.* Exod. 20: 10. So that the Sabbath was commanded and observed before any of those sacrifices were commanded to be offered upon it. But because the Jews did such a service upon the Sabbath day, as they were a typical people, it doth not follow that this was any part of the commandment; and therefore we are to rest, as those disciples did, according to the commandment. It is remarkable, that the Holy Ghost should leave this thing upon record, which would not have been, I am persuaded, had the Sabbath then been abolished. He doth not only say, they returned and rested on the Sabbath day, but, to prevent all mistakes, lest it should be thought they did it ignorantly or superstitiously, or for fear of the Jews, he saith they did it groundedly, that is, according to the commandment.

Obj. But the disciples were met together upon the first day of the week, and Christ appeared unto them. John 20: 9.

Ans. It is true, they were assembled together upon the same day at even, being the first day of the week, with the door shut; and the cause is laid down why they were so, namely, for fear of the Jews. Some of the disciples, as I said before, kept the Sabbath the day before, and I think we can not reasonably imagine but that those did who were together on the first day, for they did frequently correspond together, that is manifest. But what doth their being together on the first day evening, and Christ's appearing to them, prove for the observation of the first day, more than his appearing to them eight days after, and appearing to them the third time early in the morning when they were fishing, (John 24: 4, 5,) for the observation of those days? It was necessary that Christ should appear to his disciples on the first day of the week, that his word might be fulfilled of his rising the third day, so that they might boldly witness the same.

Obj. But the disciples came together on the first day of the week, and did break bread, and Paul preached unto them. Acts 20.

Ans. This is all the meeting or preaching that ever we find held upon the first day, except the disciples being together for fear of the Jews, mentioned before, at evening. So this seemed to be, because when they came together Paul preached with them, continuing his speech until midnight. It is not likely, then, that they observed the day and came together in the morning, seeing he continued his speech so long. And, as we have the cause of the disciples being together with their doors shut, so we have the cause of this meeting. Paul was ready to depart on the morrow upon an extraordinary occasion, and he had many things to communicate to them, as appears by his discoursing with them till midnight, and talking till break of day. But that which makes the objectors lay such stress upon this text, is because the disciples came together to break bread, which they judge to be the Lord's Supper. Suppose it were so, what doth this make for the observation of the first day, more than Christ's first instituting the Supper upon the fifth day of the week, (as is generally conceived,) doth make for the observation of it? But we have no proof that this was the Supper of the Lord that they came to partake of, but it seems to be such breaking of bread as the margin of some Bibles refers to. Acts 2: 46. *They continued daily with one accord in the temple, and breaking bread from house to house, and did eat their meat with gladness of heart.* So in Luke 24: 30, 35. And it is explained what kind of breaking of bread it was, where it is said, when he was risen up again, and had broken bread and eaten, and talked a good while, till break of day, he departed. Here is eating and talking; it is not solemnized as the Lord's Supper. Some would have this common breaking of bread, and the other in verse 7, to be the Lord's Supper; but it is very unlikely that there should be two sorts of breaking of bread at one time, by the same persons, and yet nothing spoken distinctly by which we might know the one from the other. The most that can be said, is but a supposition; it can not be proved that this was the Lord's Supper. How weak a ground this is for the observation of this day as a Sabbath, or more than any other day, or to limit the administration of the Lord's Supper to this day, I leave to the truly wise in heart to judge.

Obj. But the church had their gatherings upon the first day of the week, by which it appears that it was the day that they met together upon. 1 Cor. 16: 2.

Ans. The words are these, *Upon the first day of the week let every one of you lay by him in store, as God hath prospered him, that there be no gatherings when I come.* Here is no proof of their meeting together, but rather the contrary, every one was to lay by him in store as God had prospered him; no public gathering, but private laying up. But be cause the Apostle saith, in the close of the verse, *that there be no gatherings when I come*, therefore it is thought the Scripture can not be so understood, because it would not prevent gatherings. But is this fair, when a text of Scripture stands alone, to put such a sense upon it as doth contradict the very letter of it—when it saith, let every one of you lay by him in store, then to say the meaning is to have public gatherings and but one store? And would not the end of the Apostle be fully answered, namely, to have no gatherings, if each of them did lay by in store, as God had prospered them in the world, ready against the Apostle came, they knowing of his coming? And when he came, was it not as easy to carry it with them to him, as for us to carry our Bibles to a meeting; and what need would there be then of gatherings? And this way of giving would not be pharisee-like, but according to the words of Christ, in Matt. 6 : 1—4, *Take heed that ye do not your alms before men, to be seen of them; otherwise ye have no reward of your Father which is in heaven. But when thou doest thine alms, let not thy left hand know what thy right hand doeth; that thine alms may be in secret; and thy Father which seeth in secret, himself shall reward thee openly.*

Obj. But John was in the spirit on the Lord's day, (and had the various revelations upon it,) which is conceived to be the first day of the week. Rev. 1: 10.

Ans. It is true, John was in the spirit on the Lord's day. But the question will be, what day that was. If any particular one of the seven, it must have been the Sabbath, for no other day is so called but that. God calls it his holy day in Isa. 58 : 13, and Christ saith he is Lord even of the Sabbath day. And if so, then it is his day, for he is Lord of it, and that by way of eminence; not, as some would have it, to show that he is Lord of every day, but as it is the Sabbath; for so it is said the Son of Man is Lord even of the Sabbath day. So that this notion that the Lord's day is the first day, is merely taken up on trust one from another, without one word of Scripture to prove it.

Obj. But it will be yet objected, by those that are for no Sabbath, in the words of the Apostle in Col. 2: 16, 17, *Let no man therefore judge you in meat, or in drink, or in respect of an holy-day, or of the new-moon, or of the Sabbath-days, which are a shadow of things to come, but the body is of Christ;* whence it is concluded that the Sabbath was but a shadow, and none are to be judged for not observing it.

Ans. There were holy-days and Sabbaths besides the seventh-day Sabbath, or the Sabbath of the Lord thy God, for so it is called in the commandment, as doth appear in Lev. 23: 39. Now, because it is implied by the words of the Apostle, that Sabbaths were shadows, to be done away by the body of Christ, doth it therefore follow that all Sabbaths were so, any more than the words of the Apostle that men shall be saved, prove that all men shall be saved? And if we consider the verses before, it will plainly appear, that the Apostle was not speaking of any of the ten commandments. In verse 15, the Apostle is speaking to the Gentiles, showing how they were dead in sins, and in the uncircumcision of their flesh, but are now quickened by Christ, and all their trespasses forgiven them. In verse 14, he shows what farther benefit they had by the death of Christ, Blotting out the hand-writing of ordinances, which was against us, and contrary to us, he took it out of the way, nailing it to his cross; and the Scripture on which the objection is founded hath its dependence upon that which comes in with, Therefore let no man judge you in meats, and drinks, &c.; as though the Apostle had said, Forasmuch as Christ hath blotted out and nailed to his cross those ordinances which are against the Gentiles, you are not to be judged for the non-performance of them. Now the ten commandments were never against the Gentiles, nor contrary to them; for the same Apostle saith the matter of them was written in their hearts, as was said before, and they did by nature the things contained in them, and therefore they were not contrary to them. But circumcision and other ordinances stood as a wall against the Gentiles, which Christ broke down, by taking them out of the way and nailing them to the cross, *having abolished in his flesh the enmity, even the law of commandments contained in ordinances, for to make in himself of twain one new man, so making peace, that he might reconcile both unto God in one body by the cross, having slain the enmity thereby.* Eph. 2: 15. So that it is clear, that the Apostle is speaking of such commandments as were contained in ordinances, and not those commandments that were eminently distinguished from ordinances; but those ordinances which were against the Gentiles, and made them and the Jews two, as did drinks, new-moons, holy-days, and Sabbath-days, Christ by his blood having taken these away, hath made them one. That the ten commandments should be struck at, there is no cover in this Scripture for, or that the Sabbath should only be taken from them and nailed to the cross with new-moons, meats, and other shadows and ordinances which were against man. But Christ saith, The Sabbath was made for man. So that in this place there is no proof for the abrogation of this command of God. But for a more full answer see my other book.

Obj. How is it that the Apostle saith, in Rom. 14 : 5, 6, *that one man esteemeth one day above another, another esteemeth every day alike*, and yet he does not reprove either of them?

Ans. I make no doubt but if the controversy here alluded to had been about the Sabbath, whether it were to be observed or not, it would have been plainly expressed, and not passed over so slightly But the Apostle is speaking of *indifferent things*, which men were not to be judged for their doing or not doing, and not of commandments. Because it is said that some esteem every day alike, therefore some conclude that this takes away the Sabbath day; but we must compare Scripture with Scripture, adopt such a sense as may bring them into harmony, and sometimes explain general terms by restrictive Scriptures. For instance, Christ says to his disciples, *Go preach the gospel to every creature;* we must understand it to mean to every creature that is in a condition to hear the gospel. The Apostle saith, that every creature of God is good, and nothing to be refused. But some are poison, and are to be refused. So is every day alike, that is, every working day, which God hath made alike; but the seventh day he hath sanctified and made a Sabbath of rest, and so not like the others. This interpretation is according to that Scripture in Exod. 16 : 4, *Behold, I will rain bread from heaven for you, and the people shall go out and gather a certain rate every day;* and in verse 12, *They gathered every morning every man according to his eating, yet on the Sabbath day there was none to gather.* And in our common speech it is so; we call the six days every day. Men say, we work every day, or we travel so far every day, when they mean only the six days that they count working days. So the Apostle, speaking to them that kept the Sabbath, speaks in the same language, and we have no ground to think otherwise; for there is no Scripture that we find before this that hath any seeming dislike against the observation of the Sabbath, but the contrary.

Obj. Ye observe days, and years, and times, and months; I am afraid of you, lest I have bestowed upon you labor in vain. Gal. 4: 10, 11.

Ans. This cannot be understood that the Apostle here strikes at the mere observation of days, a thing of such dangerous consequence, for he would not have them judged that observed one day above another. In Rom. 14: 5, 6, and in this place, he himself judges these as persons that had so far degenerated, that he was afraid he had bestowed upon them labor in vain; but it is manifest that these Galatians were gone back to circumcision, and so were debtors to the whole law, seeking justification thereby. Gal. 5: 2—4. So they observed days and years, according to the law that was a shadow of good things to come, solemnizing the days, and months, and years, with those things that were appointed for them, as burnt-offerings, meat-offerings, the waving of the sheaf, the Passover, and Feast of Unleavened Bread, and the like, as may be seen at large in Lev. 23: 8—11; for they could not be said to observe times, and months and years, according to the law, except they did such service. And this gave the Apostle just ground to fear that he had bestowed on them labor in vain. But to imagine that to observe the Sabbath according to the commandment, or to observe a day voluntarily to the Lord, is so dangerous, is contrary both to Scripture and reason.

Obj. We who believe are entered into rest, of which the Sabbath was but a type, as appears by the words of the Apostle in Heb. 4 : 3.

Ans. If eternal rest by faith be the antitype of the Sabbath, the Sabbath ceased to be in force to every man so soon as he believed; which is ridiculous to think, and contrary to the current of Scripture. But the Apostle saith, *We who believe do enter into rest; for he that is entered into his rest is ceased from his own works, as God did from his. Let us labor therefore to enter into that rest, lest any man fall after the example of unbelief.* Heb. 4: 10, 11. Mind this chapter well, and I am persuaded you will see that the drift of the Apostle, in mentioning the seventh day here, is but to amplify and set forth that perfect rest which they that believe do and shall enjoy, of which the land of Canaan was but a type; and to show that God's rest was before the land of Canaan, and that there yet remains a rest to the people of God. As God did rest the seventh day from all his works, so they that enter into rest do cease from their own works, as God did from his. And this is not as soon as men believe, for the Apostle provokes himself and others which were believers to labor to enter into it. And therefore, if you will have the Sabbath a type from this Scripture, though it is nowhere so called, it must be a type of eternal rest, which saints do enter into when they cease from their own works, as God did from his. And that will not be till they lay down this tabernacle, which will not affect the thing asserted. And indeed I cannot deny but the Sabbath is an earnest of that rest, and saints that are spiritual in the observation of it find it so, and of great use to put them in mind of that glorious rest, as the bread and wine in the Lord's Supper put us in mind of the sufferings of Christ; so this being a day of rest and delight, being striped of all worldly incumbrances, and devoted to the Lord, to pray unto him, and to praise his holy name, to meditate upon heaven and heavenly glory.

Obj. But many say, If the Sabbath be in force, then the penalty must needs be so, and then those that do not keep it must be stoned; therefore this opinion is dangerous, and will lead saints to destroy one another.

Ans. This is a very showy objection, but indeed it is a very weak one. I do not find that any more than one was stoned, and it was for presumptuous breaking of the Sabbath. But suppose that penalty be in force; every saint is not a magistrate to put it in execution. If a saint should kill a man, saints as they are saints are not to execute him; all that they can do is to endeavor his repentance, but it belongs to the true magistrate to inflict the punishment. The penal laws of God take hold of presumptuous sinners, not for sins of ignorance, and therefore it is not to be thought that any punishment will be inflicted upon any for a breach of the Sabbath till it be universally acknowledged. So then, if God hath annexed the penalty of death to the breaking of it, doubtless it will be just. But we find in Nehemiah's time, that although they had made a market-day of the Sabbath, treading of wine-presses, lading of asses, and selling of all manner of provisions upon it, yet he doth but contend with them. He contends with the Jews of Jerusalem, the nobles of Judah, and the men of Tyre, but inflicts no punishment on either. Neh. 13: 15—17, 21. But what a strange thing is this, that men should count it a dangerous opinion, to hold that the Sabbath is in force, because of the penalty! Suppose it be so; the same may be said of the rest of the commandments. For instance, the first commandment is, *Thou shalt have no other gods before me;* he that worshiped a strange god was to be put to death. Now, shall we not own this commandment, because the breakers of it were so punished? Again, *He that sheddeth man's blood, by man shall his blood be shed.* Now, is there any danger in the owning of this commandment, *Thou shalt do no murder*, because the punishment is in force? Again, the fifth commandment is, *Honor thy father and thy mother*, but he that cursed father or mother was to be put to death. Now, shall we not honor father and mother, and so shall we break this commandment, because this punishment belongs to the breakers of it? So this objection is of no weight or use at all, except it be as a bear-skin put upon the truth to frighten children away, lest they should look into it.

Obj. But we do not find any of the apostles urge this commandment in any of their epistles, namely, that the Sabbath day should be observed.

Ans. Neither do we find the apostles urging the first, second, or third commandment in particular, as laid down in the table, but they are frequently urged in the general, as in Rom. 7: 12, 13: 8—10, and generals comprehend particulars. James saith, *Whosoever shall keep the whole law, yet offend in one point, is guilty of all;* and he proves it thus, *Because he that said, Do not commit adultery, said also, Do not kill; now, if thou commit no adultery, yet if thou kill, thou art become a transgressor of the law.* The same argument may be drawn from the thing in hand. He that saith, Do not commit adultery, saith also, Keep the Sabbath; now, if thou commit no adultery, yet if thou break the Sabbath, thou art become a transgressor of the law. James 2: 10, 11.

And Paul saith, *Circumcision is nothing, and uncircumcision is nothing, but the keeping of the commandments of God.* 1 Cor. 7: 19. John saith, in his first epistle, chapter 5: 2, 3, *By this we know that we love the children of God, when we love God and keep his commandments; for this is the love of God, that we keep his commandments, and his commandments are not grievous.* And if the apostles had not spoken a word to this commandment, in general or in particular, it is no ground for us to lay it by, except the observation of it were forbidden, because it is so plainly commanded by God, explained by Christ, observed by his disciples, both before and after his death, as was said before, and will farther appear by and by.

Obj. But we do not find that any of the churches kept the Sabbath.

Ans. That is no proof that they did not keep it. But it is clear that the church of Jerusalem kept it, though it is not plainly expressed, for they were so zealous for the very customs, that Paul is counseled to purify himself, lest they should be offended at him. Acts 21: 21, 24. Now, if they were for the observation of those things that were but shadows, there is no doubt but they were very strict for the observation of the Sabbath. And there was such offence taken against Paul for preaching against circumcision and the customs, that we need not question, if the Sabbath had been preached against, but we should have heard a great noise of it in the Scriptures, and seen strong convincing reasons why it was abolished. And it is as clear that the apostles kept the Sabbath after the resurrection of Christ as before. *Paul went into the synagogue on the Sabbath day, and sat down, and after the reading of the law preached the gospel, and told them of the ignorance of those that dwelt at Jerusalem of the voice of the prophets which were read every Sabbath day. And the Gentiles besought him that these words might be spoken to them the next Sabbath. And the next Sabbath came almost the whole city together to hear the word of God.* Acts 13: 14, 15, 42, 44. So that it is clear, that the Sabbath was Paul's resting-day and preaching-day, both to the Jews and Gentiles, that being the day that the Gentiles used to hear; and though they had a desire to hear the same words again, yet it must be next Sabbath; and Paul fulfills their desire, and preaches to them the next Sabbath, and almost the whole city came to hear. Can we think, if there had been no Sabbath, that Paul would have countenanced them so in their ignorance? Or, if the first day had been a day that was observed, would he not have told them so, that they might have heard the word before the next Sabbath. And when Paul came to Philippi, a Gentile city, mind what is said in Acts 16: 12, 13, *We were in that city abiding certain days, and on the Sabbath day we went out of the city by a river side, where prayer was wont to be made, and we sat down and spake unto the women that resorted thither.* The seventh day hath its title still, as is said by the Spirit in Acts; speaking of certain days, this is singled out and called the Sabbath day, with an account how they spent it, and the blessing they received upon it; they resorted to the place of prayer, and there they preached, and the Lord opened Lydia's heart to attend to the words of Paul. And in Acts 17: 2, it is said, *That Paul, as his manner was, went in unto them, and three Sabbath days reasoned with them out of the Scriptures.* And when Paul came to Corinth, which was a Gentile city, and found Aquila, a Jew, and his wife Priscilla, and because they were of the same craft, he abode with them, and wrought, for by occupation they were tent-makers, *he reasoned in the synagogue every Sabbath day, and persuaded the Jews and Greeks.* Acts 18 : 2—4. So that it is manifest, that the Greeks kept the Sabbath as well as the Jews, and that though Paul wrought at his trade and made tents, yet he rested every Sabbath day; and as we have an account how he spent his time, namely, in working at his trade, so we have an account how he spent his time on the Sabbath. Now, if it be such a strong argument for the observation of the first day, because Paul preached upon it once; what is this for the observation of the seventh day, that Paul did not only preach constantly upon it, but wherever the Spirit speaks of it he calls it the Sabbath day, without the least hint that he did so out of condescension to the weakness of others? And let it be shown by the Scriptures that the apostles did countenance and own any shadow that was done away, as they owned and countenanced the keeping of the Sabbath, and we may follow the apostles as they followed the Lord in this matter, though we have no express word that the churches kept it. And, indeed, I think I may say in this case, as the Apostle said in another, that it would have been superfluous for the apostles to have told any people in their time that such and such a church kept the Sabbath; it being a truth not so much as questioned, that we hear of, but Jews and Gentiles both observed it. But now I cease answering objections, as I have spoken to those that are the most material of them that I have heard, and I shall proceed to another ground.

8. Consider the bondage and slavery that both man and beast would be in if this doctrine were received for truth. Would it not now, however have the tendency to bring the world more to athe

ism? Some men would not allow themselves nor their servants time to rest, or heai the word of God, if they were persuaded that there was no Sabbath; yea, and the greater part of saints are left to the mercy of merciless men, most of them being children, and wives, and servants; and they cannot challenge a day in seven, or a day in seventy, as their right to rest upon, and to worship the Lord in, from any commandment of God, if this doctrine be true, that the Sabbath is abolished. And were this but to bring a yoke of bondage upon us, that neither we nor our fathers were able to bear, we should not so much as take notice at this time how it goes in probability, for the way of numbering is by sevens.

But some will say, It is good to observe one day in seven, though it be not a constant day. This will be confessed, for one to observe one day, and another to observe another day, while others are for a seventh day to be constantly observed. But why not the seventh day which God hath commanded, for the seventh day is the Sabbath? It plainly appears, that there is something of the table-law yet upon the table of the hearts of most men, though worn by much transgression; for men generally plead to have one day in seven to rest in, and yet because of custom they contend against this holy, just law of God, that was made in mercy for man. I am persuaded in my very heart, and that not without good ground, that if the seventh day had been observed as the first day is, no man that owns the Scriptures would have questioned whether it ought to be observed or not, or at least no opposition would have been made against it; and when all is said, custom and worldly interest are the two great things that stand in opposition to it.

9. And lastly, consider those great and precious promises made to them that keep the Sabbath according to the inside and spirituality of it; not that

we are so to spiritualize it as to make void the letter, but according to the letter, as Christ doth. For instance, he saith, *Ye have heard that it hath been said of old time, Thou shalt not commit adultery; but I say unto you, Whosoever looketh on a woman and lusteth after her, hath committed adultery with her in his heart.* Now, if it be adultery to lust, doubtless it is to act, and this is forbidden in the commandment, for the commandment is, *Thou shalt not commit adultery;* but Christ unfolds this commandment, and gives such a sense of it as the scribes and pharisees understood not. Again, the sixth commandment is, *Thou shalt do no murder;* and John saith, *Whosoever hateth his brother is a murderer.* John 3: 15. Now, all murder was forbidden in the commandment, yet this was not understood to be murder; but John obeyed the spirituality of the commandment. And the same may be said of the fourth commandment, *Remember the Sabbath day to keep it holy;* all servile work is forbidden in it, and that the pharisees understood; but they did not understand that works of mercy, as curing the sick, and healing the diseased, might be done upon it. Neither did they understand that inward and spiritual rest that was held out in the commandment, as appears by the words of the Lord in Isa. 58: 13, 14, *If thou turn away thy foot from the Sabbath, from doing thy pleasure on my holy day, and call the Sabbath a delight, the holy of the Lord, honorable, and shalt honor him, not doing thine own ways, nor finding thine own pleasure, nor speaking thine own words.* So that the saints are not only to cease from outward work in their callings, but also from works that are inward and spiritually wicked, that so the Sabbath may be a delight unto them, the holy of the Lord, honorable. And mark the promise that is to such Sabbath-keepers, in the fourteenth verse, *Then shalt thou delight thyself in the Lord, and I will cause thee to ride upon the high places of the earth, and will feed thee with the heritage of Jacob thy father; for the mouth of the Lord hath spoken it.* First, they shall delight themselves in the Lord, and that will make the Sabbath a delight. Second, they shall ride upon the high places of the earth; the high places of the earth holding forth, as I conceive, the great opposition, whether of great and mighty men, or great walled cities, according to that in Deut. 1: 28, which hath an allusion to Israel's subduing the land of Canaan. Deut. 32: 13. Thou shalt ride upon them, that is, subdue and conquer them. Psalm 45: 4, 66: 12. *They shall tread upon their high places.* Deut. 33: 39. *They shall be as ashes under the soles of their feet.* Mal. 4: 3. Now, when did the Lord's people do such work as this since this prophesy? or, is it yet to be fulfilled?

Again, consider what the Lord saith in Isa. 56: 6, 7, *Also the sons of the stranger that join themselves to the Lord, to serve him, and to love the name of the Lord, to be his servants, every one that keepeth the Sabbath from polluting it, and taketh hold of my covenant, even them will I bring to my holy mountain, and make them joyful in my house of prayer; their burnt offerings and their sacrifices shall be accepted upon mine altar, for mine house shall be called an house of prayer to all people.* By the sons of the stranger, I understand is here meant Gentiles, who were strangers to the commonwealth of Israel and afar off, but are now made nigh by the blood of Christ, and so they join themselves to the Lord, and serve him, and love the name of the Lord; these are such as keep the Sabbath, and take hold of God's covenant, and it is such a Sabbath as may be polluted, and therefore not Christ's, as some would have it. Now, the promises that are made to these strangers, do look at clear gospel times.

They shall be brought into God's holy mountain.

and there be made joyful, when it is so mountainous that it is the house of prayer for all people, or for all nations, as Christ saith in Matt. 11: 17. *Blessed is the man that doeth this, and the son of man that taketh hold on it, that keepeth the Sabbath from polluting it, and keepeth his hand from doing any evil. Thus saith the Lord unto the eunuchs that keep my Sabbath, and choose the things that please me, and take hold on my covenant, even unto them will I give a name and a place better than of sons and daughters; I will give them an everlasting name, that shall not be cut off.* Isa. 56: 2, 4, 5. The eunuchs are such as care for the things that please the Lord, when the married careth for the things that please his wife. Cor. 7: 32, 33. And when two parts shall be cut off and die, the eunuchs that keep the Sabbath shall have an everlasting name, which shall not be cut off.

Now, let us not think it incredible that the Sabbath should be yet in force, because it hath been so long laid aside; it hath been so with other truths, and so with this, before now. It seemed to be so out of knowledge with Israel in the wilderness, that when the people had gathered twice as much manna on the sixth day, they did not understand the meaning of it; but the nobles came and told Moses, and he told them what the Lord had said, that to-morrow should be the rest of the holy Sabbath. And also, after their coming out of Babylon, when they had built the house of God, and set it in order, placing the priests and Levites, and had chosen faithful men to distribute the maintenance to their brethren. Neh. 13: 10, 13. In a word, their reformation was much about the light of ours, and it is confessed by the enlightened that it was a type of this reformation that the Lord hath begun amongst us in these isles, namely, in bringing his people out of Babylon, and building up of Zion; and, indeed, as their sins and ours are alike in many things, so in this, namely in breaking the fourth commandment; for Nehemiah saith, in chap. 13: 15, that in those days he saw in Judah some treading wine-presses on the Sabbath, and lading asses, and bringing in sheaves, as also wine, grapes, and figs, and all manner of burdens, which they brought into Jerusalem upon the Sabbath day; and he testified against them in the day wherein they sold victuals. Notwithstanding all the reformation, yet this was seen in Judah. They had laid by the observation of the Sabbath, and had made it a common working, market day, as may be seen at large in that chapter. It was not in vain, therefore, that the Lord said, *Remember the Sabbath*, he foreseeing how it would be slighted and forgotten, not only by those that were brought out of literal Babylon, but also by those that should be brought out of spiritual Babylon in the latter days; and when the day of the Lord burns as an oven, it will be remembered to some purpose. Mal. 4: 4. In the mean time, the Lord is stirring up some of his poor babes and sucklings. Such he is pleased usually to discover truth unto at the first breaking out of it, and they are to contend for it, though in much weakness.

But a word to the beginning and ending of the Sabbath. There are various apprehensions about it, which, for brevity's sake, I shall omit. The Scripture is plain, that from evening to evening is the set time, or from the going down of the sun to the going down of the sun. This is clear from the beginning, according to Gen. 1: 5, *The evening and the morning was the first day.* The evening and morning make a complete natural day, and the evening goeth before the morning, because the darkness was before the light.

Obj. But some will say, It is not said the evening and the morning was the seventh day.

Ans. If the evening and the morning be the sixth day, the evening and the morning must needs be the seventh day, unless we should think that the seventh day hath no night belonging to it. Some think that the reason why no mention is made of the evening of the seventh day, is, because the Sabbath is a day of joy and delight, or an earnest of the new Jerusalem state, wherein shall be no night. Rev. 21 : 25. Night doth frequently, in the Scripture, hold forth a state of affliction, but the Sabbath is a holy, sanctified time; on it the Creator rested and was refreshed, and commanded the observation of it that his creatures might be refreshed.

Nehemiah's practice is sufficient proof for the beginning of the Sabbath at evening, (chap. 13 : 19,) who, when the gates of Jerusalem began to be dark, commanded them to be shut till after the Sabbath. And if you would know when the evening begins, the evangelist Mark doth inform you in chapter 1 : 32, *At even, when the sun did set, they brought unto him all that were diseased.* When the sun doth set, then begins the evening, then begins the holy rest or seventh-day Sabbath. So the disciples of Christ began the Sabbath; and so the Lord's ancient people celebrate the Sabbath unto this day.

But what confusion are they in who say the Sabbath was changed from the seventh day to the first day, and yet observe neither, but part of the first day and part of the second day; for they begin their Sabbath at midnight, when a good part of the first day is spent, and they end at midnight, when a good part of the second day is spent; and yet they will have this to be a Sabbath, yea, and a first day Sabbath, and will highly charge a man to be an offender if he work one hour upon the first day, though themselves work five; and thus we see how anti-Christ hath changed times as well as laws; a first-day Sabbath instead of a seventh-day Sabbath; instead of from even to even, from midnight to midnight, when most are fast asleep, being insensible of the beginning of their Sabbath, or the ending of it.

But, blessed be the Lord, that he hath revealed this his ancient, useful, and honorable truth, to wit, the holy seventh-day Sabbath, notwithstanding all the inventions of anti-Christ to bury it in oblivion, and that he is pleased to separate a remnant, that are resolved to search and try their ways, and to turn unto him, to follow him in the ways of his precepts, (notwithstanding the dragon's wrath,) who will not take things upon trust, nor go upon the legs of men, but will try all things, and hold fast that which is good, for they are virgins, and they will follow the Lamb, though their company be small and their charge great. They will not be afraid of the Sabbath because it was given to the Jews, any more than they are afraid of the adoption, and the glory, and the promises, and the other nine lively oracles, which were all given to the Jews. Rom. 9: 4. And this I may modestly say, to the praise of the Lord of the Sabbath, and without boasting, that if the saints did know how the Lord delights to meet with his people in this way of obedience in celebrating the Sabbath, they would soon call the *Sabbath a delight, the holy of the Lord, honorable*, and honor him by ceasing from their own works, as God did from his, and doing those works which are suitable for the blessed season. But I shall say no more at present, save only this, that whoever they are that would follow the Lord in this appointment of his, they must labor much in the strength of his Spirit to get this world under them, for it stands in direct opposition to earthly men, and earthly principles; therefore pray with the Psalmist, *Incline my heart unto thy testimonies, and not to covetousness.*

VINDICATION

OF

THE TRUE SABBATH

IN TWO PARTS:

PART FIRST,

Narrative of Recent Events;

PART SECOND,

Divine Appointment of the Seventh Day.

By J. W. MORTON,

LATE MISSIONARY OF THE REFORMED PRESBYTERIAN CHURCH.

NEW-YORK:

PUBLISHED FOR THE AUTHOR,

AT THE SABBATH RECORDER OFFICE,

No. 9 Spruce Street.

PART I.

NARRATIVE OF RECENT EVENTS

CHAPTER I.

On the 13th of December, 1847, I landed with my family in Port-au-Prince, Haïti, the first Foreign Missionary of the Reformed Presbyterian Church in the United States. I began my labors soon afterwards, and continued them, without serious interruption, till the 21st of April, 1849, when a train of circumstances, to which I am about to advert, made it necessary that I should return home.

In the latter part of December, 1848, I was unexpectedly called upon to defend the practice of keeping holy the first day of the week, in place of the seventh. I had been taught from my infancy, that the moral law, "summarily comprehended in the ten commandments," is the only rule of moral conduct; and I had supposed, that it required me and everybody else to keep the "Christian Sabbath" on the first day of the week. On examination, however, I was forced to the conclusion, that the fourth commandment enjoins nothing else than the sanctification of the seventh day. Of course, then, I must either renounce this precept, as a part of the rule of my life, or endeavor to keep holy the seventh day of the week. The former I might not dare to do; the latter I knew I might *attempt*, without offending God, or insulting the majesty of his law.

The question then came up, Is there any scripture authority for keeping holy the first day? Does God require it? I knew very well, that if God does *not* require it, I could not, as a Reformed Presbyterian, bind my conscience to it. I took up the Bible, resolved on a prayerful and thorough search. I wished to assure myself of the divine authority of the first day, even after I was satisfied that the claims of the seventh are indisputable. But how was it possible to gain this object? Every text to which I was referred for proof seemed to lack the very thing that I most wanted, *a certain testimony to the institution of a Christian Sabbath.* I reasoned thus:—The fact that Christ appeared once or twice to his disciples on the first day of the week, and the fact that the disciples met *once* on that day to break bread, and the fact that Paul commanded the Corinthians and Galatians to 'lay by them in store' on that day, as God had prospered them—these facts, with a few others, *might* shed light on the *institution*, if *one single text* could be found, to prove its *existence.* But if this can not be found, they do not touch the question at issue. And how I did long for that *one text!* How I chided with the Apostles for not having made known more clearly what I had determined to be the will of God! Never did Rachel mourn for her children, as I mourned for that *one text:* but, like her, I could not be comforted, because *it was not!*

I was thus driven to the conclusion, that, should I make conscience of keeping holy the first day of the week, I would offer to God a service that he did not require, and could not accept at my hands.

But what was I to do? This was the great *practical* question. Could I, with my then present views, continue to preach the gospel, as I had done before, in that "land of darkness, and of the shadow of death?" Could I teach the children in the school, as I had taught them before, that God had changed the Sabbath to the first day of the week? Could I proclaim to the benighted heathen, that they might habitually break the fourth commandment with impunity? Could I, as a Protestant missionary, become the partizan of him who thought "to change times and laws,"* by assuring his blinded devotees, that his changes had been made by divine authority? Or, on the other hand, could I carry out my convictions of truth and duty, declaring the whole counsel of God, as I then understood it, and retain, at the same time, my connection with my brethren at home? Would they grant me this privilege, and, if they would, could I accept it?

A little reflection served to convince me, that all these questions must be answered in the negative. It was no small matter, to resolve upon breaking those bonds of ecclesiastical fellowship that had so sweetly bound me to the Reformed Presbyterian Church. A struggle, painful indeed, but not protracted, ensued. I resolved at once to keep the Sabbath in my family, though I feared it would not be honest to make any *public* exhibition of my views, while I continued to minister by the authority of the Synod. I know not what I should have done, had not my change of sentiments brought with it the needed consolations. Whatever were the "vexing thoughts" with which my heart was oppressed, during the first six days of the week, I found invariably, in the quiet retreat of my little family, on the seventh, that "peace of God that passeth all understanding." Yes, Haïti, when the recollection of thy brilliant skies, thy evergreen mountains, and thy

* I believe, that the prophecy in Dan. 7: 25, refers mainly to the change of Sabbath-time, and Sabbath-law. What time, of divine appointment, it may be asked, was ever changed, except the time of the Sabbath?

sweet clear rivers, shall have ceased to awaken joy in my bosom, the memory of thy Sabbaths shall be "my songs in the house of my pilgrimage!"

CHAPTER II.

Convinced as I was, that something must be done immediately to bring the subject of my change to the attention of the rulers of our church, before the next meeting of Synod, I prepared the following Circular Letter, which I transmitted to more than seventy ministers and elders, in different parts of the United States.

CIRCULAR.

PORT-AU-PRINCE, Haïti, Jan. 17, 1849.

MY DEAR BROTHER,—The mutual relation existing between us, as members of the same Synod, the glory of our common Lord, the interests of our Mission, and a sacred regard for personal character, all require, that the following statement be transmitted to you and my other co-presbyters, with as little delay as possible. If I am not actuated herein by a desire to promote God's glory and the salvation of men, may the Lord rebuke and forgive me, and "let the righteous smite me, it shall be a kindness!" May the Head of the Church grant to you, and to all the other members of Synod, a disposition to hear, with patience and candor, a narration of my recent experience, in which perhaps you *may* find things both "new and old."

My sentiments in relation to the "Sabbath of the Lord our God," have undergone an important change; to which I now wish to call your attention. Our Confession of Faith, Catechisms, and Testimony, all teach that the first day of the week is, and has been ever since the resurrection of Christ, the Christian Sabbath. This doctrine *alone*, of all those contained in our Standards, though I did believe it till lately, I can no longer receive. As to the *manner* of sanctifying the Sabbath, I believe all that you and I have always contended for; but, for the present, I am constrained to believe, that the seventh day of the week is the only weekly Sabbath that God has ever appointed.

My attention was first called to this subject by Rev. W. M. Jones, Missionary of the Baptist Church, who has recently abandoned his earlier views and practice in regard to the Sabbath. He not only argued the question with me at length, but gave me some publications of the American Sabbath Tract Society, which, as they seemed to breathe a spirit of ardent piety and zeal for God's law, I read with attention. Both in my discussion with him, and in the reading of those tracts, I struggled with all my might to convince myself, from the Scriptures, of the divine appointment of the first-day, or Christian Sabbath. But though I did not then doubt it, I was astonished to find how hard it is to prove it.

I searched all the books I could find, bearing on this question, and discovered, what I had never noticed before, that the early French and Genevan Reformers, with Calvin at their head, had taught the abrogation of the fourth commandment, as a ceremonial institution; and that they contended for a Sabbath, or stated day of worship, under the gospel, only as a wise and necessary human arrangement. I found that even Turretin, at a later period, had taught that the fourth commandment is *partly* ceremonial, and that it was necessary to change the Sabbath from the seventh day, in order to put a difference between Jews and Christians. I found also, in my books, quotations, containing similar sentiments, from the celebrated Augsburg Confession. The only authors I could find who had attempted to prove, from the Scriptures, that the Sabbath has been changed from the seventh to the first day of the week, by divine authority, were, Turretin, and the framers of our Standards. These authors appeared to depend *mainly* for proof upon three texts of Scripture:—Acts 20: 7; 1 Cor. 16: 1, 2; and Rev. 1: 10. When I came to examine these texts, I was surprised and mortified, to find that they contain neither the word "Sabbath," nor any other synonymous with it. True, I had always thought that the "Lord's day," Rev. 1: 10, was the first day of the week; but my opponents contended that the terms refer more properly to the seventh, which God styles "my holy day," Is. 58: 13; and when I remembered "his challenging a special propriety in the seventh," I could not well deny it. Moreover, I could not find a single passage asserting that the first is holier than any other day of the week, or that Christians were, in the Apostles' days, in the habit of holding religious meetings *regu-*

larly on that day. Neither could I discover that Christ or his Apostles had ever spoken, directly or indirectly, of keeping a day holy in honor of his resurrection; nor that that event, which is always held up as the occasion of the change of the Sabbath, is even once mentioned in connection with the first day, unless where it is recorded as a historical fact. On the other hand, I observed that Christ and his Apostles *were accustomed* to enter into the synagogue on the seventh day, or Sabbath, for public worship. Luke 4: 16; Acts 17: 2, and elsewhere.

Thus, my dear brother, I saw at this critical moment all Scripture evidence forsaking me, while every inch of ground on which I could set my foot was trembling. It seemed as if the thunders of Sinai were uttering anew their awful threatenings, while the "still small voice" of "Him that dwelt in the bush" was whispering in my ears, "The *seventh* day is the Sabbath of the Lord thy God." Ex. 20: 10. "I am Jehovah, I change not." Mal. 3: 6. "Verily, I say unto you, till heaven and earth pass, one jot or one tittle shall in no wise pass from the law, till all be fulfilled." Matt. 5: 18. Still I hesitated. For a moment I thought of "going down to Egypt for help." The Fathers, thought I, have fixed the interpretation of these texts in favor of the observance of the first day. But immediately I heard a voice within me, saying, "Would you then observe a holy-day, whose appointment cannot be proved from the Bible, without the aid of human tradition? Could you admit the 'testimony of the Fathers,' to set aside one of the plainest injunctions of the moral law, that law that was written upon tables of stone, 'by the finger of God,' and styled, by way of preëminence, '*the* Testimony?'" No! I replied, with an involuntary shudder; and another flood of Scriptures came rushing in, like "deep waters," to the very soul. "The law of the Lord is perfect." Ps. 19: 7. "Forever, O Lord, thy word is settled in heaven." Ps. 119: 89. "Thy righteousness is an everlasting righteousness, and thy law is the truth." Ps. 119: 142. "All his commandments are sure; they stand fast forever and ever, and are done in truth and uprightness." Ps. 111: 7, 8. "Think not that I am come to destroy the law or the prophets; I am not come to destroy, but to fulfill." Matt. 5: 17. "Do we then make void the law through faith? God forbid; yea, we establish the law." Rom. 3: 31. O my brother, "the word of God is quick and powerful, and sharper than any two-edged sword."

You have now my reasons for embracing a doctrine which is confessedly at variance with our Standards. What I entreat of you is, that you will once more examine this subject for yourself, and see whether those Standards are consistent, on this point, either with the Scriptures, or with themselves.

You perhaps think that I have forsaken the "footsteps of the flock," and that testimony which has been sealed with the blood of martyrs. But tell me candidly, was there ever a martyr who died in defense of the first-day Sabbath? Or, could *you*, my brother, collect from the Scriptures evidence of its divine appointment, clear enough to solace your soul in the midst of the flames? From my inmost soul I pity that Covenanter who may be called to testify, at the stake, to the change of the Sabbath from the seventh to the first day of the week. Remember, too, that I am now in the path that was trodden by the saints for more than four thousand years; and it is for *you* to show that that path was ever stopped up, unless by the presumption and inexcusable neglect of man. Truly, I am "compassed about by a great cloud of witnesses." I would follow the example of Jehovah himself, who "blessed the seventh day and sanctified it," and by whom "the Sabbath was made for man;" the example of Adam, Enoch, and Noah; of Abraham, Isaac, Jacob, and the twelve patriarchs; of Moses, Aaron, and those millions of Pilgrim Covenanters who united in its observance in the wilderness; the example of Samuel, David, and a host of other prophets; of Jesus Christ, our Divine Mediator, and "Lord of the Sabbath;" and of the Apostles of our Lord, together with the churches established and watered by them;—in one word, the example of all the saints, from Adam to the last Apostle; all of whom kept and honored the seventh day as "the Sabbath of the Lord their God," and, having finished their course with joy, are entered into that heavenly rest, of which that Sabbath was, and still is, an emblem.

I intend, if the Lord will, to be present at the next meeting of our Synod, and meet my brethren face to face. I expect, of course, nothing less than to be excluded from the privileges of the church; but I rejoice that I have learned to respect the discipline of the Lord's house. I desire, therefore, with a willing heart to approach the altar, and, if the Head of the Church require it, to be "offered upon the sacrifice and service of your faith," that God may be glorified in my salvation, and not in my destruction. God forbid, that either prejudice, willful ignorance, passion, or personal resentment, should fan the flames of that altar!

In conclusion, rest assured of my continued and unabated attachment to the cause of the Reformation, in general, and to the interests of the Reformed Presbyterian Church, in particular; and allow me to repeat what I have already intimated, that with every other doctrine contained in our Standards I am, so far as I understand my profession, entirely satisfied; nor have I abandoned *this one*, but from a firm conviction that it is not taught in God's Word. I know well, that trials sore and many await me. God doth know, that my heart delighteth not in contention; but, my brother, have we not all "entered into a curse, and into an oath, to walk in God's law, which was given by Moses, the servant of God, and to observe and do all the commandments of the Lord our God?" Neh. 10: 29.

Your Brother in Gospel bonds,
J. W. MORTON,
Missionary of the Ref. Presb. Church

CHAPTER III.

On the 21st of April, 1849, I set sail, with my family, from Port-au-Prince, bidding farewell to Haïti and her children, whom perhaps we shall never see again in this vale of tears. We arrived at Boston, all in good health, on the first Sabbath in May.

On the evening of Tuesday, May 22, the Synod was convened in Philadelphia; and the next morning I appeared and took my seat with the other members.

After noon, the same day, Rev. David Scott stated to Synod, that I had made known a change of views in relation to the Sabbath, and moved that a committee of three be appointed to confer with me, and report what farther action should be taken in the case.

While this motion was pending, I stated, in substance, that, as I was alone in a Synod of more than sixty members, without a single man to plead my cause, I thought I had a right to *demand* that the proceedings should be instituted in strict accordance with the letter of the law. I was here interrupted by the Moderator, who, having informed me that I had no right to dictate to the Court the method of proceeding with its own business, peremptorily ordered me to take my seat. I obeyed, of course, though I could not see what dictation there was in demanding a legal trial, according to the printed rules of Synod. The motion was carried, and the committee appointed.

Next morning, May 24, I had a conference of half an hour with this committee, and at noon another, that lasted about the same time. Their principal object seemed to be, to ascertain whether I was ready to *recant*, and submit to censure for my past errors. I assured them, that while I had not the slightest wish to withdraw from the communion of the Reformed Presbyterian Church, I adhered to every word in my Circular, and must continue to do so, till convinced of error by the infallible scriptures. The committee quoted several texts, and advised me to read several authors, after which our conference was closed.

After noon they presented their report, recommending that the following Libel be preferred against me by Synod:—

LIBEL PREFERRED AGAINST J. W. MORTON.

Whereas, denying that the first day of the week is the day on which the Christian Sabbath should be kept, is a heinous sin and scandal, contrary to the Word of God, and the Profession of the Reformed Presbyterian Church, founded thereon —(*Acts* 20: 7, " And upon the first day of the week, when the disciples came together to break bread," &c.; *Shorter Catechism*, " From the beginning of the world to the resurrection of Christ, God appointed the seventh day of the week to be the weekly Sabbath, and the first day of the week ever since to continue to the end of the world, which is the Christian Sabbath."

Yet true it is, that you, Rev. J. W. Morton, are guilty of the scandal above stated, in so far as you, the said J. W. Morton, at Port-au Prince, Haïti, 17th of January, 1849, did publish a Circular, in which you oppugned and denied that the first day of the week is the Christian Sabbath, which being found relevant, and proved against you, you ought to be proceeded against by the censures of the Lord's House.

A true copy. By order of the Synod.
[Signed] JOHN WALLACE, Ass't Clerk.

After some discussion, the above Libel was decided to be relevant, and the Clerk was directed to serve a copy on me, with citation to appear for trial the next day, after noon.

I went to my lodgings that evening with a heavy heart. I was convinced, from the spirit of determined opposition that had been manifested by many of the brethren, when the Libel was under consideration, that the majority had already determined that I should not be permitted to "speak for myself." True, I knew very well that the Apostle Paul had once enjoyed this liberty, through the cool civility of a Roman Governor, and afterwards, through that of a Roman King; but I knew just *as* well, that Felix and Aggrippa were heathens, while my brethren are Christians; and that the dignity of a court, composed of "worms of the dust," has been much better understood, since the famous "Diet of Worms," than ever before.

Still, I could not forbear asking myself, Why is there now such bitter opposition to an Institution that was once the delight of both God and man? Why do men hate with such perfect hatred what Jehovah made, and blessed, and sanctified, before sin had entered into the world? Why should *this* daughter of Innocence be spurned from every door, and loaded with the damning reproach of Judaism, while her twin sister, Marriage, sucks the breasts, and is dandled upon the knees of Orthodoxy? Why should I be ranked with thieves and murderers, for believing that "the seventh day is the Sabbath of the Lord my God?" Bitter were the tears that flowed; and more bitter still was the reflection, that "when I wept, that was to my reproach."

I was hedged in round about, and what could I do? I could only exclaim, with the "sweet Singer of Israel," "Let not them that wait on thee, O Lord God of Hosts, be ashamed for my sake; let not those that seek thee be confounded for my sake, O God of Israel. Because for thy sake I have borne reproach; shame hath covered my face. I am become a stranger unto my brethren, and an alien unto my mother's children. For the zeal of thy house hath eaten me up; and the reproaches of them that reproached thee are fallen upon me." Never shall I forget the sensation experienced while the last sentence was passing through my mind: "*And the reproaches of them that reproached thee are fallen upon me.*" I know not how often, during that night, I repeated these words, and compared them with the exhortation of the Apostle: "Let us go forth therefore unto him without the camp, bearing his reproach." These were the comforts, that, "in the multitude of my thoughts within me," then delighted my soul. I was about to go forth "without the camp;" and it was indeed refreshing, in that hour of trial, to believe, that I was bearing a portion of the same burden that had once bowed down the 'Man of Sorrows."

2

CHAPTER IV.

My trial came on after noon, May 25th. The following extract from the published Minutes of Synod is, I believe, a correct, and sufficiently full, account of the final issue; only it makes no mention of the fact that I protested against the proceedings, and appealed to the head of the Church, for reasons to be given in afterwards. Why this fact was not recorded, I have not been able to ascertain.

EXTRACT FROM MINUTES OF SYNOD.

Order of the day, viz., the case of Mr. Morton, called for. The libel was then read by the Clerk; when Mr. Morton having, in reply to the Moderator, answered that he was prepared for trial, the substance of the libel was again stated in his hearing. Mr. Morton was then called upon, according to the rule provided for in such cases, either to confess the charge or put himself upon his trial. Mr. Morton in return acknowledged that he had denied that the day commonly called the Christian Sabbath is so by Divine appointment, and then proceeded to plead the irrelevancy of the charge by endeavoring to prove the perpetuity of the law for the observance of the seventh day. While so doing, he was arrested by the Moderator, who informed him that the charge contained in the libel was such that Mr. Morton could only prove its irrelevancy to censure by proving that the appropriation of the first day of the week, known as the Christian Sabbath, to secular employments, or teaching so to do, is not relevant to censure, which attempt the Moderator would consider disorderly, and would not allow.

From this decision J. M. Willson appealed, when the Moderator's decision was unanimously sustained. Upon this Mr. Morton declined the authority of the court.

Resolved, That Mr. Morton's appointment as missionary to Haïti be revoked.

Resolved, That inasmuch as Mr. Morton has now publicly declined the authority of this court, he be suspended from the exercise of the Christian ministry, and from the privileges of the Reformed Presbyterian Church.

The Moderator then publicly pronounced the sentence of suspension on Mr. Morton, agreeably to the above resolution

Not long afterwards I presented to the Moderator the following Reasons of Protest and Appeal, with a request that he would allow them to be laid before the court, which he utterly refused to do.

REASONS OF PROTEST AND APPEAL.

I do respectfully protest against the action of Synod in my case, on the 24th of the present month, and appeal therefrom to the Lord Jesus Christ, the King and Head of the Church, for the following reasons :—

1st. Because I was not allowed to prove the irrelevancy of the charge made against me, by an appeal to the Bible, " the only rule of faith and manners. "

2nd. Because I believe that the statements, on the subject of the Sabbath, set forth in our subordinate standards, are inconsistent with one another, and in part contrary to the Word of God : yet it was by these unscriptural portions, that I was tried and condemned.

Brethren, I entertain no hard feelings towards you. My daily prayer to God is, that you may be saved, and led into all truth. I did hope that you would hear and consider the claims of the Lord 's holy Sabbath, when presented in a mild and affectionate manner. But either I have failed to present the question with sufficient tenderness, or you have determined to avoid all discussion in regard to it.

It grieves me to the soul to bid you farewell. Both God and man will bear witness, in the day of final reckoning, that you have trampled down, by the resistless force of an overwhelming majority, one who was endeavoring with both hands to hold up the standard of the great Covenant God of our fathers. But though for the present cast down, I am not dismayed. The Sabbath of the Lord God is a richer treasure than the richest you can either give or take away. " Rejoice not against me, O mine enemy ; when I fall, I shall arise ; when I sit in darkness, the Lord will be a light unto me. I will bear the indignation of the Lord, because I have sinned against him, until he plead my cause, and execute judgment for me ; he will bring me forth to the light, and I shall behold his righteousness."

Brethren, I shall meet you before the judgment seat of Christ, on that day when he shall come "with ten thousand of his saints." "Behold, he cometh with clouds ; and every eye shall see him, and they also which pierced him ; and all kindreds of the earth shall wail because of him. Even so, amen."

J. W. Morton

Philadelphia, May 29th, 1849.

REFLECTIONS.

I did believe, and believe yet, that, had I been sustained by twenty ministers and as many congregations, I should have had leave to defend myself to my heart's content. But it was very evident to the Synod, that I stood alone. They knew that I could do them no harm, by fomenting discord ; and —may I not add?—they knew that I was not the man to be found employed in such a work. The only loss they could sustain, in cutting me off, with all my adherents, was that of two adults and as many little children. Indeed, many of the members *seemed* to regret the *trouble* far more than the *necessity* of executing the law ; and one aged father has remarked to me since, that till then he never witnessed a trial, before a church court, in which *there was not one atom of mercy.*

Now, is there not a reason for all this? Unquestionably there is. The loose and unpresbyterial doctrine, that a majority has a right to determine what *is*, and what *is not* truth, and that the greater the majority in favor of any dogma, the more firmly its truth is established, has leavened, sadly and extensively, even the Reformed Presbyterian Church. This is the reason why one who represents a lean minority cannot be heard, even in defense of ecclesiastical life. The majority have said, that the first day is the Sabbath, and who dare call in question the assertion? A man may be denounced as a covenant-breaker; yet, because he belongs to a small minority, he may not attempt to prove his innocence of the crime. Thus the right of the minority to vindicate themselves from the Scriptures, in defense of which many of the old Covenanters bled, is practically denied by their descendants. "O Lord, how long!"

Brethren, are you really so wedded to this *majority principle?* Know, then, that *God is a majority;* and that those that are with *me* are more than those that are with *you.* God's testimony is worth more than that of all men. What though millions *have* affirmed, that the seventh day is NOT the Sabbath? *He* hath left us this imperishable testimony: "The seventh day IS the Sabbath of the Lord thy God." And this is the testimony of the *greatest majority* that ever gave utterance to truth. But God hath not left himself without other witnesses. Where are those myriads of angels who were present when "the Sabbath was made for man?" Where are those "morning stars" who "sang together," and those "sons of God" who "shouted for joy," when our Father "laid the foundations of the earth?" They are not *now* present with us, 't is true, to bear their testimony; but they *will be* present, when you and I shall appear before the judgment seat of Christ, to hear the decision of this controversy. And do you think that you will then dare, on the authority of what is said in Acts 20: 7, to lift up your hands, and swear "by Him that liveth forever and ever," that the Sabbath has been "changed into the first day of the week"—and that, too, in presence of those who saw the foundations of the ancient Sabbath, like those of the earth itself, laid and balanced upon God's eternal decree, and inwrought with the very stones of "the everlasting hills?" No! No!! The Sabbath was one of those *pillars* of the ancient earth, which Christ, the Mediator, seized with the hand of his omnipotence, and bare up, when "the earth and all its inhabitants" were sinking into nothing. I repeat it —and who dare gainsay it?—the Lord of Hosts is an overwhelming *majority!*

But this is not all. There is, indeed, no *greater* witness than these; but there is *other* witness. Look into your own hearts, ye children of God, redeemed by the blood of the Lamb, and you will find recorded there: "The seventh day is the Sabbath of the Lord thy God; in it thou shalt not do any work." "For this is the covenant that I will make with the house of Israel, after those days, saith the Lord; I will put *my laws* into their mind, and write them in their hearts." Here there is not the least hint of any exception. The same moral law that was written "with the finger of God," on tables of stone, is now written "by the Spirit of the living God," on the fleshly tables of *your* hearts. Yes, brethren, turn your eyes inward, and you will read, "The seventh day is the Sabbath of the Lord thy God; in it thou shalt not do any work." If you say, We have sought this law, but find it not—O brethren, you have not "sought it carefully with tears." It is hidden among the rubbish, and you will never find it, till that be removed. But I speak what I do know, when I assure you, that it *is* recorded there; and in the day of the Lord Jesus, if not sooner, you will find it there, to your unspeakable joy and satisfaction. O Lord, "open thou our eyes, that we may behold wondrous things out of thy law."

PART II.

DIVINE APPOINTMENT OF THE SEVENTH DAY

INTRODUCTION.

The following pages, containing a brief discussion of a small but intensely interesting portion of the Sabbath controversy, are designed especially for the perusal of those Christians, styled orthodox, who do not keep holy the seventh day of the week.

Dear brethren, this is a subject of fearful importance. If the views herein advocated are correct, *you* are guilty both of breaking and of teaching men to break one of God 's holy commandments ; if they are incorrect, I am no less guilty. Need I say any thing more to convince you that you ought to give this subject a candid and prayerful examination? " Ye are the light of the world ;" take heed, brethren, that your light be not darkness ! You know—you cannot but know—that there is much, *very much*, said in the Bible about the Sabbath, and that men are very often commanded to keep it holy. You must know, also, that God has said in the fourth commandment, "The *seventh day* is the Sabbath of the Lord thy God ; in it thou shalt not do any work ; " and that, for more than four thousand years, no other day of the week ever claimed to be holy. Moreover, you cannot but know, if you have read the Bible carefully, that the first day of the week, which you call " the Christian Sabbath," is *very seldom* mentioned ; that there are only six passages in which the name occurs, and that four of these may be viewed as one, being the records of the same events, by different Evangelists; and how can you have failed to notice the fact, that in not one of these six passages are we, or any of our fellow-creatures, commanded to keep the first day holy? Yet you are convinced that the first day of the week is *the very Sabbath-day*, while among all those Scripture commands, before referred to, you find nothing to sustain the claims of the seventh. O brethren, you "put darkness for light, and light for darkness." Let us bow before the mercy-seat of Him who is the Author of life and light, and, renewing our personal covenant with him, plead his precious promise: "If ye continue in my word, then are ye my disciples indeed; and ye shall know the truth, and the truth shall make you free."

I shall endeavor, in the following pages, to establish the truth of the following proposition :—

That the seventh day of the week is the only weekly Sabbath of God's appointment.

I intend to present and enforce *four reasons* for believing this proposition :—

First—Because the original Sabbath law requires the sanctification of no other day.

Second—Because Adam and all his posterity have solemnly covenanted to keep holy the seventh day.

Third—Because Christ and his Apostles honored this day; and did not intimate that it would ever cease to be the Sabbath, but the contrary.

Fourth—Because God has never blessed and sanctified any day of the week but the seventh.

As the discussion is limited by design to a narrow range, you will please to bear in mind, that the following points are assumed as true :—

First—The Sabbath was instituted before the fall of man.

Second—Adam represented all his posterity in the covenant of works.

Third—The Sabbath law is perpetual, "binding all men in all ages."

Fourth—The seventh day was the *only* weekly Sabbath for at least four thousand years.

Lord, sanctify us by thy truth. May the Holy Ghost, the Comforter, whom thou sendest in the name of thy Son our Lord, abide in us and preside in this controversy. May he teach us all things, and bring all things to our remembrance. May all bitterness, and wrath, and malice, and evil-speaking, be far from us; and may we love one another with pure hearts fervently—for Christ's sake. Amen.

CHAPTER I.

PROPOSITION.

That the seventh day of the week is the only weekly sabbath of God's appointment.

First Reason.

My first reason for believing this proposition is, That the original Sabbath law, referred to in Genesis 2 : 2, 3, and embodied in Exodus 20 : 8—11, requires the sanctification of no other day.

Genesis 2: 2, 3.—"And on the seventh day (*on day the seventh*) God ended his work which he had made; and he rested on the seventh day (*on day the seventh*) from all his work which he had made. And God blessed the seventh DAY (*the day the seventh*,) and sanctified it: because that in IT he had rested from all his work which God created and made."

Exodus 20: 8, 11.—"Remember the Sabbath-DAY, (*the day of the rest, or Sabbath*,) to keep it holy. Six days shalt thou labor, and do all thy work; but the seventh day (*day the seventh*) is the Sabbath (*rest*) of the Lord thy God: *in it* thou shalt not do any manner of work, thou, nor thy son, nor thy daughter, thy man-servant, nor thy maid-servant, nor thy cattle, nor thy stranger that *is* within thy gates: for in six days the Lord made heaven and earth, the sea, and all that in them *is*, and rested the seventh day (*on day the seventh*;) wherefore the Lord blessed the Sabbath-DAY (*the day of the rest, or Sabbath*,) and hallowed IT."

The only object, direct or indirect, of this commandment, is "*the day*." What are we commanded to remember? "The day." What are we required to keep holy? "The day." What did the Lord bless and hallow? "The day." In what are we forbidden to work? In "the day." Now let us inquire—

1. What day? *Not* the day of Adam's fall; nor the day Noah went into the ark; nor the day of the overthrow of Sodom; nor the day of the Exodus; nor the day of the Provocation; nor the day of the removal of the ark; nor the day of Christ's birth; nor the day of his crucifixion; nor the day of his resurrection; nor the day of his ascension; nor the day of judgment. It may be, and certainly is, proper, that we should remember all these; but we are not told to do so in this commandment. Neither is it some one day of the week, but no one in particular; for how could we remember "*the* day," that is no day in particular?—how could we keep holy "*the* day" that has not been specified?—and how could we say that God had blessed and hallowed "*the* day," that was no one day more than another? What day, then? God says, Remember *the Sabbath-day*, or *the day of the Sabbath;* Keep holy *the*

day of the Sabbath; The Lord blessed and hallowed *the day of the Sabbath.* He also says, *The seventh day* is the Sabbath of the Lord thy God ; *in it* thou shalt not do any work. This day, therefore, is " the seventh day," or " the day of the Sabbath."

2. What Sabbath? Not "*a* Sabbath," or any Sabbath that man may invent, or that God may hereafter keep ; for that would be " some Sabbath," but no one in particular. Not some institution yet undetermined, that God may require man to observe weekly ; for the command is not, " Remember the Sabbath institution," but, " Remember the *day* of the Sabbath ;" not, " Keep holy the Sabbath institution," but, " Keep holy the *day* of the Sabbath." The Lord did not bless and hallow " the Sabbath institution," but " the *day* of the Sabbath." We are not forbidden to do work in " the Sabbath institution," but in " the *seventh day.*" In fact, the phrase " the Sabbath," in this commandment, means neither more nor less than " the rest." It is not *here* the name of any institution at all, though it is often thus used in other parts of the Bible. Hence, this Sabbath is " the Sabbath or rest of the Lord thy God."

3. Which day of the week is "the day of the Sabbath?" No other than that day on which the Lord rested ; for the command refers to God's Sabbath. On which day of the week did he rest? " And he rested on the seventh day." Genesis 2 : 2. Therefore, " the day of the Sabbath" is the same day of the week on which God rested from the work of creation ; and as he rested on the seventh day of the first week, and on no other, the seventh and no other day of every other week must be the only " day of the Sabbath."

Let it be particularly observed, that God does not say, Remember the Sabbath, or, Remember the Sab batic institution, though this is necessarily implied in the command ; but, Remember "the day of the Sabbath"—the day on which I have ordained that the Sabbatic institution be observed. As if he had said, There is little danger, *comparatively*, that you will forget the fact of my having kept Sabbath ; nor is it likely that you will altogether neglect to observe *some day* of rest from your arduous toils, for you will be driven to this by the ever returning demands of your exhausted bodies ; but you are, and always will be, in especial danger of forgetting the proper day of the week for honoring me in my own institution. Satan, who takes infinite delight in all kinds of "will-worship," while he hates with a perfect hatred every act of strict obedience to my law, will do all he can to persuade you that some other day will do just as well, or even better. Remember, therefore, the day of my Sabbath, and keep the same day holy in every week ; for—mark the reason—I have myself rested on the seventh day, and on that account I have blessed and sanctified that and no other day of the week, that you may observe it, and keep it holy, not because it is in itself better than any other day, but because I have blessed and sanctified it.

But you say that the phrase, "the Sabbath-day," or "the day of the Sabbath," does not mean any particular day, but "one day in seven," or some one of the days of the week. You alledge that "the day of the Sabbath," like "the Pope of Rome," "the Emperor of Russia," or "the King of Denmark," is a generic term, alike applicable to all the members of the same class. The phrase, "the Emperor of Russia," you say, refers alike to Peter, to Alexander, and to Nicholas, though only one of them could be Emperor at any given time ; so "the day of the Sabbath" refers alike to the seventh and to the first day of the week, though there never was but one Sabbath at any one time. This is a very ingenious and plausible method of evading the force of the Divine testimony; but, as the reasoning by which it is sustained appears to be entirely sophistical, I cannot but look upon the whole thing as a fabrication. I believe that any man, possessing the requisite qualifications, *may* become "Emperor of Russia," but deny that any day but one *can* be the day of God's Sabbath, inasmuch as God had never kept, at that time, but one Sabbath, and that occupied only one day. There is only one day of American Independence; only one day of the Resurrection of Christ; only one day of the birth of any one man; and only one day of Judgment. And why? Because American Independence was declared on but one day; Christ rose on but one day; the same man cannot be born on two different days; and God hath appointed only one day in which he will judge the world. Now, on the same principle, there can be but one "day of the Sabbath" of the Lord our God. If I should say that the day of Christ's Resurrection is not any particular day of the week, but only "one day in seven," you would not hesitate to call me a fool, while my ignorance would excite your deepest sympathy; but when *you* say that "the day of the Sabbath" does not mean that particular day on which the Lord's Sabbath occurred, but only "one day in seven," you expect me to receive your assertion as the infallible teaching of superior wisdom. I cannot, however, so receive it, for the following reasons:—

1. If God had meant "one day in seven," he would have said so. His first and great design, in writing his law on tables of stone, was to be understood by his creatures; but, for more than two thousand years after he gave the law, no human being

ever suspected that "the day of the Sabbath" meant anything else than the seventh day of the week, because it was commonly known that that day alone was in reality "the day of the Sabbath." Indeed, this "one-day-in-seven" doctrine is known to have been invented within a few hundred years, with the pious design of accounting for a change of Sabbath, without the necessity of repealing a portion of the moral law. It is matter of great surprise, that those pious theologians, who first substituted "one day in seven" for "the day of the Sabbath," did not shudder at the thought of presuming to mend the language of the Holy Ghost. "The words of the Lord are pure words; as silver tried in a furnace of earth, purified seven times." Ps. 12 : 6. Brethren, are you prepared to enter into judgment, and answer for the liberties you have taken with God's word? In substituting the vague and indefinite expression, "one day in seven," for the definite and unequivocal terms, "the Sabbath-day," and "the seventh day," you have as truly taken "away from the words of the prophecy of this book," as if you had blotted the fourth commandment from the Decalogue; while your leading object has been, to make way for the introduction of a new command that, for aught the Scriptures teach, it never entered into the heart of the Almighty to put into his law. "A faithful witness will not lie," and when the world asks, Which day of the seven hath God appointed to be the weekly Sabbath? God expects that you, as faithful witnesses, will not only "not lie," but that you will not equivocate, or give with the gospel trumpet "an uncertain sound." He does not expect that you will quote a text from the Acts of the Apostles, that says not one word about Sabbath-keeping, to prove that the fourth commandment enjoins the keeping holy of "one day in seven," but of "no day in particular."

2. God never blessed "one day in seven," without blessing a particular day. He either blessed some definite object, or nothing. You *may* say, indeed, without falsehood, that God blessed "one day in seven;" but if you mean that this act of blessing did not terminate on any particular day, you ought to know, that you are asserting what is naturally impossible. As well might you say of a band of robbers, that they had killed "one man in seven," while in reality they had killed no man in particular. No, brethren, yourselves know very well, that God had not blessed and sanctified any day but *the seventh of the seven*, prior to the giving of the written law. You know, that if God blessed any day of the week at all, it was a definite day, distinct from all the other days of the week. But this commandment says, that "the Lord blessed the Sabbath-day." Therefore the Sabbath-day must be a particular day of the week. Therefore "the Sabbath-day" is not "one day in seven," or an indefinite seventh part of time. Therefore it is not "one day in seven" that we are required to remember, and keep holy, and in which we are forbidden to do any work; but "the seventh day" of the week, which was then, is now, and will be till the end of time, "the day of the Sabbath" of the Lord our God.

3. No day of the week but the seventh was ever called "the day of the Sabbath," either by God or man, till long since the death of the last inspired writer. Search both Testaments through and through, and you will find no other day called "*the* Sabbath," or even "*a* Sabbath," except the ceremonial Sabbaths, with which, of course, we have nothing to do in this controversy. And long after the close of the canon of inspiration, the seventh day, and no other, was still called "the Sabbath." If you can prove that any one man, among the millions

of Adam's children, from the beginning of the world till the *rise of Anti-Christ,* ever called the first day of the week "*the Sabbath,*" you will shed a light upon this controversy, for which a host of able writers have searched in vain.

But, farther; the first day of the week was not observed by any of the children of men, *as a Sabbath,* for three hundred years after the birth of Christ. Do you ask proof? I refer you to Theodore de Beza, who plainly says so. If you are not satisfied with the witness, will you have the goodness to prove the affirmative of the proposition?

I infer, therefore, that "the day of the Sabbath," or "the Sabbath-day," is the proper name of the seventh day of the week, as much so as "the day of Saturn;" and that to attach this proper name *now* to some other day of the week, and to affirm that God meant that other day, as much as he did the seventh, when he wrote the law on tables of stone, is as unreasonable as it is impious. If you say, that when God speaks of "the Sabbath-day," he means "one day in seven, but no day in particular," you are as far from the truth as if you said that, when he speaks of Moses, he does not mean any particular man, but "some one of the Israelites." Moses *was* one of the Israelites, just as the Sabbath-day *is* one day in seven. But when God says Moses, he means Moses the son of Amram; and when he says "the Sabbath-day," he means the seventh day of the week. You *may* give different names to the same object, without interfering with its identity; but to apply the same name to two different objects, and then to affirm that these two objects are identically the same, so that what is predicated of the one must be true of the other, is as though a navigator should discover an island in the Southern Ocean, and call it "England," and then affirm that the late work of Mr. Macaulay, entitled "The History of England," is a veritable and authentic history of his newly-discovered empire. Which would you wonder at most, the stupidity or the effrontery of that navigator?

I cannot close this chapter without reminding you that, in attempting to refute the above reasoning, the main thing you will have to show is, that "the Sabbath-day," or "the day of the Sabbath," is an indefinite or general expression, applicable alike to at least two different days of the week, and that it is used indefinitely in this commandment. If it has been proved, that "the day of the Sabbath" refers, and can refer, *only* to the seventh day of the week, then it is true, and will remain forever true, that the original Sabbath law requires the sanctification of no other day. This is the truth which I undertook to exhibit in this chapter, and is my first reason for believing the proposition under consideration.

CHAPTER II.

Second Reason.

My second reason for believing this proposition is, That Adam and all his posterity have solemnly covenanted to keep holy the seventh day.

Genesis 2: 15—17—"And the Lord God took the man, and put him into the Garden of Eden, to dress it, and to keep it. And the Lord God commanded the man, saying, Of every tree of the garden thou mayest freely eat; but of the tree of the knowledge of good and evil, thou shalt not eat of it; for in the day that thou eatest thereof thou shalt surely die."

Romans 5: 12, 19—"Wherefore, as by one man sin entered

into the world, and death by sin, and so death passed upon all men, for that all have sinned." "For as by one man's disobedience many were made sinners; so by the obedience of one many shall be made righteous."

Galatians 3: 10—"For as many as are of the works of the law, are under the curse: for it is written, Cursed is every one that continueth not in all things which are written in the book of the law to do them."

On these passages it may be remarked—

1. "God gave to Adam a law, as a covenant of works, by which he bound him, *and all his posterity*, to personal, exact, *entire*, and *perpetual* obedience."

2. "This law, after his fall, continued to be *a perfect rule of righteousness;* and, *as such*, was delivered by God upon Mount Sinai in ten commandments, and written in two tables." Therefore, the fourth commandment and the Sabbath law of the covenant of works are *one and the same law;* and all believers in Christ are now bound by this law, *as a rule of life*, to remember and keep holy the *same Sabbath-day* that Adam and all his posterity covenanted to remember and keep holy.

3. You admit that Adam, *and all his posterity*, pledged themselves to keep holy the seventh day of every week, *and no other*. Therefore, *we* are all born under a solemn obligation, our own obligation in Adam, to keep holy that same seventh day of every week as long as we remain on earth: "*Neither doth Christ in the gospel any way dissolve but much strengthen this obligation.*"

4. It is now too late to alter the covenant of works, by substituting some other day of the week for the seventh, for the following reasons:—

First—Because the whole transaction was finished, in the person of our representative, nearly six thousand years ago. The covenant was made, the obligation assumed, the deed of transgression consummated, the curse pronounced, and the bitter *death* experienced, in *kind*, though not *in degree*, and all this before the first revelation of the mercy of God in Christ. We are, therefore, all of us, the very moment we are born, accursed of God, for not having kept holy the seventh day of the week, according to our covenant. And all who are not redeemed therefrom by Christ, remain forever under this curse. From which it is plain, that to substitute some other day for the seventh, since the fall of man, is as impossible as it would be to substitute *some other tree* for the "tree of knowledge." To all who admit that God made a covenant of works with all mankind *in Adam*, these truths ought to be self-evident. Brethren, *we* acknowledge that we are all guilty before God of having eaten of the fruit of the tree of knowledge, while we disclaim *any guilt whatever* in regard to the fruit of every other tree ; so are we guilty of violating the rest of the seventh day of the week, while we are not by nature guilty of polluting any other day.

Second—Because such substitution would destroy an integral part of the moral law. The law written on the heart of man said nothing about keeping holy any other day than the seventh ; for all admit that, had Adam not fallen, there never would have been any other holy day. If, then, this law does *not now* require the sanctification of the seventh day, *the fourth commandment must have been annihilated ;* and if another day is *now* the Sabbath, a new commandment, requiring *for a new reason* the sanctification of a different day, must have been substituted in its place. But this new law can be *no part of the moral law,* because it was *not written on man's heart,* nor did any human being know of its existence till thousands of God's people had been taken home to glory. God gave to Adam *free permission* tc labor and do work on every day but the seventh, and he, as a free moral agent, accepted the proffered boon. Therefore, to labor on any one of the first six days of the week is, under the covenant of works, *as innocent in itself* as to pray to the Creator of the Universe. It is as much a natural and inalienable right, as "life, liberty, and the pursuit of happiness." Now, if there is a law that requires the keeping holy of some other day, it must have its origin in the new-covenant grace of God; and if that other day, and not the seventh, is *now* the Sabbath, men are *now* no more under a *natural* obligation to keep a Sabbath than to be baptized, or to celebrate the Lord's Supper. The obligation to keep it *must*, on your principle, grow out of their new-covenant relation to God in Christ.

Let us now look for a moment at the consequences flowing from the doctrine, that some other day—the first, for example—has been substituted for the seventh. "Try the spirits." "By their fruits ye shall know them."

1. If this doctrine be true, the doctrine *that Adam represented all his posterity, must be false;* for, if Adam covenanted, as you admit he did, to keep holy the seventh day of every week, and *we* are not bound to do so, he certainly did not represent us, neither in that nor in any other part of the covenant; for, if we did not promise in Adam to keep holy the Sabbath-day, we did not promise to keep any thing else.

2. If this doctrine be true, *there is now no such thing as original sin.* This follows as a matter of course; for, if Adam did not represent us, we are not *born sinners.* The fact might be proved in another way, but this is enough.

3. If this doctrine be true, and the law of the new Sabbath bind "all men," as you say it does, it must

kind *the heathen*, who are a part of " all men." But if there is a new Sabbath instituted, it can only be made known through the written word of God, of which the heathen *can know nothing*. This new Sabbath has never been made known to them, nor to any of their ancestors. Nevertheless, you say that they are bound to observe it, *according to the written word*, and that they shall be punished to all eternity for breaking it; which is contrary to the teaching of the Apostle, (Rom. 2: 12,) that the heathen shall be judged and condemned, not by the written word, but by *the law of nature*, which you know can reveal no Sabbath but that of the seventh day; for Adam, who understood the law of nature better than any other mere man, never thought of keeping holy any other day. And, moreover, the heathen have, on your principle, only nine commandments to obey or disobey; for they are under the law of nature, which says, " Keep holy the seventh day:" but you say that God does not *now* require this: therefore they are released from the obligation. And, what is stranger still, the heathen have no means of knowing that to keep the seventh day *is a work of supererogation*. These are *a few* of the consequences of your doctrine of a change of Sabbath. What must be the character of that tree which yields such fruits!

Let us now attend for a moment to your objections.

Do you say, Those who believe in Christ are redeemed, not only from the curse of the Sabbath law, but also from the obligation to obey it in future? If so, who can tell but we are redeemed from *every other* moral obligation?

Or, do you alledge, that Christ makes a new contract with the sinner, saying, If you keep holy the first day, I will release you from the obligation to sanctify the seventh? "Do we then make void the law through faith? God forbid: yea, we establish the law." Rom. 3: 31. But perhaps you say, To change the Sabbath from one day to another is not to make void the law;" it is only to vary its application. I reply, It *is* to make void, to *annul*, to *annihilate*, one tenth part of that law that God wrote on Adam's heart; for, as has been shown already, that law required him to keep no day holy but the seventh.

Or, do you plead that, as God *has* substituted the Lord Jesus Christ for the sinner, without violating the moral law, so he *may* have substituted some other day for the seventh? I reply, The cases are not parallel; for—

1. The substitution of Christ does not render a change of any part of the law necessary; but the other does. Christ "came not to destroy" the law, but to fulfill it; and in fulfilling it, he honored the seventh day: but the substitution of some other day for the seventh, had it taken place before Christ came, would have released him, as well as us, from the obligation to obey a part of the law of the covenant of works.

2. A change of Sabbath is not, like the substitution of Christ, *necessary* to the salvation of sinners; for God had saved thousands before this change is alledged to have taken place.

3. The substitution of Christ changes the moral condition *of the church only;* but the change of Sabbath would affect the moral relations of all men; for the Sabbath was made, not for the church, but "for man."

4. The evangelical doctrine of the substitutionary sacrifice of Christ, of itself, proves the impossibility of a change of Sabbath. All evangelical Christians hold, that believers are delivered, through

Christ, from the *curse* of the law—the law of the covenant of works—*but not from the obligation to obey it.* If, therefore, that law required *Adam and his posterity* to keep holy the seventh day of the week, Christ has never redeemed them from the obligation to render " *exact obedience*," in this particular, as in every other.

Do you plead, as a last resort, that, as the command not to eat of the fruit of the tree of knowledge has passed away, so it may be with the law of the seventh-day Sabbath ? I reply, The cases are not parallel ; for that command never was a part of the moral law. It was never written, either on man's heart, or on tables of stone ; but this was. Besides, the tree of knowledge has been destroyed from the face of the earth, so that to eat of its fruit is now impossible ; but the seventh day will continue to return " while the earth remaineth."

Brethren, you bewilder yourselves and others, by adopting, as a moral axiom, the false principle, that whatever is in its nature positive, is, *for that reason*, changeable. There is no principle more deadly than this. Do you not know, that all our hopes, as Christians, for time and for eternity, are suspended on the *immutability* of that *positive arrangement* between the Father and the Son, which we call the covenant of grace ? Are not the decrees of God all *positive*, yet, at the same time, immutable ? So, also, the *Sabbath law*, though in its nature positive, has been made unchangeable, by a solemn covenant arrangement, " in which it was impossible for God to lie." If God had not made the law, requiring the sanctification of the seventh day, an essential part of the covenant of works, your doctrine of a change of Sabbath would not be so preposterous. As it is, how can serious, thinking men, help viewing it as a monstrous and impious absurdity !

CHAPTER III.

Third Reason.

My third reason for believing this proposition is, That Christ and his Apostles honored this day; and did not intimate that it would ever cease to be the Sabbath, but the contrary.

1. Christ honored this day.

Luke 4: 16—"And he came to Nazareth, where he had been brought up: and, as his custom was, he went into the synagogue on the Sabbath-day, and stood up for to read."

Luke 4: 30, 31; (See also Mark 1: 21)—"But he, passing through the midst of them, went his way, and came down to Capernaum, a city of Galilee, and taught them on the Sabbath-days."

Luke 13: 10—"And he was teaching in one of the synagogues on the Sabbath."

Mark 3: 1, 2—"And he entered again into the synagogue; and there was a man there which had a withered hand. And they watched him whether he would heal him on the Sabbath-day."

Mark 6: 2—"And when the Sabbath-day was come, he began to teach in the synagogue."

2. The Apostles honored this day. Read carefully the following passages and their contexts.

Acts 13: 14—"But when they departed from Perga, they came to Antioch in Pisidia, and went into the synagogue on the Sabbath-day, and sat down."

Acts 13: 44—"And the next Sabbath-day came almost the whole city together to hear the word of God." (That is, to hear Paul and Barnabas preach.)

Acts 14: 1—"And it came to pass in Iconium, that they Paul and Barnabas) went both together into the synagogue of the Jews, and so spake, that a great multitude, both of the Jews, and also of the Greeks, believed."

Acts 16: 23—"And on the Sabbath we went out of the city by a river side, where prayer was wont to be made; and we sat down, and spake unto the women which resorted thither."

Acts 17: 2—"And Paul, as his manner was, went in unto them, and three Sabbath-days reasoned with them out of the Scriptures."

Acts 18: 4—"And he (Paul) reasoned in the synagoguge every Sabbath, and persuaded the Jews and the Greeks."

Brethren, if you produce one solitary apostolic example of unnecessary labor performed on the seventh day, I will at once give up the argument in its favor.

3. Neither Christ nor his Apostles intimated that the seventh day would cease to be the Sabbath.

This being a negative assertion, I am not bound to prove it, of course. If you assert that they did, I demand the proof of it.

4. Christ has very plainly intimated the contrary.

Matthew 24: 20—"But pray ye that your flight be not in winter, neither on the Sabbath-day."

The "flight" here spoken of was to take place about the time of the destruction of Jerusalem; and the Saviour admonishes his disciples to pray that it might not happen on the Sabbath-day. Now, if he knew that the Sabbath-day would be changed into the "Lord's day," forty years before the event he had just alluded to, why did he speak of it as a thing that would be then in existence? Many are the efforts that have been made to evade the force of the argument from this text; but they are all unavailing.

Matthew 5: 17, 19—"Think not that I am come to destroy the law, or the prophets: I am not come to destroy, but to fulfill. For verily I say unto you, Till heaven and earth pass, one jot or one tittle shall in no wise pass from the law, till all be fulfilled. Whosoever therefore shall break one of these least commandments, and shall teach men so, he shall be called least in the kingdom of heaven: but whosoever shall do and teach them, the same shall be called great in the kingdom of heaven."

It is almost universally admitted, that the Saviour, in these verses, refers principally to the ten commandments, which were then, as now, called, by way of preëminence, "*the* law." That he may have referred also to the ceremonial code, which he came to fulfill, we do not deny. But this has nothing to do with our present purpose.

That the fourth commandment enjoins the sanctification of the seventh day of the week, no man in his senses denies. But you alledge that that part of it has been taken away, so that it does not now bind us.

Now, in making this assertion, you either affirm what is positively denied in the above quotation, or you make this commandment at least *partly* ceremonial, and *peculiar to the Jews*. This will appear evident from the following considerations:—

First—The command to keep holy the seventh day of the week, is far more than "one jot or one tittle" of this law. It could be no less, but it is much more. Indeed, it is very certain, that Adam considered it a very important part of the law; and so did Christ, when he uttered these words, for he kept the Sabbath as devoutly as Adam ever did.

Second—Heaven and earth have not yet passed away; but you say that this seventh-day law has; therefore, much more than "one jot or one tittle" has passed from the law—which is contrary to Christ's assertion.

Third—If you say that Christ has fulfilled this law, and so taken it away, you make it a ceremony, like the Passover. You know that Christ never fulfilled, *so as to take away*, any law but those that he "nailed to his cross," and that he never nailed to his cross any law that bindeth "all men in all ages." If, then, the law requiring the sanctification of the seventh day of the week has been nailed to the cross of Christ, it must have been a ceremony peculiar to the Jews, and to which the Gentiles were never bound. Was Adam a Jew? Was Enoch a Jew? Were Noah and his sons Jews? But these all kept the seventh day, *and no other*.*

Brethren, it has been proved, in the first chapter of this treatise, that the fourth commandment requires simply the observance of the seventh day of the week. I will not repeat what is there said. I now ask you, as candid inquirers after truth, to place this commandment and our Saviour's declarations, quoted above, side by side, and see if *your* conduct is not at war with both. You neglect the only day that God's law requires you to remember, while Christ assures you, in the most solemn manner, that "one jot or one tittle" shall in no wise pass from the law, "till heaven and earth pass," or till time shall be no more.

* Some of my Reformed Presbyterian brethren appear to be as far from believing "the whole doctrine of the Westminster Confession of Faith" as myself, only they are a little more guarded in the choice of words. That Confession says, (ch. 21, sec. 7,) "—so, in his word, by a positive, moral, and perpetual commandment, *binding all men in all ages*, he hath particularly appointed one day in seven for a Sabbath, to be kept holy unto him." But Rev. Andrew Stephenson, in a letter to me, speaking of the seventh-day Sabbath, styles it, "This relict of Judaism;" and Rev. James Milligan, in a recent letter, asks me, "Why has not the Lord's day as good a right to take the place of the seventh day, as the Lord's Supper has to take the place of the Passover?" Query—Are Reformed Presbyterians, who hold such sentiments, any better qualified to judge their brethren for Sabbath-breaking, than I would be to judge them for a like offense?

There is a little commandment in that law that says, "The seventh day is the Sabbath of the Lord thy God; in it thou shalt not do any work." Christ says, that whosoever doeth and teacheth this commandment "shall be called great in the kingdom of heaven." But this hath been my only crime. God knows, and you know, that the only thing I have done to offend you is, that I endeavor to refrain from doing work on the seventh day, and to "teach men so." Yet for this I am declared to be the "least in the kingdom of heaven," and no longer worthy of a seat at the table of Him who said, that "one jot or one tittle" should *in no wise* pass from the law.

Blessed be God! it is a light thing to be judged of man's judgment. But I confess that sometimes my blood runs cold, when I think of this solemn declaration of the same "Lord of the Sabbath," (John 12: 48,) "He that rejecteth me, and receiveth not my words, hath one that judgeth him: the word that I have spoken, the same shall judge him in the last day." "Never man spake like this man." O, brethren, are you ready for that awful judgment day? Nothing but God's *word* will avail you there. If you are determined to go on, appropriating the seventh day to secular purposes, and "teaching men so," I cannot help it; but I call heaven and earth to witness, that, in regard to every reader of these pages, my skirts are henceforth clear. On your own souls will rest the responsibility of rejecting these solemn words of Christ. And you who are ministers—how will you answer for the wanderings of those lambs of Christ's fold, whom you are leading into strange pastures?

CHAPTER IV.

Fourth Reason.

My fourth reason for believing this proposition is, That God has never blessed and sanctified any day of the week but the seventh.

In sustaining this reason, as I occupy negative ground, I shall simply defend it against your usual scripture arguments in defense of your favorite doctrine, that God blessed and sanctified the first day of the week, in commemoration of the resurrection of Christ.

In arguing this doctrine, you do not pretend to offer *positive*, but only *inferential* proof. You quote certain texts, and say, Hence we infer that the first day of the week is the Sabbath. Now, as there are many possible, and even plausible, inferences, that are not necessarily true, I intend to be governed, in the examination of your scripture proofs, by the following rule of interpretation :—

" The whole counsel of God, concerning all things necessary for his own glory, man's salvation, faith, and life, is either expressly set down in scripture, or *by good and necessary consequence* may be deduced from scripture."

Brethren, I intend, with God's help, to show that, according to the above rule, which you admit to be correct, all your inferences in favor of a first-day Sabbath are *unnecessary*, and some of them wholly inadmissible.

YOUR FIRST PROOF.

Hebrews 4: 9, 10—" There remaineth, therefore, a rest (sabbatism) to the people of God. For he that is entered into his rest, he also hath ceased from his own works, as God did from his."

Your premises consist of four assertions :—First, That the rest, or sabbatism, that remaineth, is something different from the ancient Sabbath. Second, That the person who "hath ceased from his own works, as God did from his," is the Lord Jesus Christ. These two assertions I most cheerfully admit. Third, That Christ entered into his rest on the day of his resurrection. Fourth, That the sabbatism of God's people is enjoyed in this life. These last two assertions I utterly deny.

Your inference is, That the first day of every week, that being the day of the week on which Christ rose, is the sabbatism of God's people. Of course, if I prove that the last two assertions are false, your inference will be shown to be inadmissible.

I assert, then,—

1. That Christ did *not* "enter into his rest" on the day of his resurrection; for the following reasons :—First, Because the Scriptures do not say so. Second, Because this earth is not the place of his rest. He was, to the last day he spent here, "a pilgrim and a stranger in the earth," and had not therein "where to lay his head." But his resurrection took place on earth, and he continued on earth for "forty days" afterwards. Third, Because the scriptures plainly teach, that the Mediator *did* "enter into his rest," when he "sat down on the right hand of the Majesty on high." Heb. 1 : 3. "Arise, O Lord, into thy rest; thou and the ark of thy strength." Ps. 132 : 2. This was the prayer of David and the congregation of Israel, when they removed the ark from the house of Obed-Edom to the place "that David had pitched for it." When Solomon and the Elders of Israel brought up the ark from the city of David, and placed it in the holy of holies, in the temple "made with hands," they pray

ed in like manner, "Now therefore arise, O Lord God, into thy resting-place, thou, and the ark of thy strength." 2 Chron. 6 : 41. Now the ark was a type of Christ, while "heaven itself" is the true "holy of holies," "whither the forerunner is for us entered, even Jesus, made a high priest forever after the order of Melchizedek." Heb. 6 : 20. If, then, the ark entered into its rest, when it was placed in the holy of holies, Jesus Christ, the anti-typical ark, entered into *his* rest when he sat down on the right hand of God, in the anti-typical holy of holies. Fourth, Because the Apostle's great design, in this epistle, was to convince the church, and especially the Hebrews, that Christ, having "by himself purged our sins," as they all admitted he had done, "sat down on the right hand of the Majesty on high," (ch. 1 : 3,) as our ever-living Intercessor. Yes, the "one idea," that runs through the whole Epistle, is to illustrate and magnify the doctrine of the glorious intercession of Christ the Mediator, who, "after he had offered one sacrifice for sins, forever sat down on the right hand of God." Do you ask proof? Take, then, the apostle's own assertion, (ch. 8 : 1,) "Now, of the things which we have spoken, this is the sum : We have such a high priest, who is set on the right hand of the throne of the Majesty in the heavens ; a minister of the sanctuary, and of the true tabernacle, which the Lord pitched, and not man." All that is said in the third and fourth chapters, about the rest of Christ and the sabbatism of the people of God, is included in this summary ; so that it is to Christ's eternal rest in the heavens that the verses under consideration refer. Indeed, we have evidence of this fact, satisfactory enough, in the immediate context, (ch. 3 : 4,) "Wherefore, holy brethren, partakers of the heavenly calling, consider the Apostle and High Priest of our profession, Christ Jesus"—compared with ch. 4 : 14—"Seeing, then, that we have a great High Priest, that is passed into the heavens, Jesus the Son of God, let us hold fast our profession." Fifth, Because there is not, in this epistle, one solitary reference to the resurrection of Christ, except in the concluding benediction; but it abounds in references to his ascension and intercession.

2. If I have reasoned correctly above, your assertion, that the sabbatism of God's people is enjoyed in this life, scarcely needs refutation. As Christ entered into his rest, when he received the crown of glory from the Father; so believers shall enter into his rest, when they "shall be glorified with him." Moreover, as Christ did not enter into his rest on the first day of the week, your inference, that that day is the Sabbath, is not only *unnecessary*, but wholly inadmissible.

Bear in mind also, brethren, that, if Christ did not enter into his rest on the first day of the week, then your great philosophical argument for the first-day Sabbath, founded upon the fact, that the work of redemption is greater than that of creation, vanishes at once into smoke, or, at least, becomes useless for your purpose.

YOUR SECOND PROOF.

Psalm 118 : 22, 24—"The stone which the builders refused is become the head-stone of the corner." "This is the day which the Lord hath made, we will rejoice and be glad in it."

Acts 4: 10, 11—"Be it known unto you all, and to all the people of Israel, that by the name of Jesus Christ of Nazareth, whom ye crucified, whom God raised from the dead, even by him doth this man stand here before you whole. This is the stone which was set at nought of you builders, which is become the head of the corner."

You premise, that "the day which the Lord hath made" is the day of the resurrection of Christ.

Whence you infer, that the first day of the week is the Sabbath.

1. If what you premise were true, the inference does not follow. The prophet does not say, We will rejoice and be glad in the same day of every week; but, We will rejoice and be glad *in it*, that is, in that day, whatever it may be. Now Christ did not rise on the first day of every week, but on one single day; and we may very well rejoice and be glad in that one day, without keeping any Sabbath in connection with it. Abraham rejoiced and was glad in the day of Christ; but he kept no Sabbath in honor of it. So, doubtless, *you* rejoice and are glad in the day of his crucifixion, though you do not celebrate it on any particular day of the week. But—

2. You are evidently mistaken in referring this language of the Psalmist to the resurrection of Christ—for the following reasons:—

First—Because "the day which the Lord hath made" is the same in which Christ went in by the gates of righteousness. Verses 19 and 20. "Open to me the gates of righteousness: I will go into them, and I will praise the Lord. This gate of the Lord, into which the righteous shall enter." Now, though Christ *did* come up from "the gates of death" on the day of his resurrection, he *did not* formally "enter" by "the gates of righteousness," till that day when he ascended from Mount Olivet, which was not the first day of the week. His almighty power and eternal Sonship were declared most gloriously on the day of his resurrection; but it was on the day of his ascension that his mediatorial righteousness was formally approved by the Father; while it was visibly manifested, in the presence of the universe, that the door of heaven had been opened to all true believers. Then shouted the seraphim, and all the host of heaven, while the door-posts of the New Jerusalem trembled at the voice, "Arise, O Jehovah, into thy rest, thou, and the ark of thy strength. Let thy priests be clothed with righteousness; and let thy saints shout for joy!" Therefore, this is not the day of Christ's resurrection, but that of his ascension.

Second—Because "the day which the Lord hath made" is the same in which "the stone which the builders refused" became "the head-stone of the corner," (verse 22.) Christ did not become "the head of the corner," till he "sat down on the right hand of God." You assert that he did, and refer to Acts 4: 10, 11, quoted above, as proof. From what the apostle there sets forth, you draw the inference, that, as he was set at nought by the builders, when he was crucified, so he became the head of the corner, when God raised him from the dead. The apostle does not say, however, that this took place on the same day that he rose from the dead; and all that we must *necessarily* infer from what he *does say*, is, that he became the head of the corner since his resurrection, which is cheerfully admitted. But whether it was on the same day, or two, or ten, or forty days after, the apostle saith not. Still your inference would be entirely natural and proper, if it were not contrary to the analogy of faith, and to the teachings of the same spirit in other parts of the Scriptures.

I suppose it will be admitted, that when Christ became the head of the corner, he became "the head over all things to the church," and that then "all things were put under his feet." Now the apostle clearly teaches, that these things took place when he sat down on the right hand of God, as appears from the following texts:—

Ephesians 1: 20—22—"Which he wrought in Christ, when

he raised him from the dead, (or, having raised him from the dead,) and set him at his own right hand in the heavenly places, far above all principality, and power, and might, and dominion, and every name that is named, not only in this world, but also in that which is to come: and hath put all things under his feet, and gave him to be head over all things to the church."

Hebrews 2: 8, 9—"But now we see not yet all things put under him (man;) but we see Jesus, who was made a little lower than the angels, for the suffering of death, crowned with glory and honor." Observe, that the Apostle's great object in this epistle is, to show that Christ is *in heaven*, forever interceding for the church.

Now, is it not manifest from these texts, that Christ became the head of the corner when he ascended to his Father and our Father, to his God and our God? Nor is there any thing in Acts 4: 10, 11, that contradicts this idea.

Brethren, the glorious building of grace has its foundation, not on earth, where we are pilgrims and strangers, but in heaven, where Jesus, the corner-stone, "elect and precious," sitteth at the right hand of God, and is constantly occupied in gathering from afar the "lively stones" of the glorious edifice. Blessed forever be his holy name!

YOUR THIRD PROOF.

John 20: 19, 26—"Then the same day at evening, being the first day of the week, when the doors were shut where the disciples were assembled for fear of the Jews, came Jesus and stood in the midst, and saith unto them, Peace be unto you." "And after eight days again his disciples were within, and Thomas with them; then came Jesus; the doors being shut, and stood in the midst, and said, Peace be unto you."—See also Luke 24: 26.

You premise, that the disciples, on the two days referred to above, one of which certainly was, and the other may have been, the first day of the week, had met together for public or social worship, when

Christ appeared to them. Whence you infer, that the first day of the week is the Sabbath.

Now, what you premise *seems* to be a mere assumption, for which there is not a shadow of proof, either in the text or context. No one of the Evangelists says that they met for worship ; nor did they worship, so far as we know, when met together. In regard to the first of those occasions, we are told, that they " were assembled for fear of the Jews ;" and, as to the second, we are simply informed, that they "were within," which means, probably, that they were *at home ;* for Luke tells us, that, on the day of the ascension, the eleven "abode" in an upper room. Acts 1 : 13.

Again, your inference is not *necessary ;* for the matter may be explained thus : On the day of the resurrection, the eleven, having procured a common lodging-room, "assembled for fear of the Jews ;" and Christ appeared to them before the close of the same day, in order that they, who were to be witnesses of his resurrection, might have ocular demonstration of the fact, that he rose "according to the scriptures." On the other occasion, "after eight days," he met them, probably, " as they sat at meat," (Mark 16 : 14,) because Thomas, who had not seen him since his resurrection, was then with them.

These reasons are surely sufficient to account for his appearing on those occasions. But why demand reasons at all ? Had he not a right to meet his disciples on any day of the week that he chose, without telling us why ? Can you tell us why he appeared to the brethren when they were fishing ? Christ has done many things for which the only reason we can give is, that it seemed good to him.

YOUR FOURTH PROOF.

Acts 2 : 1—" And when the day of Pentecost was fully come, they were all with one accord in one place."

Your premises are—1. That the Feast of Pentecost fell that year on the first day of the week. 2. That the disciples were, *for that reason*, with one accord in one place." Whence you infer, that the first day of the week is the Sabbath. I reply—

Whether the Feast of Pentecost fell that year on the first day of the week, or not, the disciples did not meet to keep the Sabbath, but to celebrate Pentecost. They would have been, in like manner "with one accord in one place," if it had been the fourth day of the week, because it was the day of Pentecost. Therefore, your inference is not only *unnecessary*, but wholly inadmissible.

YOUR FIFTH PROOF.

Acts 20: 7—"And upon the first day of the week, when the disciples came together to break bread, Paul preached unto them, ready to depart on the morrow; and continued his speech until midnight."

You premise, that the disciples came together, in this instance, to celebrate the Lord's Supper, and to hear the word. Whence you infer, that the first day of the week is the Sabbath.

What you premise is very uncertain; for—

1. There is no evidence that they met to hear the word. The object of the meeting was "to break bread;" and the preaching of Paul seems to have been *incidental*, and not by appointment.

2. It is not certain that "to break bread" means to partake of the Lord's Supper. The Greek word, translated, *to break*, is used very often in the New Testament in reference to ordinary meals. An instance occurs in Luke 24: 35—"And they told what things were done in the way, and how he was known of them *in breaking of bread*."

But if what you assert were true, your inference is not *necessary*; for—

1. It is entirely proper, for aught we know to the

contrary, to celebrate the Lord's Supper and hear preaching on any day of the week.

2. Perhaps this meeting was held at that particular time, because the Apostle and his company were "ready to depart on the morrow." It was probably a farewell meeting, as many learned men think, and the text itself *seems* to hint.

3. There is not one word said in the text about Sabbath-keeping; nor is there the least intimation, either in the text or context, that the disciples were *accustomed* to meet on the first day of the week for any purpose whatever.

But you say, Paul waited there seven days, and we have no account of his preaching till the last night of his stay, which was the first of the week. We reply, This is no evidence that he did not preach during the other six days. Luke tells us, in this same chapter, verses 2 and 3, that "he came into Greece, and there abode three months;" and he does not say that he preached once during that time. But a small part, indeed, of the doings of the Apostles is recorded.

It is a remarkable fact, that this text, which is the only one in the New Testament that speaks of public religious exercises on the first day of the week, is, at the same time, the only one in the Bible that directly proves, that this day is *not* the Sabbath. I have already proposed to give up the argument in favor of the seventh day, if you produce one apostolic example of unnecessary labor performed therein. Will you give up your argument for the first day on the same condition? I believe this verse furnishes such an example.

The text proves nothing for you, if Paul's sermon and the breaking of bread were not on the first day. The sermon was preached between evening and midnight, and the bread was broken between midnight and break of day, and then Paul set out on his journey. According to the Roman method of computing time, the breaking of bread, at least, was in the morning of the same day in which Paul traveled from Troas to Assos, and thence to Mitylene; and, according to the Jewish method, the sermon, the breaking of bread, and the journey from Troas to Mitylene, were all within the compass of the same "first day of the week." That Luke should follow the unnatural Roman method, is so unlikely as hardly to be supposable. Now, if Paul traveled unnecessarily from Troas to Mitylene, as it seems he did, on the first day of the week, surely that day was not then the Sabbath of the fourth commandment. This text, therefore, *proves positively that the first day is not the Sabbath*, on which account it is of no little value in this controversy.

YOUR SIXTH PROOF.

1 Corinthians 16: 2—"Upon the first day of the week, let every one of you lay by him in store, as God hath prospered him, that there be no gatherings when I come."

Your premises are—1. That the Apostle here commands the Corinthians to make public collections on the first day of the week. 2. That, therefore, public assemblies were accustomed to be held on that day. Whence you infer, that the first day of the week is the Sabbath.

I deny both your premises. The apostle simply orders, that each one of the Corinthian brethren should lay up *at home* some portion of his weekly gains on the first day of the week. The whole question turns upon the meaning of the expression, "by him;" and I marvel greatly how you can imagine that it means "in the collection box of the congregation." Greenfield, in his Lexicon, translates the Greek term, "*by one's self, i. e. at home.*" Two Latin versions, the Vulgate and that of Castellio, render it, "*apud se,*" with one's self, at home. Three French translations, those of Martin, Osterwald, and De Sacy, "*chez soi,*" at his own house, at home. The German of Luther, "*bei sich selbst,*" by himself, at home. The Dutch, "*by hemselven,*" same as the German. The Italian of Diodati "*appresso di se,*" in his own presence, at home. The Spanish of Felipe Scio, "*en su casa,*" in his own house. The Portuguese of Ferreira, "*para isso,*" with himself. The Swedish, "*nær sig sielf,*" near himself. I know not how much this list of authorities might be swelled, for I have not examined one translation that differs from those quoted above. Now, if your premises are false, your inference is not only *unnecessary*, but wholly inadmissible.

YOUR SEVENTH PROOF

Revelations 1: 10—"I was in the spirit on the Lord's day."

You premise, that the "Lord's day" is the first day of the week. Whence you infer, that the first day of the week is the Sabbath.

You here assume the principal point in dispute, namely, that God has appointed the first day of every week to be kept in commemoration of the resurrection of Christ. Is every Friday the "Lord's day," because he was crucified on Friday? You answer, No. Is every Thursday the "Lord's day," because he ascended on Thursday? You answer, No. So, when you ask, Is every first day of the week the "Lord's day," because he rose on the first day? I answer, No. And is it too much that I should ask you to prove your assumption? I have never yet met with an attempt to prove it.

But, were this even proved, your inference would not be *necessary*. The first day *might* be the "Lord's day," and yet not the Sabbath. Would the bare mention of this day by the Apostle John, even if it were certain that he referred to the first day of the week, repeal or alter the fourth commandment? Certainly not. But you ask, What day did he mean? I reply, Most probably he meant the seventh, since we know from several scriptures that this *is in fact the Lord's day*. See Nehemiah 9 : 14, and Isaiah 58 : 13. But you ask again, Why did he not say "the Sabbath," if he meant it? I reply by asking you, Why did he not say "the first day," if he meant it?

Brethren, who can say, that, from any or all of the texts commented upon above, the inference is *necessary*, that the first day of the week *is*, and that the seventh *is not*, *holy?* But this is precisely what *you* infer from them. On the sole authority of these passages, together with that one in which Christ says, that he is "Lord of the Sabbath," you have no hesitation in affirming that the first day of the week is the very Sabbath day spoken of in the fourth commandment, and that the seventh day of the week is not *now* more holy than any other; or, in other words, that the blessing which God put upon it in the beginning, (Gen. 2 : 21,) has been taken from it, and given to another day. What! because "there remaineth a sabbatism to the people of God," therefore the seventh day *must* have ceased to be the Sabbath! Because "we will be glad and rejoice" in "the day which the Lord hath made," therefore the seventh day *must* have ceased to be holy! Because Christ showed himself to his disciples once or twice on the first day of the week, therefore the seventh day *cannot* be the Sabbath! Because the Pentecostal effusion of the Holy Ghost happened on the first day of the week, as is clearly demonstrated by arithmetical calculation, therefore the seventh day *cannot* claim to be the Sabbath! Because the disciples met *once* "to break bread" on the first day of the week, therefore God *must* have unsanctified the seventh day! Because the Corinthian and Galatian Christians were commanded to "lay by them in store" on the first day of the week, for the relief of the poor saints, therefore the seventh day *can be nothing more* than a working day! Because John was "in the spirit on the Lord's day," therefore the seventh day *cannot* be "the Lord's day," as it used to be! Because Jesus Christ is "Lord of the Sabbath," and has the right to change it, or even to annihilate it, (?) therefore the seventh day *must* have ceased to be a day of rest! O brethren, you dare not say, that any of these inferences flow from the Scriptures as *necessary consequences.* But if they are not *necessary*—if there is any way of avoiding them, without doing violence either to the text or context—how *can* you ask me to believe that the first day *is*, and that the seventh *is not*, holy?

CONCLUSION.

"The Sabbath was made for man." I am a man; therefore, the Sabbath was made for me. God has blessed and sanctified *the seventh day* of the week, and commanded me to keep it holy *for that reason;* therefore, as long as the seventh day continues to be divinely blessed and sanctified, I am bound to keep it holy. But it is nowhere said in the Bible that God has removed the blessing from this day, or that he has unsanctified it. *You* say so, indeed; but you are neither the authors nor the finishers of my faith; nor will your unsupported assertion, a thousand times repeated, amount to a divine revelation. If you assert that it is the will of God that I should cease to regard the seventh day as holy, I ask, Where is this revealed? What Prophet or Apostle has said so, *directly or indirectly?* It is not enough for you to answer, that the first day has been blessed and sanctified, as a memorial of the work of redemption. That assertion, if it were true, would not prove that the seventh day *is not holy.* No, brethren, your own conscience must tell you, that there is not one syllable in the Bible on which to ground the doctrine that God has *unsanctified* the seventh day of the week.

But one of your ministers has told me, that God did not bless and sanctify any particular day of the week, but only the Sabbath Institution. To this I have only to say, "Let God be true, and every man a liar." The Holy Ghost says, (Gen. 2: 2,) "And God blessed the *seventh day*, and sanctified it;" and again, (Exod. 20: 11,) "Wherefore the Lord blessed the Sabbath DAY, and hallowed it." Now, if you assert, with these scriptures staring you in the face, that God never blessed and sanctified any particular day, but only the Sabbath Institution, do you not make God a liar, in order to excuse your own rebellion? O brethren, I perceive that these texts are an eye-sore to you, and that in your hearts you wish they were out of the Bible. If you loved them you would not flatly contradict them. I appeal to your own consciousness, is it not your great effort, when you take up the fourth commandment, to convince yourselves and others, that God's Spirit *does not mean* what he says, in as plain language as any Sabbatarian could employ; that is, that 'the seventh day is the Sabbath of the Lord thy God.' And, when you take up these passages in the New Testament, which have been considered above, do you not labor to convince yourselves, that the same Spirit *does mean* what he *does not say;* that is, that the first day is the Sabbath ?

You do not believe that what God says a dozen times, or more, *can* be true ; but you are sure, that what he *does not say even once* is infallibly true ; and that nothing but stupidity or scepticism would presume to doubt it. When you are told that the seventh day is the Sabbath, and the testimony of God's Spirit, plainly uttered in one dozen passages, together with the uniform practice of the church as long as we can trace the inspired history of the Sabbath, is offered in proof of the assertion, you shut your eyes, and declare that you can see nothing, and that all this proves nothing. But when you tell me, that the first day *is*, and that the seventh *is not*, the Sabbath, and quote, as proof, Acts 20 : 7, and a few other passages, not one of which says one word about the Sabbath, or the seventh day, or a day of rest, or holy time, or exercises which are proper only on the Sabbath, you affirm, that you have proved your position beyond all doubt, and that the only reason why I cannot see the evidence is because the vail of Judaism is over my eyes. The moral law says, " The seventh day is the Sabbath ;" but you say, " No, the seventh day is not the Sabbath ; you do not understand the law ; you mistake its meaning." Neither that law, nor any other in the Bible, says, " The first day is the Sabbath." Notwithstanding, you dare to lift up your hands, and swear by the living God, that the first day *is* the Sabbath. But this is not all. Oh ! that it were ! The Holy Ghost has said, not only in the record that God made on Adam's heart, and in the covenant of works, but also in the written law given at Mount Sinai, and in several other passages of Scripture, " The seventh day is the Sabbath of the Lord thy God." But you have repeatedly sworn by the infinite, eternal, and unchangeable Jehovah, that *this assertion is not true* — that the seventh day is *not* the Sabbath of the Lord our God — that it is a common working day. Because I can no longer join you in this heaven-daring oath, you have declared me unworthy of the confidence of a Christian people, and forbidden me to perform any longer the functions of a missionary of the cross. You have told the church, that, having violated my ordination vows, I have forfeited my ministry, and that my seat at the Lord's table is vacant. You have thus flung upon the heedless winds the mad-dog cry of " suspended minister," " covenant-breaker," and " disturber of the church's peace."

But think not, brethren, beloved in the Lord, that the treatment which I have received at your hands shall deter me from proclaiming what I believe to be God's truth, as God may give me utterance. That you wish to do what is right, I do not doubt. That you believe you do God service in thrusting me from your Christian embraces, is evident enough. That many of you love me yet, and pray for me, I can but hope. But that you all sin in not searching the Scriptures daily to see whether these things are so, I do firmly believe.

And now, brethren, I cannot close this treatise without uttering a word of warning to every one of you, which will, I fear, be very generally disregarded by you. Yet " wo is me" if I utter it not! Do not, I beseech you, be angry at any thing I have written, or refuse to hear my parting words because I am a " suspended minister." You have loaded me with reproach, not because I have committed any crime, but because I have plead for the integrity and immutability of the moral law. I am neither a thief, nor a murderer, nor a robber of churches, but I do most firmly believe, that the seventh day is the Sabbath of the Lord my God, and that you, and all others who do not keep it holy, are guilty before God of a gross violation of the moral law. And can I, under those circumstances, regard your reproaches as a legitimate expression of the Divine displeasure? No. That I am really unworthy of the gospel ministry, I confess. That I am not sufficient for these things, I know. But, after having been regularly called to this responsible work, I will not be driven from it, for such a cause. Know then, ye rulers in the house of God, that I am still a minister of Jesus Christ, sent forth to proclaim the terrors of God's law to the rebellious and impenitent, and to promise the grace of the gospel to the penitent and believing. Know also, ye professors of the Christian religion who neglect the sanctification of the seventh day, and especially ye ministers of Jesus who "teach men so," that you make dark what God has made plain; that you pluck out of the hand of God's schoolmaster one of those rods wherewith he would lash the carnal heart; that you hide one of God's candles under a bushel, and compass yourselves about with sparks, and a fire of your own kindling; that you provoke the Holy Spirit, in rejecting his testimony, and teaching for doctrine the commandments of men. Yes, brethren, though my words fall upon your ears as an idle tale that you believe not, I declare to you, in the name of Him whom your doctrine dishonors and your philosophy insults—in the name of that *suspended Minister*, to whom all the ends of the earth shall look for salvation—that, if you repent not, the Holy Ghost will bear witness against you, in the awful day of retribution, that you have refused his words, and that you have "put darkness for light, and light for darkness!"

Think not that I am your enemy, because I thus speak. Think not that I have no confidence in your piety, because I rebuke you sharply. Think not that I am proud, boastful, and self-confident, because I dare to approach *you*, who are vastly my superiors in knowledge, and remind you of your duty. I would gladly have avoided this public exhibition of my sentiments. Had it been possible to withhold my testimony, you would never have seen these pages. But "necessity is laid upon me." And think not, I beseech you, that I am against the church of our Redeemer, or would hinder her prosperity, because I oppose a human institution which Christians very generally observe. "If I forget thee, O Jerusalem, let my right hand forget her cunning. If I do not remember thee, let my tongue cleave to the roof of my mouth; if I prefer not Jerusalem above my chief joy."

www.ingramcontent.com/pod-product-compliance
Lightning Source LLC
LaVergne TN
LVHW020121110826
845151LV00001B/238

* 9 7 8 1 4 2 5 5 4 2 0 7 8 *